AF352694

Dialect Contact

Dialect Contact

From Speaker to Community-Based Perspectives

Víctor Fernández-Mallat and Jennifer Nycz, Editors

Georgetown University Press
Washington, DC

The publisher is not responsible for third-party websites or their content. URL links were active at time of publication.

Library of Congress Cataloging-in-Publication Data

Names: Georgetown University Round Table on Languages and Linguistics (2022), author. | Fernández-Mallat, Víctor, 1981- editor. | Nycz, Jennifer, editor.
Title: Dialect contact : from speaker to community-based perspectives / Victor Fernández-Mallat and Jennifer Nycz, editors.
Description: Washington, DC : Georgetown University Press, 2025. | Series: Georgetown University Round Table on Languages and Linguistics | Papers originally presented at the Georgetown University Round Table on Languages and Linguistics, held online in March 2022. | Includes bibliographical references and index.
Identifiers: LCCN 2024019049 (print) | LCCN 2024019050 (ebook) | ISBN 9781647125011 (hardcover) | ISBN 9781647125028 (paperback) | ISBN 9781647125035 (ebook)
Subjects: LCSH: Languages in contact—Congresses. | Dialectology—Congresses. Sociolinguistics—Congresses. | LCGFT: Conference papers and proceedings.
Classification: LCC P130.5 .G46 2022 (print) | LCC P130.5 (ebook) | DDC 306.44/6—dc23/eng20240522

LC record available at https://lccn.loc.gov/2024019049
LC ebook record available at https://lccn.loc.gov/2024019050

♾ This paper meets the requirements of ANSI/NISO Z39.48-1992 (Permanence of Paper).

25 24   9 8 7 6 5 4 3 2   First printing

Printed in the United States of America

Cover design by Nathan Putens
Interior design by Westchester

Contents

Chapter 1

A Multi-level Approach to Understanding the Dynamics of Dialect Contact

VÍCTOR FERNÁNDEZ-MALLAT AND JENNIFER NYCZ, EDITORS
Georgetown University

LINGUISTICS IS OFTEN DEFINED as "the scientific study of language":[1] linguists take a systematic approach to describing and explaining existing and possible human languages and linguistic patterns. As scientists, we recognize the importance of controlling as many variables as possible in our studies and constraining our empirical reach to a manageable scope; as *social* scientists, we know it's difficult in practice to meet these ideals when real people are involved. One approach to exerting some measure of control over our datasets is to focus our observations on as homogenous a participant set as possible. For instance, the formal theoretician may ask just one or two prototypical speakers for grammaticality judgments or for citation form readings, while the descriptively oriented sociolinguist might limit their community recruitment efforts to lifelong, nonmobile residents whose vernaculars have presumably not been influenced by other language varieties.

Studies that have narrowed their scope in this way have certainly expanded our knowledge of how language patterns, similar to the way in which working a physics problem with the assumption of zero friction can lead to some understanding of the way objects move in space. In the actual world, however, objects rub together, and people are rarely linguistically isolated in the way our simplifying assumptions may imply. Even individuals who are functionally monolingual regularly come into contact with others who use mutually intelligible yet saliently different varieties of their language. Exposure to new dialects can occur as the result of (one's or another's) geographic or social mobility, or even via the media. These cases of *dialect contact* can have measurable and enduring effects on the language of individual people, and when such contact occurs among a significant number of people over time, we can observe long-lasting effects on dialects at the community level. A comprehensive theory of language, whether focusing on representations of linguistic structure in the mind or patterns of language variation and change in society, must be able to account for contact effects. A prerequisite for effectively modeling these phenomena is a solid empirical understanding of the dynamics of dialect contact across different languages and sociolinguistic scenarios.

Accordingly, many types of linguists have engaged with the topic of dialect contact at varying levels of analysis and time spans. For example, phoneticians and laboratory phonologists have conducted studies on short-term exposure to new accent variants in laboratory settings, investigating the extent to which phonetic imitation is an automatic process or socially driven, as well as the linguistic constraints on phonetic shift (e.g., Babel 2010; Nielsen 2011). This work has found that phonetic convergence is mediated by various factors, including linguistic category boundaries and word frequency (Goldinger 1998; Nielsen 2011), social factors like gender and interactional role (Namy, Nygaard and Sauerteig 2002; Pardo 2006), attitudes about speaker groups (Babel 2010), and initial distance between the speaker's variety and the target voice (Kim, Horton and Bradlow 2011; Nycz and Mooney 2017). Interestingly, interaction is not always a prerequisite for convergence: talkers will also mimic disembodied voices presented over headphones or speakers (Delvaux and Soquet 2007; Goldinger 1998; Nielsen 2011), although convergence is facilitated by a visible interlocutor (Dias and Rosenblum 2011). Sociolinguists, meanwhile, have documented longer-term changes in people who have experienced extended exposure to new dialect input in the non-laboratory world—a phenomenon often referred to as *second dialect acquisition*, or SDA (Nycz 2015; Siegel 2010). This research has identified the many interacting developmental, linguistic, social, and attitudinal factors that influence whether people adopt new dialect features. These include age of arrival in a new dialect region (Chambers 1992; Kerswill 1996; Payne 1980; Tagliamonte and Molfenter 2007), the linguistic status or complexity of specific features (Chambers 1992; Kerswill 1996; Payne 1980), characteristics of the person's native dialect (Payne 1980), the composition of a person's social network and levels of exposure to other forms (Evans 2004; Foreman 2003; Walker 2014), and their attitudes toward different varieties (Nycz 2013; Sankoff 2004; Walker 2014). Sociolinguists and applied linguists have also investigated how language learners acquire new regional or social dialects of their second language (e.g., Drummond 2012; Geeslin and Gudmestad 2008; Gnevsheva, Szakay and Jansen 2021; Salgado-Robles 2018), and the extent to which SDA in an second language (L2) is subject to the same constraints as SDA in a first language (L1).

Other sociolinguists and historical linguists study language change at the community or variety level and have examined the linguistic and social conditions that underlie contact-induced changes over generations (e.g., Hinskens 2000; Kerswill and Trudgill 2005; Otheguy and Zentella 2012). Researchers with this focus typically examine scenarios involving group migration, such as the dynamics of new dialect formation in *new towns* (Britain 1997; Kerswill and Williams 2000) and postcolonial settings (Trudgill 1986; Trudgill 2008). These studies reveal how dialect mixture and feature competition ultimately lead to the creation of new local varieties. Alternatively, some researchers examine cases in which migrants enter regions where a variety of their language is already established. A common scenario involves groups of rural speakers relocating to urban areas in search of economic and social opportunities (Bortoni-Ricardo 1985; Trudgill 1974); in such cases, the rural features typically do not persist over time. More recent studies have explored the emergence of US-based dialects of Spanish like New York Spanish (Erker and Otheguy 2016; Otheguy and Zentella 2012; Otheguy, Zentella and Livert 2007) and Chicago Spanish (O'Rourke and Potowski 2016) resulting from dialect contact between speakers of different Latin American varieties. This body of research demonstrates how long-term accommodation, dialect leveling, koineization, reallocation, and simplification processes shape synchronic and diachronic variation (Britain and Trudgill 1999; Dodsworth 2017). Moreover, it emphasizes how factors like salience, linguistic complexity, and social evaluation impact which features persist over time (Auer 2006; Dodsworth 2017).

To summarize, there are two significant perspectives to consider in the study of dialect contact: one focuses on the individual while the other considers the community system. The first approach investigates how an individual's dialect as a cognitive system changes due to exposure to new input. In contrast, the latter treats dialects as social objects, shared by the communities in which they are spoken. It is essential to recognize that these two perspectives are not entirely separable, as an individual's linguistic system is shaped by their social context and the broader linguistic dynamics of the community. Similarly, community dialects are ultimately spoken by individual speakers. Therefore, it is crucial for scholars working from each of these perspectives to collaborate and communicate with each other to fully comprehend the mechanisms and outcomes of dialect contact.

Recognizing the importance of this communication, we decided to host a conference to bring together scholars working on all aspects of dialect contact, as an instantiation of the Georgetown University Round Table on Language and Linguistics (GURT). GURT is an annual conference held in Washington, DC; while the specific topic of GURT varies from year to year, each meeting shares a commitment to examining some aspect of language from multiple, interdisciplinary perspectives and invites scholars from various linguistic subfields to speak and submit papers. Due to the ongoing COVID pandemic, our GURT was held online in March 2022, in the virtual meeting space of Gather.town. At first, we ruefully acknowledged the irony of hosting a contactless conference on the topic of dialect contact (!), but any worries we had about the quality of the meeting were quickly dispelled by the engagement of nearly a hundred meeting attendees from around the world, who cheerfully ran their 8-bit avatars around the virtual conference center, gave insightful and thought-provoking presentations, and contributed to energetic and fruitful discussions after and between talks.

The chapters in this volume, most of which are based on papers delivered during GURT, provide a wide-ranging exploration of dialect contact across a diverse set of languages and varieties spanning five continents. Together they exhibit a rich and nuanced understanding of the complexities involved in studying contact, highlighting theoretical and methodological considerations at different levels of analysis. Through their empirical contributions, they not only validate existing findings but also shed light on unique contact dynamics that are specific to particular communities or groups of speakers.

For example, a typical outcome of dialect contact at the level of the community is *leveling* towards a supraregional, more standard form (Britain 2010; Dodsworth 2017;

Trudgill 1986). Torrano-Moreno and Hernández-Campoy observe such leveling in their study of affricate variation in the Spanish spoken in Ricote, a rural town in the province of Murcia, Spain, which has become increasingly connected to larger cities where the use of standard linguistic features is common. Torrano-Moreno and Hernández-Campoy draw on spontaneous speech data and rapid-anonymous surveys to show that the autochthonous voiced variant of (ch) has given way to the voiceless supralocal variant over five generations in apparent-time, with today's adolescents having totally adopted the standard form. While the overall trend toward the standard may be unsurprising in this case, the fact that adolescents are leading initially seems to be at odds with decades of sociolinguistic research, which has consistently demonstrated that adolescents tend to favor the use of non-standard linguistic features (Cheshire 1982; Coates 2015), whether in cases of stable variation, changes from below, or changes from above due to contact from outside the community. In the last case, adolescents typically lag behind adults because they are not (yet) directly exposed to the new prestige variants or subject to relevant marketplace pressures. In Ricote, however, adolescents (unlike their elders) are the ones who frequently commute to the city for education and leisure and are therefore regularly exposed to standard linguistic features. As a result, the authors argue, these adolescents are orienting their language practices toward the standard linguistic market.

Local dialect attrition is also the focus of Beaman's chapter, which presents both apparent-time and real-time trend study data to examine the use of dialect features by Swabian speakers in the face of regular contact with Standard German. Beaman's quantitative analysis shows community-level patterns that are familiar to anyone who works on dialect contact between local and standard varieties: Swabian features are generally on the decline, both generationally and over the lifespan. That said, closer examination of speaker and variable attributes, as well as a qualitative analysis of speakers' metalinguistic commentary, reveal nuance in this generalization: younger, educated speakers with a high local orientation use more Swabian features to index pride in their Swabian identity, especially those features salient as local features per se. The contrast between young speakers of Ricote Spanish (who have completely turned their backs on at least one local feature) and young speakers of Swabian German (who have held onto certain features) drives home the importance of understanding the social circumstances, constraints, and needs of the individuals who instantiate the community-wide changes we observe.

Of course, leveling and simplification of dialect features are not the only potential outcome of contact. Al-Wer and Al-Hawamdeh argue that another possible outcome is *complication*, wherein the new dialect has more forms than those contributed by the dialects originally involved in the contact situation. Their chapter focuses on a morphological feature of the dialect of Arabic spoken in Amman, Jordan. Despite Amman's historical significance as one of the oldest inhabited places in the region, it shares similarities with what Kerswill and Williams (2005) refer to as "New Towns." This characterization stems from the fact that Amman's current sociolinguistic configuration can be traced to two founder populations of Arabic-speaking migrants from two nearby cities who arrived in the early to mid-twentieth century. The contact dynamics in new towns often result in the formation of new dialects; typically, these new dialects emerge over generations, with an initial phase characterized by extreme variability of linguistic forms, followed by a later stage where the variability decreases and the dialects start to focus. During this focusing phase, some variants are adopted by the community as a whole, while others become obsolete. If the variability persists over time, certain variants may be reallocated and become associated with specific groups of individuals of a particular national or regional heritage. In the case of Amman, however, Al-Wer and Al-Hawamdeh observe that great variability of forms is present regardless of the generation of the members of Amman's Arabic-speaking community and that regional heritage is no longer associated with the use of the variants available to speakers. Overall, their study invites us to rethink the principles of new-dialect formation and explore the mechanisms through which contact between dialects may lead to additional complexity in certain areas of the grammar.

As we have seen, dialect contact often results in convergence of forms between one or both varieties. Typically, people purposefully adopt the dialect patterns of socially prestigious groups they are in contact with, resulting in a *change from above*. However, convergence does not always occur in the direction of the higher-status group. Shapp, Marinaccio, and Singler argue that a change from *below* has occurred in Liberia, due to contact between speakers of Kolokwa English and speakers of Liberian Settler English. By all accounts, the Settlers have higher social status: the authors document relevant attitudes both in the historical record and in the metalinguistic commentary of their research participants. Yet Shapp et al.'s study reveals that the Settlers are assimilating their vowel system toward that of the Kolokwa speakers. The authors suggest that this "downward" convergence is possible due to the low perceptual salience of vowels: while other features may be consciously avoided by Settlers due to their awareness of them as Kolokwa, their realizations of vowels quietly shift toward those of the other variety, presumably due to the general tendency for speakers to converge phonetically (Babel 2010; Pickering and Garrod 2013). Their findings encourage further exploration of how factors interact in dialect contact situations, particularly the role of salience as a variable that may moderate the otherwise influential role of group social prestige.

In a similar vein, Kang considers how factors such as linguistic complexity, salience, and attitudes influence the adoption of new dialect forms by adults moving within South Korea. Previous studies of speakers migrating within-nation typically focus on movement in one direction: people from a rural region (characterized by a less prestigious, or even stigmatized dialect) relocating to a more urban one, whose dialect is relatively prestigious (e.g., Bortoni-Ricardo 1985; Kerswill 1994). Kang's chapter investigates speakers of this kind, namely, natives of the rural Korean province of Kyungsang who move to Seoul, the country's cultural and economic center, for education and employment opportunities. She is also, however, able to examine movement in the opposite direction: because several large companies also have a presence in Kyungsang, people from Seoul move to the province for jobs. Kang's study reveals an overall expected asymmetry in the use of new dialect features among these groups: the native, mobile Kyungsang speakers generally show more use of Seoul features than the native, mobile Seoul speakers do of Kyungsang features. But the reasons for this asymmetrical behavior are myriad and difficult to tease apart.

For example, Kang finds (like Shapp et al.) that less-salient features are more likely to be acquired by even the Seoul speakers in Kyungsang, though in practice salience cannot be easily disentangled from factors such as linguistic complexity, and its effect may be influenced by speaker identity and attitudes.

The difficulty of teasing apart the effects of individual variables in SDA studies is the focus of Oushiro's chapter, which draws from her extensive work on mobile speakers of Brazilian Portuguese within Brazil to illustrate how the complex social reality of mobile populations often problematizes our attempts to apply straightforward quantitative analyses. As Oushiro notes, the social characteristics of mobile speaker populations exhibit some of the same quantitative challenges as the non-mobile populations who have traditionally been the focus of sociolinguistic work. The effects of social factors are often not independent of each other but may interact in various ways: the specific effect of education level, for example, may depend on gender. Yet mobile speaker samples also present somewhat unique challenges for analysis. Factors such as Length of Residence (LoR) and Age of Arrival are often confounded in SDA studies, as speakers with long LoRs often (but not always) have them by virtue of arriving to their new region early in life. Carefully designed speaker samples can address this particular problem, but other factor relationships may be harder to tease apart. LoR and speaker attitude may be highly correlated, for example, reflecting some essential connection between these factors.

The challenges to analysis and to our ability to draw replicable conclusions are enhanced in cases when language contact occurs alongside dialect contact. Erker's contribution engages with these challenges head on via his study of dialect and language contact among Spanish speakers in two cities, New York City and Boston. Erker designed his Boston study to replicate, as closely as possible, previous work carried out in New York City (Erker and Otheguy 2016; Otheguy and Zentella 2012); both studies compare subject personal pronoun use (among other features) among immigrants and US-born Spanish speakers with origins in either Mainland Latin America or the Caribbean. On the one hand, his results show structural continuity across studies, with the same linguistic constraints conditioning linguistic phenomena in both cities. On the other hand, he finds that the two study sites are not fully comparable: the New York speakers exhibit both convergence with English structures and regional dialect leveling within Spanish, while in Boston, only a subset of speakers show convergence toward English, and speakers of different Spanish varieties do not converge toward each other. Erker's chapter highlights the intricacies of linguistic contact and the difficulty of replicability even with similarly designed studies.

Lincoln and Starr's chapter reminds us, meanwhile, that not all cases of dialect change that look contact-induced are necessarily attributable to contact. Their chapter examines t-flapping in Singapore English (SgE), an "Outer Circle" variety that has traditionally oriented toward British English for its norms but whose speakers are increasingly in contact with American English (AmE) via direct interaction with AmE speakers as well as through media exposure. T-flapping is not yet an established feature of Singapore English, but the authors have noticed some use of it, particularly in informal speech, and an intuitively appealing hypothesis is that the feature comes "from" AmE. To test whether such an account is correct, Lincoln and Starr gathered data on speakers' intuitions regarding the likelihood of flapping in various phonological contexts and lexical items, both in AmE and in the participants' own speech. The authors find that these speakers have reasonably accurate intuitions regarding the patterning of flapping in AmE—and yet, their intuitions about their *own* use of the feature departs from these patterns, suggesting that flapping has developed independently in SgE. Which is not to say that contact plays no role in the ongoing development of this feature: SgE users who have greater interpersonal contact with AmE speakers report own-usage that aligns more with AmE patterns. However, Lincoln and Starr's chapter drives home the importance of examining the fine-grained patterning of what may appear to be "the same" feature on the surface, especially when trying to make claims about the origin of those features.

Finally, Walker's chapter raises many programmatic issues around the approach to studying SDA, including the key distinction (often not engaged in SDA work) between "knowing" and "doing" in contact scenarios. In several publications Walker (2014, 2018, 2019) has examined the production and perception of new dialect forms by mobile individuals—specifically, expat Americans living in England and English expats living in the United States. These works use quantitative methods to assess the influence of factors often examined in the SDA literature—such as type of linguistic feature, topic, and amount of contact with the ambient dialect (D2)—on the use or accurate perception of D2 forms. As Walker points out in her contribution to this volume, however, "the migrant is not just a receptacle for D2 input" whose behavior is determined by linguistic and input constraints but an agent in the social world with needs and goals. Drawing on interviews she carried out with the same expats whose data she has quantitatively analyzed, here she explores the motivations of individual mobile speakers to use (or not use) features of a new dialect, observing that migrants can consciously alter their productions to achieve communicative goals—such as being understood, or avoiding judgment—in the moment.

The following chapters in this volume have made significant contributions to the study of dialect contact in various ways. They have validated previous findings that emphasize how dialect contact can lead to linguistic change, whether through leveling, reallocation, simplification, or other mechanisms. They have also shed light on the many factors influencing the direction of these changes and the nontrivial issue of how to properly disentangle their effects in actual datasets. Ultimately, they all highlight the importance of considering contact dynamics specific to the communities and individuals under investigation. Accordingly, we stress the need for further research encompassing a broader range of languages, including signed dialects, in more regions, and in communities representing a range of sociolinguistic scenarios. We hope that the valuable insights provided by the chapters in this volume will inspire other linguists, particularly early-career researchers, to contemplate how the approaches outlined here can be extended to the examination of communities they are interested in or have special access to. By doing so, we can enhance our comprehension of the intricate dynamics and linguistic results that unfold when people who speak differently communicate with one another.

Acknowledgments

We have many to thank for making this volume possible, starting with the institutions and people who supported our GURT conference. We are very grateful to the Department of Linguistics and the Faculty of Languages and Linguistics at Georgetown University for financial and administrative support of the 2022 GURT. A conference grant from the National Science Foundation (award #BCS-2017415) also provided crucial funding that enabled us to offer free registration for all conference presenters, increasing the accessibility of the meeting. The conference also benefited from the work of several excellent graduate student assistants—Yoojin Kang, Ping Hei Yeung, and Yilun Zhu—who built the Gather.town environment, supervised registration, and provided AV support (among myriad other tasks). We thank graduate student Abby Killam for her work on formatting and other assistance in polishing each chapter for publication. Last but not least, we appreciate Hope LeGro at Georgetown University Press for stellar communication and support throughout the process of preparing this volume. We also express our gratitude to the press for hosting full-resolution versions of select figures included in this volume on their website, which are accessible at the following link: press.georgetown.edu/Book/Dialect-Contact

Note

1. E.g., by the Linguistic Society of America, whose website tagline is "Advancing the Scientific Study of Language Since 1924" (https://www.linguisticsociety.org/).

References

Auer, Peter. 2006. Mobility, contact and accommodation. In Carmen Llamas, Louise Mullany and Peter Stockwell (eds.), *The Routledge companion to sociolinguistics*. London: Routledge, 2006, 109–15.

Babel, Molly. 2010. Dialect convergence and divergence in New Zealand English. *Language in Society* 39 (4): 437–56.

Bortoni-Ricardo, Stella Maris. 1985. *The urbanization of rural dialect speakers: A sociolinguistic study in Brazil*. Cambridge: Cambridge University Press.

Britain, David. 1997. Dialect contact, focusing and phonological rule complexity: The Koineisation of Fenland English. *University of Pennsylvania Working Papers in Linguistics* 4 (1): 141–69.

Britain, David. 2010. Contact and dialectology. In Raymond Hickey (ed.), *The handbook of language contact*. Oxford: Blackwell, 208–29.

Britain, David and Peter Trudgill. 1999. Migration, new-dialect formation and sociolinguistic refunctionalisation: Reallocation as an outcome of dialect contact. *Transactions of the Philologica Society* 97 (2): 245–56.

Chambers, J. K. 1992. Dialect acquisition. *Language* 68 (4): 673–705.

Cheshire, Jenny. 1982. *Variations in an English dialect: A sociolinguistic study*. Cambridge: Cambridge University Press.

Coates, Jennifer. 2015. *Women, men and language: A sociolinguistic account of gender differences in language* (3rd ed.). London: Routledge.

Delvaux, Véronique and Alain Soquet. 2007. The influence of ambient speech on adult speech productions through unintentional imitation. *Phonetica* 64 (2–3): 145–73.

Dias, James W. and Lawrence D. Rosenblum. 2011. Visual influences on interactive speech alignment. *Perception* 40 (12): 1457–66.

Dodsworth, Robin. 2017. Migration and dialect contact. *Annual Review of Linguistics* 3 (1): 331–46.

Drummond, Rob. 2012. Aspects of identity in a second language: ING variation in the speech of Polish migrants living in Manchester, UK. *Language Variation and Change* 24 (1): 107–33.

Erker, Daniel and Ricardo Otheguy. 2016. Contact and coherence: Dialectal leveling and structural convergence in NYC Spanish. *Lingua* 172–73: 131–46.

Evans, Betsy E. 2004. The role of social network in the acquisition of local dialect norms by Appalachian migrants in Ypsilanti, Michigan. *Language Variation and Change* 16 (2): 153–67.

Foreman, Annik. 2003. *Pretending to be someone you're not: A study of second dialect acquisition in Australia*. Unpublished PhD dissertation, Monash University, Melbourne.

Geeslin, Kimberly L. and Aarnes Gudmestad. 2008. The acquisition of variation in second-language Spanish. *Journal of Applied Linguistics and Professional Practice* 5 (2): 137–57.

Gnevsheva, Ksenia, Anita Szakay and Sandra Jansen. 2021. Lexical preference in second dialect acquisition in a second language. *International Journal of Bilingualism* 26 (2): 163–80.

Goldinger, Stephen D. 1998. Echoes of echoes? An episodic theory of lexical access. *Psychological Review* 105 (2): 251–79.

Hinskens, Frans. 2000. Dialect levelling: A two-dimensional process. *Folia Linguistica* 32 (1–2): 35–51.

Kerswill, Paul. 1994. *Dialects converging: Rural speech in urban Norway*. Oxford: Clarendon.

Kerswill, Paul. 1996. Children, adolescents, and language change. *Language Variation and Change* 8 (2): 177–202.

Kerswill, Paul and Peter Trudgill. 2005. The birth of new dialects. In Peter Auer, Frans Hinskens and Paul Kerswill (eds.), *Dialect change: Convergence and divergence in European languages*. Cambridge: Cambridge University Press, 196–220.

Kerswill Paul and Ann Williams. 2000. Creating a new town koine: Children and language change in Milton Keynes. *Language in Society* 29 (1): 65–115.

Kerswill, Paul and Ann Williams. 2005. New towns and koineization: Linguistic and social correlates. *Linguistics* 43 (5): 1023–48.

Kim, Midam, William S. Horton and Ann R. Bradlow. 2011. Phonetic convergence in spontaneous conversations as a function of interlocutor language distance. *Laboratory Phonology* 2 (1): 125–56.

Namy, Laura. L., Lynne C. Nygaard and Denise Sauerteig. 2002. Gender differences in vocal accommodation: The role of perception. *Journal of Language and Social Psychology* 21 (4): 422–32.

Nielsen, Kuniko. 2011. Specificity and abstraction of VOT imitation. *Journal of Phonetics* 39 (2): 132–42.

Nycz, Jennifer. 2013. New contrast acquisition: Methodological issues and theoretical implications. *English Language and Linguistics* 17 (2): 325–57.

Nycz, Jennifer. 2015. Second dialect acquisition: A sociophonetic perspective. *Language and Linguistics Compass* 9 (11): 469–82.

Nycz, Jennifer and Shannon Mooney. 2017. Variable vowel convergence in a cooperative task. Poster presented at New Ways of Analyzing Variation 46, Madison, WI, November 3.

O'Rourke, Erin and Kim Potowski. 2016. Phonetic accommodation in a situation of Spanish dialect contact: Coda /s/ and /r̄/ in Chicago. *Studies in Hispanic and Lusophone Linguistics* 9 (2): 355–99.

Otheguy, Ricardo and Ana Celia Zentella. 2012. *Spanish in New York: Language contact, dialectal leveling and structural continuity*. New York: Oxford University Press.

Otheguy, Ricardo, Ana Celia Zentella and David Livert. 2007. Language and dialect contact in Spanish in New York: Toward the formation of a speech community. *Language* 83 (4): 770–802.

Pardo, Jennifer S. 2006. On phonetic convergence during conversational interaction. *The Journal of the Acoustical Society of America* 119 (4): 2382–93.

Payne, Arvilla. 1980. Factors controlling the acquisition of the Philadelphia dialect by out-of-state children. In William Labov (ed.), *Locating language in time and space*. New York: Academic Press, 143–78.

Pickering, Martin J. and Simon Garrod. 2013. An integrated theory of language production and comprehension. *The Behavioral and Brain Sciences* 36 (4): 329–47.

Salgado-Robles, Francisco. 2018. *Desarrollo de la competencia sociolingüística por aprendices de español en un contexto de inmersión en el extranjero*. Bern: Peter Lang.

Sankoff, Gillian. 2004. Adolescents, young adults and the critical period: Two case studies from "Seven Up." In Carmen Fought (ed.), *Sociolinguistic variation: Critical reflections*. Oxford: Oxford University Press, 121–39.

Siegel, Jeff. 2010. *Second dialect acquisition*. Cambridge: Cambridge University Press.

Tagliamonte, Sali A. and Sonja Molfenter. 2007. How'd you get that accent?: Acquiring a second dialect of the same language. *Language in Society* 36 (5): 649–75.

Trudgill Peter. 1974. *The social differentiation of English in Norwich*. Cambridge: Cambridge University Press.

Trudgill, Peter. 1986. *Dialects in contact*. Oxford: Blackwell.

Trudgill, Peter. 2008. Colonial dialect contact in the history of European languages: On the irrelevance of identity to new-dialect formation. *Language in Society* 37 (2): 241–80.

Walker, Abby. 2014. *Crossing oceans with voices and ears: Second dialect acquisition and topic-based shifting in production and perception*. Unpublished PhD dissertation, The Ohio State University Columbus.

Walker, Abby. 2018. The effect of long-term second dialect exposure on sentence transcription in noise. *Journal of Phonetics* 71: 162–76.

Walker, Abby. 2019. The role of dialect experience in topic-based shifts in speech production. *Language Variation and Change* 31 (2): 135–63.

Chapter 2

Dialect Leveling and Supralocalization in a Rural Community: Generational Change from 7:35 P.M. to 8:30 P.M. in Ricote

LAURA TORRANO-MORENO
Comunidad Autónoma de Murcia

JUAN M. HERNÁNDEZ-CAMPOY
Universidad de Murcia

ONE OF THE MOST common outcomes in contact situations between standard and non-standard varieties is dialect leveling and supralocalization, with subsequent linguistic erosion and obsolescence. This study observes the attrition of a vernacular feature currently in action in Ricote, an isolated rural town in Murcia, as part of the process of vertical convergence toward Castilian Spanish through leveling: variable (ch) in prevocalic position, with the autochthonous realization [dʒ], and the standard one [tʃ]. The apparent-time study correlating this linguistic feature with sociodemographic groups and levels of formality showed age-, gender- and style-based patterns of behavior. We account for these patterns via a new conception of people's spatiality after an increase in education and mundane mobility. The evidence suggests that the vernacular feature is nearing its loss, with dialect contact potentially being one of the main causes.

Supralocalization and Dialect Attrition

Rural dialect attrition constitutes a typical linguistic outcome of leveling in contact situations between rural and standard dialects. In horizontal and vertical processes of dialect convergence (Auer 2018, 161–62), the competition between varieties in terms of preference, choice, and usage has been traditionally unbalanced in favor of the powerful one because of status, prestige, social functions, written version availability, and codification: "Since one product of convergent linguistic accommodation is levelling, highly local dialect forms are often beginning to be eroded, levelled away in favor of spatially more widely distributed variants" (Britain 2010, 197; see also Røyneland 2011; Siebenhaar 2011).

Additionally, increased geographical mobility and urbanization lead to contact between rural and urban dialects and thus to leveling and koineization (Britain 2018; Trudgill 1986): "Dialect levelling involves the eradication of socially marked variants (both within and between linguistic systems) in conditions of social or geographical mobility and resultant dialect contact" (L. Milroy 2002, 7). Dialect leveling may also be accelerated by conceptions of people's spatiality, as mundane mobility is currently blurring the urban-rural dichotomy (Adey 2010; Champion 2009; Cresswell 2006; Merriman 2012; Urry 2000, 2007): socially, increased commuting is breaking down local networks and routines, and, linguistically, greater transience is bringing increased contact and the leveling of autochthonous dialect forms, along with the reinforcement of supralocalization in traditionally isolated communities (Britain 2009a, 2010, 2013a, 2016, 2017; Milroy and Llamas 2013; Vandekerckhove 2011).

As Haugen (1972, 266) stated, with the exception of uncommon cases of monocentric selection (Britain 2009a), many standard languages—especially those involving dominant ones, such as Spanish, English, French—have developed as the result of dialect leveling and koineization or supralocalization through polycentric selection (Deumert 2003, 2004). In these cases, "linguistic variants with a wider sociospatial currency become more widely adopted at the expense of more locally specific forms" (Britain 2010, 195), with the subsequent dialect attrition and obsolescence as a price to pay after the leveling of varieties (see also Auer and Hinskens 1996; Auer, Hinskens and Kerswill 2005; Cheshire and Stein 1997; Kerswill and William 1999, 2000; Trudgill 1986). Dialect obsolescence is thus inextricably linked to mobility and contact (Britain 2009a, 2010). But particularly isolated rural dialects are also under the potential threat of attrition through "the erosion of a traditional locally embedded dialect (including accent) feature or features in favour of one originating either from outside the community or from another group within the same community" (Britain 2009a, 123). The eradication of local marked linguistic features in favour of majority, unmarked, or simpler forms is the most reliable symptom of attrition leading to supralocalization (Britain 2013b, 176; 2018, 149).

The macroscopic process of dialect leveling is inevitably implemented through the microscopic agency of speakers at the individual level, where factors such as age, aging, and lifespan are crucial for the actuation and development of the intermediate stages of variation and change in the long run (see Beaman and Buchstaller 2020; Britain 2011; Labov 1994; Sankoff and Blondeau 2007; Wagner and Buchstaller 2018). Language change, its constancy over an individual's lifespan, and its reflection on the local community have provided us with different explanatory models in variationist sociolinguistics: age-grading, generational change, communal change, and both progressive and retrograde lifespan change. In longitudinal and cross-sectional approaches to language variation and change, the individual's age has become a key factor for the detection of change in progress. In fact, the assumption of grammar fixation in early adult speakers may cause age-related variation in the community to be interpreted as indicative of diachronic change (Labov 1994; MacKenzie 2014;

Wagner and Buchstaller 2018). Typical results in the industrialized Western World have demonstrated adolescents' adherence to the vernacular world and its local values through their use of non-standard features: Cheshire (1978, 1987) and Cheshire and Stein (1997) in Reading (England), Rampton (1995, 2006) in the south Midlands and London (England), Labov (1973) in South Central Harlem (New York City), Eckert (1989) in Belten High (Michigan), Mendoza-Denton (2008) in California gangs, Bailey (2002) in Providence (Rhode Island), or Johnstone and Kiesling (2008) in Pittsburgh (Pennsylvania), among others. As we will show, however, adolescents in contact situations may also abandon the local vernacular in favor of the standard.

Objectives

In the small rural Spanish town of Ricote, the local realization of the consonantal variable (ch) in prevocalic position has two variants: the voiced palatal affricate [dʒ], as in *ocho* (['o.dʒo]), which constitutes the non-standard local realization; and the voiceless palatal affricate [ʧ], as in *ocho* (['o.ʧo]), which comes from Standard Castilian Spanish. The latter is expanding in the local community. The voiced realization of the palatal affricate is typical in the Spanish of the Canary Islands (Almeida 1994), while fricativization of this palatal affricate consonant (realized as [ʃ]) is found mostly in western areas of Andalusian and Caribbean Spanish (Fernández de Molina Ortés and Hernández-Campoy 2018; Harjus 2018; Hernández-Campoy and Villena-Ponsoda 2009; Villena-Ponsoda 2008). However, the realization found in Ricote is not a typical dialectal feature currently characterizing Murcian Spanish nor has it been mentioned in traditional dialectological descriptions of the region (Alvar 1996; Lapesa [1942] 1988; Penny 1991, 2000; Zamora-Vicente [1960] 1989). In fact, the voiced variant is probably a remnant of an old feature that did not change until recently given the isolation of the community in Ricote. That is, in medieval times, the voiced affricate was a phoneme and started to compete with its voiceless counterpart in the fourteenth century, with the voiced variant losing ground in the fifteenth century.

In this context of rural dialect attrition through dialect leveling, as a result of contact, the aim of this study is the observation of this linguistic change in progress within the local community of Ricote and its sociogeographically oriented account. We also measure the sociolinguistic vitality and esteem of this variant, to reveal the nature of this change (if any), as well as its origin, its motivations, any socially and/or stylistically conditions, and the leaders of the change.

Methodology

Area under Research: Ricote

Ricote is a small agriculture-based town located on a quiet isolated mountain valley plain in the heart of the Region of Murcia in southeastern Spain, with a fertile landscape of citrus fruit and palm trees watered by the Segura River. Outward migration of younger people since the mid-twentieth century after the Spanish Civil War (1936–39) and especially during the 1980s has negatively affected Ricote's demography and economy. After a peak of 2,999 inhabitants in 1910, the town had a population of

1,275 Ricoteños in 2022; when this study was carried out, between 2014 and 2015, there were 1,398 inhabitants. Interaction with non-residents decreases with the friction of distance and population size (Hernández-Campoy 2003), and Ricote is highly constrained by these factors. Migration, together with its geographically isolated location due to physical barriers (mountains and river), and the subsequent low contact with urban areas and Murcia city, make Ricote a highly endocentric and conservative community (Andersen 1988).

Linguistic Situation

With the exception of the voicing of the affricate palatal consonant, the Spanish spoken in Ricote is essentially Murcian, a non-standard Spanish variety. Murcian is a predominantly southern transition dialect, sharing features with Valencian Catalan, Castilian, Aragonese, and Andalusian Spanish (Hernández-Campoy 2008; Monroy-Casas and Hernández-Campoy 2015). Sociolinguistically, Murcian Spanish has traditionally been stereotyped as a highly vernacular accent, with connotations of ruralness and unfavorable attitudes for both outsiders and insiders (Hernández-Campoy 2008). The dialect also carries covert prestige (Jiménez-Cano 2001), as sometimes found in communities of linguistic insecurity among local speakers with a strong double-consciousness situation (Labov [1966] 2006). The two researchers of the present study are Murcian, and one of them originally comes from and lives in Ricote, which has an important advantage for the selection of the variables, the obtainment of data, and the analysis of results and their interpretation, as advocated by Trudgill (1983, 41): "Wherever possible, field-workers should be native of the area, or people familiar with the local dialect."

Dependent and Independent Variables

The sociolinguistic variable under study is the realization of consonant (ch) in onset position,[1] with its two variants in Ricote: the voiceless palatal affricate [ʧ], as found in *chocolate* [ʧo.koˈ.la.te] 'chocolate', *lechuga* [leˈ.ʧu.ɣa] 'lettuce', or *coche* ([ˈko.ʧe]) 'car', which comes from Standard Castilian Spanish and is now increasingly expanding in the local community; and the voiced palatal affricate [ʤ], realized as [ʤo.koˈ.la.te], [leˈ.ʤu.ɣa], and ([ˈko.ʤe]), which constitutes the non-standard autochthonous realization and is currently receding in local speech. For a reliable binary coding of data into voiced and voiceless, spectrograms of the recordings containing this variable were visually inspected in Praat (version 5.4.04; Boersma and Weenink 2014).

Given that the linguistic feature under observation seems to be a change in progress within the local community, according to the fieldworker's native knowledge of the speech area, the study focuses on "age" and "gender" as sociodemographic predictor variables. Sociolinguistic studies carried out in the industrialized Western World have demonstrated that young female informants are recurrently in the vanguard of innovations, thus evidencing the role of gender-based (and even age-based) variation in patterns of language change, when these take place in the direction of the prestige variety. Despite following a traditional Western sociolinguistic approach, the role of the typical factor of socioeconomic status was not examined because of the small size of the town, its eminently rural economy, and the endocentric and conservative characterization of the community. These factors mean that social class (a sociologically linear construct) as applied here would be blurred at the edges, methodologically inaccurate, and thus less relevant for the correlation of linguistic and non-linguistic data.[2]

Data Collection

Sociolinguistic variability involves not only some causal relationships between sociodemographic factors and a particular linguistic realization but also different linguistic realizations within the same sociodemographic group according to the situational context and formality: i.e., inter-speaker and intra-speaker variation (Bell 1984). Assuming that careful language production increases progressively with formality and degree of speech self-monitoring, as suggested by Labov ([1966] 2006), two styles were used in this research: casual speech (informal) and emphatic (formal) through uncontrolled observation. Therefore, the data collection process consisted of two steps: a sociolinguistic interview (Test-1) and a rapid and anonymous interview (Test-2), allowing us to examine stylistic differentiation.

Test-1 was based on the observation of natural and spontaneous speech produced in casual situations of family conversations but part of a sociolinguistic interview. The context allowed informants' attention to be generally diverted away from how they speak—requiring the lowest amount level of conscious self-monitoring—which is assumed to be closest to the vernacular: "the style in which they argue with their nearest and dearest, scold their children, or pass the time of day with their friends" (Labov [1966] 2006, 64). Forty-three samples of 10 minutes of average length were recorded by the native Ricote coauthor. Recordings were made using an Olympus PCM digital recorder (LS-P1) with a sampling rate of 44.1 kHz and an internal microphone. A total number of 305 tokens were used (213 standard forms and 92 non-standard ones).

Test-2 consisted of the observation of variable (ch) in different styles elicited through rapid and anonymous surveying, as Labov ([1966] 2006, 40–57) pioneeringly designed in his study on the use of postvocalic /r/ by employees at three department stores of New York City. That is, we examined the sociolinguistic behavior of informants when employing variable (ch) in two distant levels of formality. But given that there are no department stores in Ricote, the native Ricote fieldworker, Laura, adopted Labov's procedure for eliciting samples of natural speech for both styles (casual/informal and emphatic/formal) through a rapid and anonymous survey adapted to the circumstances and characteristics of a small locality where everybody knows each other. During the experiment and in a relatively simple situation, every evening, from 7:35 P.M. to 8:30 P.M., Laura went for a walk through the town accompanied by a family member (usually her mother) and selectively approached neighbors to ask them casually what the time was: *¡Hola! ¿Me puede(s) decir la hora?* 'Hello! Can you tell me what time it is?'. Obviously, the answer was forced to include the numeral *ocho* 'eight' in Spanish that contains the consonant under research: from approximately *Las ocho menos veinticinco* 'Twenty-five to eight' to *Las ocho y media* 'Half past eight'. Like Labov, after the first and most uncareful answer, the fieldworker pretended not to hear well, which provoked a repetition of the phrase: *¿Perdón?* 'Excuse me?'. This way, she would usually obtain an additional utterance spoken in a more careful style under emphatic stress.

Like Labov ([1966] 2006), this approach allowed the collection of tokens of the (ch) variable in two stylistic contexts (the initial utterance and the more careful repetition) while, in turn, overcoming the difficulties of the observer's paradox when entering the local community. Particularly useful was the collaboration of an accompanying person in order to make the situation for the diagnostic query more relaxed, casual, and trivial. The fieldworker carried a notebook to take note of the pronunciation immediately after the question, as well as the age, gender, and other characteristics of the respondents as Labov did. A total number of 80 tokens were used (57 standard forms and 23 non-standard ones). Supplementing the spontaneous speech data was desirable given the low frequency of the variable in natural speech, as we will see below.

Informants

Fifty native Ricote residents participated in Test-1: 25 males and 25 females (table 2.1). They were arranged in five age groups, which provided us with 43 samples and 305 tokens from those 50 informants.[3] The number of tokens is constrained by the low presence of this variable in Spanish words: while vowels represent 46.2% and consonants 53.8% of the sounds in Spanish, the frequency of appearance of <ch> is just 0.32% (Pérez 2003). In Test-2, 40 native residents participated: 20 males and 20 females, also classified in five age groups, yielding 80 tokens. The smaller number of informants and tokens here is due to the characteristics of data gathering in a rapid and anonymous survey: (1) the difficulties in avoiding the repetition of the question about the time to the same reduced number of native informants met in the few streets of such a small town, and (2) the use of a specific diagnostic word. With some exceptions and given the random nature of encounters, participants in Test-1 were not the same as in Test-2, where the small size of the community made the age of informants easy to gather—especially with the assistance of the coauthor's mother.

The correlation of linguistic, sociodemographic (age and gender), and stylistic (careful/uncareful speech) variables allowed us to analyze the sociolinguistic behavior of Ricoteños and measure the supralocalization process (adoption of the Castilian Spanish feature [ʧ]), if any, and hence dialect attrition, or, conversely, the maintenance of the non-standard local form [ʤ] and their tendencies diachronically.

Results and Analysis

Test-1: Casual Conversation

Detecting Language Change

Figure 2.1 and table 2.2 show the use of the standard, voiceless variant of (ch) by speakers in Test-1 according to the independent parameters of age and gender. Inferential statistics through a non-parametric Pearson's chi-square test of significance confirms that the different scores in our Ricote informants by age, gender, and also pooled did not occur by chance: the relationship is significant among males ($\chi^2 = 36.411$; df $= 4$;

Table 2.1. Informants and age groups used in Ricote to study variable (ch)

			Informants		
Test	**Tokens**	**Age groups**	**Gender**	**Number**	**Total**
Test-1	305	**Group 1: 10–19**	*Male*	5	50
			Female	5	
		Group 2: 20–34	*Male*	5	
			Female	5	
		Group 3: 35–49	*Male*	5	
			Female	5	
		Group 4: 50–64	*Male*	5	
			Female	5	
		Group 5: 65+	*Male*	5	
			Female	5	
Test-2	80	**Group 1: 10–19**	*Male*	4	40
			Female	4	
		Group 2: 20–34	*Male*	4	
			Female	4	
		Group 3: 35–49	*Male*	4	
			Female	4	
		Group 4: 50–64	*Male*	4	
			Female	4	
		Group 5: 65+	*Male*	4	
			Female	4	

$p \leq 0.01$), females ($\chi^2 = 27.478$; df $= 4$; $p \leq 0.01$), and combined ($\chi^2 = 62.689$; df $= 4$; $p \leq 0.01$). While there are only 305 total tokens for a great number of 50 participants (balanced by age/gender) for Test-1 ($n = 50$), the homogeneous distribution of tokens counts across age and gender prevented the results from being driven by a few individuals with relatively high token counts.

As figure 2.1 and table 2.2 show for pooled results (both males and females together), the group with lowest frequencies in the use of the standard variant is Group 5 (older than 65: 48.8%), followed by Group 4 (ages 50–64) with 50.7%, with no significant statistical difference between these two age groups (Fisher's exact test: $p > 0.05$ [two-tailed test: 0.1388]). It is then with Group 3 (ages 35–49) that frequencies of the local standard variant start to increase in use notably (80%, and significantly at $p \leq 0.05$), then G2 (ages 20–34) with 92.7%, until the full use of the standard form in the youngest generation (G1: ages 10–19 with 100%), which means total attrition of the local form and the subsequent completed dialect leveling. The Pearson correlation coefficient indicates that the use of the innovative form [ʧ] and the age of informants are very strongly correlated, showing a monotonic negative relationship

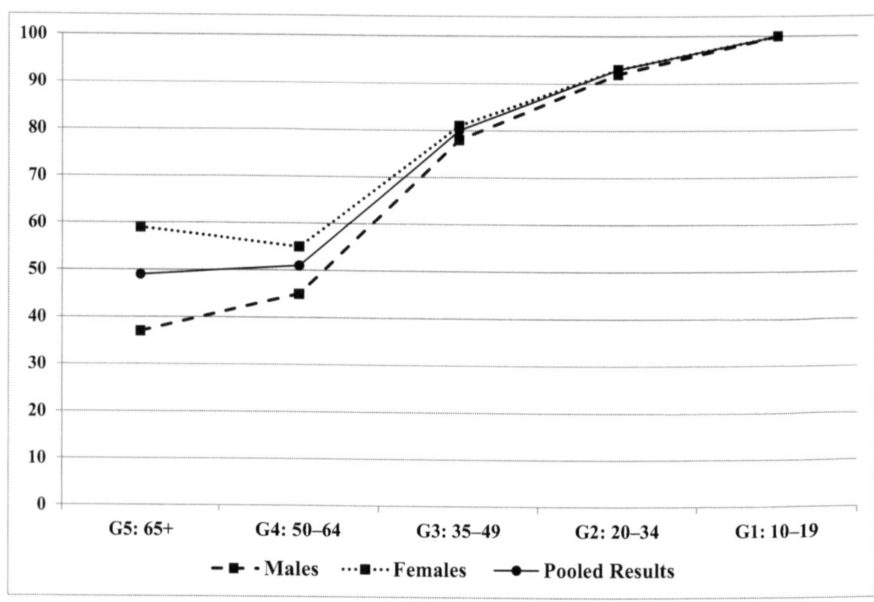

Figure 2.1. Percentages for the standard variant [t͡ʃ] in the y-axis in Ricote according to age, gender, and pooled results (Test-1)

Table 2.2. Scores for the use of variable (ch) in Ricote per age and gender: casual conversations (Test-1)

Age	Gender	Total token count	Rate of standard variant	Rate of standard variant (both genders)
G1: 10–19	Male	17	100%	100%
	Female	22	100%	
G2: 20–34	Male	24	91.7%	92.7%
	Female	31	93.4%	
G3: 35–49	Male	23	78.3%	80%
	Female	37	81.1%	
G4: 50–64	Male	29	44.8%	50.7%
	Female	38	55.3%	
G5: 65+	Male	38	36.8%	48.8%
	Female	46	58.7%	
Total	Male	131	64.1%	69.8%
	Female	174	74.1%	

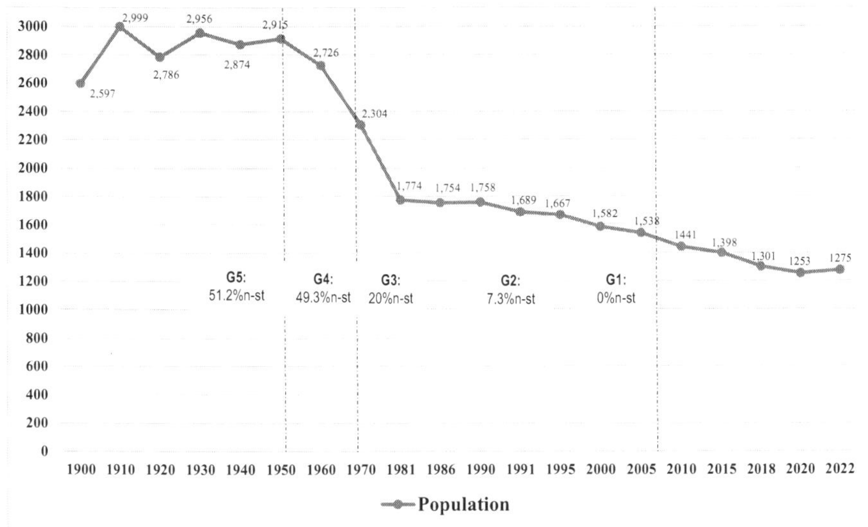

Figure 2.2. Evolution in Ricote population from 1900 to 2022 and year of birth and childhood of informants (data from Instituto Nacional de Estadística; n-st = non-standard usage)*

between age and the use of the standard Castilian form (with a R very close to−1: in pooled data, $R = -0.9706$; p value $= 0.006$; in males, $R = -0.9798$; p value $= 0.003$; in females, $R = -0.9516$; p value $= 0.012$). This means that there is an age-based inverse function here shown by a predictive model of dependency between variables in an implicational scale ordering: the younger the speaker is, the higher the frequency of the prestige variant [ʧ] coming from the national standard variety, and vice versa. The apparent-time approach allows us here to perceive that change is occurring within the local community of Ricote as for this variable: rural dialect attrition and dialect leveling. These processes are realized through a slow-but-steady progress in the use of the innovative variant individually and collectively, suggesting an age-based pattern for generational change. Each successively younger generation employs the new form more than the previous one, because "it is not only the variants but also their frequencies that are acquired during the formative years" (Nevalainen and Raumolin-Brunberg [2003] 2017, 83). The driving force for the change (the prestige of the new variant) seems to be the same after different decades and in the direction of the ongoing process taking place in the community generation after generation.

The pattern exhibited by the generational change in figure 2.2 follows a typical S-shaped curve model of diffusion (Rogers [1962] 1995, 257–63) that affects its rate: a pattern with a slow initial spread due to the still low contact frequency between users of the new and the old forms, followed then by a rapid middle stage when contact is greatest, and then a slower final phase again due to saturation (see also Labov 1994, 65–66; Nevalainen and Raumolin-Brunberg [2003] 2017, 53–55). In Ricote, while intermediate age groups (G3 and G4) accelerate the process of diffusion of the linguistic change through the rapid adoption of the standard form, G5 (at the start of the change) and G1 and G2 (near the end of the change) show slower rates of change. Obviously, during the situation of variability between the standard variety and the local dialect there was a moment when the shift from heterogeneously non-standard to homogeneously standard accelerated. In fact, in combined data, a comparison of the range of variation within the sociolinguistic behavior of Ricoteños (see Cantos 2013, 9–10) allows us to see that the oldest generations (G5 and G4) exhibit, by far, a much higher range of variation (62.08 and 49.29 respectively) than the youngest informants (G1:–8.07 and G2:–3.7). Similar patterns of variation are obtained in results for males and females. This means that the process of change for dialect leveling consists of a gradual shift from a heterogeneously non-standard sociolinguistic behavior in the oldest groups G5 and G4 to a homogeneously standard sociolinguistic practice in the youngest generations (G1 and G2), following the usual sequence of categorical use of the conservative form to the categorical use of the innovative one after intermediate stages of covariation with both.

This age-based pattern of functional relationship also occurs in both male ($R=0.96$) and female ($R=0.90$) groups separately, as the Pearson correlation coefficients suggest. However, the application of a logistic regression analysis reveals that a combination of factors—specifically age and gender—does not collectively have any effect on the use of the innovative form [ʧ], with both sociodemographic groups running in the same direction: statistically it is only age that is a significant predictor for the use of the standard form, not gender. The only statistically significant gender-based difference occurs in the frequencies of the oldest informants (Group 5), with higher use of the standard variant in females (G5: 58.7%) than in males (G5: 36.8%), as the chi-square tests also indicates ($\chi^2 = 3.9775$; df$= 1$; $p \leq 0.05$).

As shown in table 2.3, a fixed-effects analysis confirmed that "Age group" is a significant conditioning factor in the use that informants from Ricote make of the standard variant ([ʧ]) of variable (ch). More specifically, G2 is the age group that will favor most the use of the standard variant, followed by G3. On the contrary, G4 and G5 will operate as disfavoring effects in said use, being the non-standard variant more prone to emerge in G5.[4] Our analysis also indicated that "Gender" just barely failed to reach significance as a conditioning factor for use of the standard variant of (ch). However, it is noteworthy to point out that female informants will favor most the use of this variant. This result suggests that female speakers were leading the change until male speakers joined them sometime later, probably as a result of (1) the leveling effect of education, (2) the increasing contact with the standard variety, and thus (3) the greater social pressure to conform to the national prestige model.

Evaluating Language Change

The apparent loss of the vernacular variant [ʤ] traditionally used in Ricote instead of the standard [ʧ], as well as the erosion of other dialectal features,[5] is thus part of the general process of dialect leveling toward Castilian Spanish that is occurring in Murcia. The acceleration of the ongoing linguistic change can be accounted for given the changing sociohistorical circumstances of Ricote (figure 2.2). The population born by the 1950s (G5) suffered the direct and immediate consequences of the

Table 2.3. Fixed effects analysis: contribution of "Age group" (9.14e–10) and "Gender" (0.0505) to the probability of the standard variant ([tʃ]) of variable (ch) being used by informants from Ricote (Test-1)

Variable	Log odds	N	% Standard use	Factor weight
Age group				
G2	1.592	55	0.927	0.831
G3	0.393	60	0.800	0.597
G4	−0.958	67	0.507	0.277
G5	−1.026	84	0.488	0.264
Gender				
Female	0.277	152	0.704	0.569
Male	−0.277	114	0.588	0.431
Misc. 1	$N = 266$; df = 5; Intercept = 0.951; Overall proportion = 0.654; Centered input probability = 0.721.			
Misc. 2	Log likelihood = −147.081; AIC (Akaike information criterion) = 304.161; AICc (corrected AIC) = 304.392; Dxy = 0.485; $R^2 = 0.266$.			

Spanish Civil War (1936–39) as a prolonged postwar period, with severe famine, poverty, and illiteracy spread throughout the country. Group 4 was also affected by this situation, though less intensively. A good number of this population left the town of Ricote and migrated to other places, searching for better conditions and prosperity; this migration caused a dramatic decrease in the local demography, which did not have contact with the outside, nor access to education. Group 3 consists of people who grew up with access to primary and secondary education and without experiencing the direct effects of postwar insecurity and impoverishment. In fact, the intensity of population loss became much slower in the early 1980s, which had a clear linguistic impact. Between the late 1970s and early 1980s, when the new generations (G3) were between the ages of 5 and 10 and in their teens, is the moment when this group adopted the standard realization more regularly—chiefly through schooling—as also reflected in the decrease in their frequencies of the local form from 49.3% to 20%. Educational, social, and economic factors played a crucial competing influence in favor of the leveling process of the non-standard areas, as suggested by Hernández-Campoy and Jiménez-Cano (2003): (1) a rise in the educational level achieved, with a subsequent notable decrease in illiteracy during the last 40 years, which fosters standardization as writing exerts a decisive potential and prescriptivist control of speech (Milroy 2001, 531; Penny 2000, 194); and (2) the close relationship between spelling and pronunciation in Spanish. Age, therefore, is a determining factor at this stage since those informants who grew up in the 1960s and early 1970s (G4: 49.3%) had their training fully during the Franco period, while those in the 1980s and 1990s (G3: 20% and G2: 7.3%) enjoyed a different educational system and policy that made a considerable difference in their relative sociolinguistic behavior. Later, in the early 2000s, the community progressively became more middle class: education and prosperity flourished, and the working-class social space was increasingly filled by immigrants; mobility increased thanks to improvements in road connections and transportation provisions; and access to higher education expanded to a more universal range for G1. All these societal changes were inevitably leading to the full obsolescence of the local variant [ʤ] (0%).

Test-2: Rapid and Anonymous Survey
Linguistic Change from Sociodemographic Perspectives: Age and Gender
Figure 2.3 and table 2.4 show the results for Test-2, with combined scores for both the casual and emphatic answers registered in rapid and anonymous surveying through uncontrolled observation, plotting the standard and non-standard variants of variable (ch) as a function of age and gender in Ricote.

As figure 2.3 shows, both male and female informants exhibit a steady increasing relationship between age (youth) and the use of the national prestige form. Rates appear to be slightly higher in females across the generations. This pattern might be reflecting the values in gender-based sociolinguistic behavior, with women's speech tending to be more self-conscious and class-conscious than that of men's (Trudgill 1972, 183), and suggesting that women appear to be the leaders of the linguistic change in Ricote. Additionally, as Holmes (1997, 199) points out, "Women are often

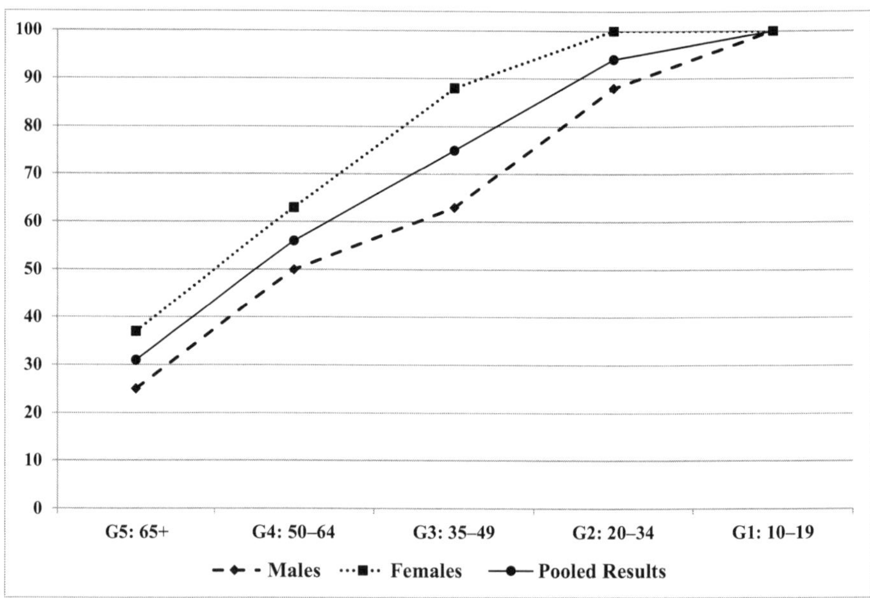

Figure 2.3. Results in percentages for the standard variant [ʧ] in Ricote according to age, gender, and pooled results in rapid and anonymous survey (Test-2)

Table 2.4. Use of the standard variant in the rapid and anonymous survey

| Groups | Gender | Answer Type | | Subtotal | Total |
		Spontaneous answer	Emphatic answer		
G1: 10–19	*Male*	100%	100%	100%	100%
		4/4	4/4	8/8	16/16
	Female	100%	100%	100%	
		4/4	4/4	8/8	
G2: 20–34	*Male*	75%	100%	88%	94%
		3/4	4/4	7/8	15/16
	Female	100%	100%	100%	
		4/4	4/4	8/8	
G3: 35–49	*Male*	50%	75%	63%	75%
		2/4	3/4	5/8	12/16
	Female	75%	100%	88%	
		3/4	4/4	7/8	
G4: 50–64	*Male*	25%	75%	50%	56%
		1/4	3/4	4/8	9/16
	Female	50%	75%	62%	
		2/4	3/4	5/8	
G5: 65+	*Male*	25%	25%	25%	31%
		1/4	1/4	2/8	5/16
	Female	0%	75%	37%	
		0/4	3/4	3/8	
Subtotal	*Male*	55%	75%	65%	71%
		11/20	15/20	26/40	57/80
	Female	65%	90%	78%	
		13/20	18/20	31/40	
Total		60%	83%	71%	
		24/40	33/40	57/80	

the family brokers in interaction with outsiders: it is more often women than men who interact with others in shops and neighborhood interactions, as well as in communications with schools, and between institutional bureaucracies and the family . . . women's social activities and jobs often involve them in interaction with a wider range of social contacts than men's."

Linguistic Change from Stylistic Perspectives: Intra-speaker Variation
The main motivation for the application behind Test-2 was to stimulate our informants to produce answers using variable (ch) under different levels of formality—in

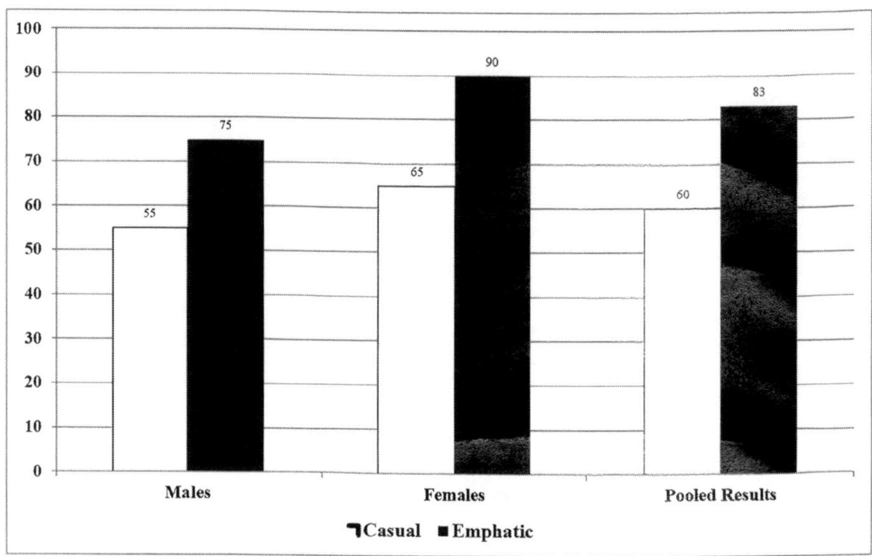

Figure 2.4. Results for the standard use ([ʧ]) of variable (ch) in both casual and emphatic answers in Ricote according to gender and pooled results: rapid and anonymous survey (Test-2)

the Labovian sense—in order to observe their sociolinguistic behavior: spontaneous answers (uncareful casual speech) versus emphatic answers (careful speech).

According to figure 2.4, style has a strong influence on the sociolinguistic behavior of Ricoteños, with use of the Castilian form reaching 60% in spontaneous answers and 83% in emphatic answers. Similar patterns are seen when observing the behavior of age groups and style (figure 2.5). The more careful the speech is, the higher the frequencies of the prestige standard variant [ʧ], revealing the vertical process of convergence and dialect leveling, which is most advanced in the local community in formal styles and appears later in informal ones.

As shown in table 2.5, a fixed-effects analysis confirmed that "Age group" is a significant conditioning factor in the use that informants from Ricote make of the standard variant ([ʧ]) of variable (ch). More specifically, G2 is the age group that will favor most the use of the standard variant, followed by G3. On the contrary, G4 and G5 will operate as disfavoring effects in said use, the non-standard variant being more prone to emerge in G5. Furthermore, our analysis also indicated that "Answer type" significantly affects the odds of using the standard variant of (ch)— spontaneous answers elicit significantly lower rates of [ʧ] than emphatic responses— whereas "Gender" failed to reach significance. Nevertheless, it is noteworthy to point out that male informants giving spontaneous answers will still favor most the use of the non-standard variant. This suggest that Ricoteñas are leading this change in the direction of the standard, albeit moderately, as claimed by Trudgill (1972) for the linguistic communities of Western societies: for all age groups in this study (except in

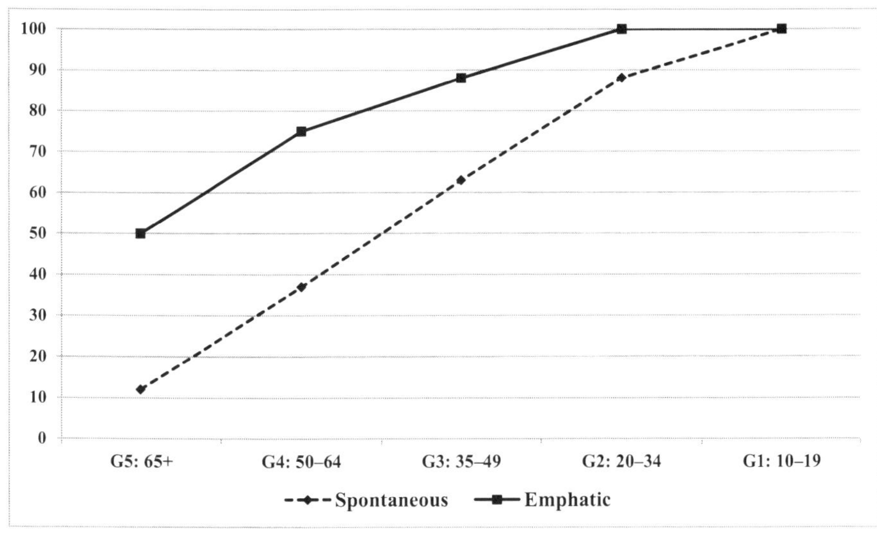

Figure 2.5. Results in percentages for the standard variant [ʧ] in Ricote according to age and styles (Test-2)

the youngest generation where the change is complete), women consistently exhibit higher frequencies of the prestige form coming from the standard Castilian Spanish variety.

Although the different age groups and gender groups exhibit different levels of usage of the variable observed, the stylistic evaluation of the different variants follows the same sociolinguistic pattern: speakers of all sociodemographic groups change their pronunciation in exactly the same direction, i.e., increasing the use of the prestige form ([ʧ]) in their speech as the stylistic context becomes more formal, as Labov ([1966] 2006, 141) found in New York.

If anything, the style effect is most easily seen among oldest speakers (women, chiefly), because the younger speakers are already using so much standard in the spontaneous utterances that they cannot go much higher in the emphatic. But this transition is not so clear in the groups of older speakers (men, mostly), probably due to their lack of education and thus high illiteracy rate, as well as less contact with the standard. Crucially, for the implementation of the standard form, age-, gender-, and style-based differences in use of the Castilian form are fully leveled among youngest informants (G1 and G2) at the expense of the local variant.

Although the apparent-time approach does not allow us to examine the progress over individuals' lifetimes, this change is not a case of age-grading. Instead, it seems to be a clear case of generational change given the linearity rather than cyclicity of the patterns exhibited and the robustness in frequencies by the leaders of change (the youngest generations), with each generation progressively increasing the use of the innovating variant within the local community. In fact, the dissimilar sociolinguistic behavior between the most distant age groups (G1 and G5) is a piece of evidence that

Table 2.5. Fixed effects analysis: contribution of "Age group" (0.000285), "Answer type" (0.00511), and "Gender" (0.107), the standard variant ([ʧ]) of variable (ch) being used by informants from Ricote (Test-2)

Variable	Log odds	N	% Use of the standard	Factor weight
Age group				
G2	2.196	16	0.938	0.9
G3	0.400	16	0.750	0.599
G4	−0.645	16	0.562	0.344
G5	−1.950	16	0.312	0.125
Answer type				
Emphatic	0.919	40	0.781	0.715
Spontaneous	−0.919	40	0.500	0.285
Gender				
Female	0.529	40	0.719	0.629
Male	−0.529	40	0.562	0.371
Misc. 1	$N = 64$; df $= 6$; Intercept $= 0.963$; Overall proportion $= 0.641$; Centered input probability $= 0.724$.			
Misc. 2	Log likelihood $= 2$–8.601; AIC (Akaike information criterion) $= 69.201$; AICc (corrected AIC) $= 70.675$; Dxy $= 0.717$; $R^2 = 0.514$.			

this linguistic situation in Ricote is not age-grading, i.e., the lack of gender- and style-based variation in the youngest group (G1), without malleability as for this linguistic feature. The independent variable "age," therefore, has been demonstrated here to be an indicator of the loss of the vernacular variant in the local community as part of the general process of dialect leveling. In both tests, the oldest informants (G5 and G4) are the most conservative, which suggests they are more attached to local values and thus the use of local features, whereas the youngest informants (G1 and G2) are leading the adoption of the prestige national standard form.

Despite typical results in the industrialized Western World (Eckert 1997) demonstrating the adolescents' adherence to the vernacular world and its non-standard features (Cheshire 1978), these data suggest that the new generations of Ricoteños may be more aware of the status and prestige of the standard variant and lead the dialect leveling process. Although the results do not provide explicit evidence of this, as native speakers of the area we know that they are likely motivated by the opportunities that the national Castilian Spanish sociolinguistic variety provides Ricoteños as opposed to their isolated linguistic and economic environment. The adoption of the standard feature becomes a way of combating geographical isolation through linguistic "onlineness," as opposed to "loneliness," especially after the new possibilities developed for mobility, connectivity, and exocentrism with commuting and hence contact (see Taylor 2003). According to human geographers, the urban-rural dichotomy is becoming blurred after the new conception of people's spatiality in late modernity (Adey 2010; Champion 2009; Cresswell 2006; Merriman 2012; Urry 2000, 2007);[6] and the resulting increased contact through intra-regional mundane mobility is breaking down local networks and routines, as well as causing the leveling of autochthonous dialect forms and the reinforcement of supralocalization (Britain 2009a, 2010, 2013a, 2017; Milroy and Llamas 2013). In fact, "intraregional mobility, whilst breaking down networks and routines at the very local level, reinforces *supralocal* structure" (Britain 2009b, 142). Education is also undoubtedly crucial for this new practice and inextricably linked to mobility, given that local adolescents from Ricote have to travel every day to the nearest town (Archena) for secondary schooling and to the capital (Murcia) for higher education, where they come into increasing contact with the standard form [ʧ]: "With improvements in transportation routes, the shift from primary and secondary to tertiary sector employment as the backbone of the economy, the expansion in higher levels of education (at sites often well away from the local speech community), the normalization of long(er)-distance commuting, labor market flexibility and the consequent geographical elasticity of family ties and other social network links have meant that these supralocal functional zones are probably larger than ever before" (Britain 2009b, 142). In this way, even in the rural communities, contact through increased routinized mobility has structural, geographical, and, crucially, linguistic consequences in everyday practices at all levels, so that, for example, the delocalization of our social life and geographical space also conveys the subsequent delocalization of sociolinguistic practices (Britain 2010, 2013b; see also Auer 2009).

Conclusion

The results obtained in this study show the dramatic and inevitably advanced case of obsolescence of a dialectal form currently in action in the Murcian isolated rural town of Ricote as part of the general process of dialect leveling after increased mundane mobility and contact. The apparent-time study correlating variable (ch) with sociodemographic groups and levels of formality uncover age-, gender-, and style-based patterns of behavior and provide us with a measurement of the variable's sociolinguistic health and esteem within the local community. But, unlike the usual adherence to the vernacular world and its sociolinguistic behavior by younger generations, in Ricote youngsters are leading a change toward the standard form that enjoys overt prestige. The ongoing sound change reflecting dialect leveling is also geolinguistically conditioned by the new conception of people's spatiality, which is currently making the dichotomy of urban-rural become blurred: socially, commuting is disintegrating local networks and routinization, and, linguistically, increased contact is resulting in the leveling of autochthonous dialect forms and the reinforcement of supralocalization in this traditionally isolated community.

Notes

*Some figures in this chapter are available on the publisher's website (press.georgetown.edu) to make it easier to view the data.

1. Consonant <ch> is always onset in Spanish, and its phonotactics and syllabification rules do not allow it to be in coda position within a syllable (except in loanwords, such as *sandwich*, whose post-vocalic <ch> would be silent in Murcian).

2. Class as a relational concept, and its relation to economic incomes and its serving as a signifier of success and social stratification, on the one hand, and the urbanites' bourgeois values and conception of the way of living, on the other, have no place in a rural world, where local people are more "preoccupied with making a living rather than creating a lifestyle" (Fawcett 2000, 167; Jensen 2018).

3. The dissimilar number of samples (43) and informants (50) is due to the fact that there were some sociolinguistic interviews where more than one informant could be observed while taking part in the same conversation.

4. Note that G1 is a knockout category, in that tokens elicited from this age group were categorically realized with the standard variant. Accordingly, it was excluded from the fixed-effects analysis, as this is the usual practice in variationist analysis.

5. These features include postvocalic consonant elisions, intervocalic /d/-dropping, regressive assimilation of consonant clusters, or permutation of liquid consonants (see Hernández-Campoy 2003, 2008, 2010; Hernández-Campoy and Jiménez-Cano 2003; Hernández-Campoy and Trudgill 2002; Hernández-Campoy and Villena-Ponsoda 2009; or Monroy-Casas and Hernández-Campoy 2015).

6. The concepts of space and spatiality, or the spatial properties, and their necessary integration within the sociolinguistic theory have performed a marginal role in the evolution of linguistic thought (Britain 2013a, 2013b). The traditional perception of space has been rather static so far, ignoring the existing inter-relationship and dynamism among the social and spatial settings, on the one hand, and linguistic processes, on the other.

References

Adey, Peter. 2010. *Mobility*. London: Routledge. doi: 10.4324/9781315669298

Almeida, Manuel. 1994. Sociolinguistic mechanisms of phonetic change: /tʃ/ in Santa Cruz de Tenerife. *Journal of Spanish Research* 3: 45–56.

Alvar, M. (ed.). 1996. *Manual de dialectología hispánica: El español de España*. Barcelona: Ariel.

Andersen, Henning. 1988. Center and periphery: Adoption, diffusion and spread. In J. Fisiak (ed.), *Historical dialectology: Regional and social*. Berlin: De Gruyter, 39–93. doi: 10.1515/9783110848137.39

Auer, Peter. 2009. Dialect levelling and the standard varieties in Europe. *Folia Lingüística Histórica* 32 (1–2): 1–9. doi: 10.1515/flin.1998.32.1-2.1

Auer, Peter. 2018. Dialect change in Europe—Leveling and convergence. In Charles Boberg, John Nerbonne and Dominic Watt (eds.), *The handbook of dialectology*. Malden, MA: Wiley-Blackwell, 159–76. doi: 10.1002/9781118827628.ch9

Auer, Peter and Frans Hinskens. 1996. The convergence and divergence of dialects in Europe: New and not so new developments in an old area. *Sociolinguistica* 10 (1): 1–30. doi: 10.1515/9783110245158.1

Auer, Peter, Frans Hinskens and Paul Kerswill (eds.). 2005. *Dialect change: Convergence and divergence in European languages*. Cambridge: Cambridge University Press. doi: 10.1017/CBO9780511486623

Bailey, Benjamin H. 2002. *Language, race, and negotiation of identity: A study of Dominican Americans*. El Paso, TX: LFB Scholarly Pub. https://works.bepress.com/benjamin_bailey/44/

Beaman, Karen and Isabelle Buchstaller (eds.). 2020. *Language variation and language change across the lifespan: Theoretical and empirical perspectives from panel studies.* London: Routledge. doi: 10.4324/9780429030314

Bell, Allan. 1984. Language style as audience design. *Language in Society* 13: 145–204. https://www.jstor.org/stable/4167516

Boersma, Paul and David Weenink. 2014. Praat: Doing phonetics by computer. Version 5.4.04, http://www.praat.org/

Britain, David. 2009a. One foot in the grave?: Dialect death, dialect contact and dialect birth in England. *International Journal of the Sociology of Language* 196/197: 121–55. doi: 10.1515/IJSL.2009.019

Britain, David. 2009b. Language and space: The variationist approach. In P. Auer and J. Schmidt (eds.), *Language and space: An international handbook of linguistic variation.* Berlin: Mouton de Gruyter, 142–62. doi: 10.1515/9783110220278.142

Britain, David. 2010. Supralocal regional dialect levelling. In C. Llamas and D. Watt (eds.), *Language and identities.* Edinburgh: Edinburgh University Press, 193–204. doi: 10.1515/9780748635788-021

Britain, David. 2011. Conceptualisations of geographic space in linguistics. In Alfred Lameli, Roland Kehrein and Stefan Rabanus (eds.), *Language and space: An international handbook of linguistic variation II: Language mapping.* Berlin: Mouton de Gruyter, 69–102. doi: 10.1515/9783110219166.1.69

Britain, David. 2013a. Space, diffusion, and mobility. In J. Chambers and N. Schilling (eds.), *The handbook of language variation and change.* Malden, MA: Wiley-Blackwell, 471–500. doi: 10.1002/9781118335598.ch22

Britain, David. 2013b. The role of mundane mobility and contact in dialect death and dialect birth. In D. Schreier and M. Hundt (eds.), *English as a contact language.* Cambridge: Cambridge University Press, 165–81. doi: 10.1017/CBO9780511740060.010

Britain, David. 2016. Sedentarism, nomadism and the sociolinguistics of dialect. In Nikolas Coupland (ed.), *Sociolinguistics: Theoretical debates,* 217–41. Cambridge: Cambridge University Press. doi: 10.1017/CBO9781107449787.011

Britain, David. 2017. Which way to look?: Perspectives on "urban" and "rural" in dialectology. In E. Moore and C. Montgomery (eds.), *A Sense of place: Studies in language and region.* Cambridge: Cambridge University Press, 171–88. doi: 10.1017/9781316162477.010

Britain, David. 2018. Dialect contact and new dialect formation. In Charles Boberg, John Nerbonne and Dominic Watt (eds.), *The handbook of dialectology.* Malden, MA: Wiley-Blackwell, 143–58. doi: 10.1002/9781118827628.ch8

Cantos, Pascual. 2013. *Statistical methods in language and linguistic research.* Sheffield, UK: Equinox Publishing.

Champion, Tony. 2009. Urban-rural differences in commuting in England: A challenge to the rural sustainability agenda? *Planning, Practice and Research* 24: 161–83. doi: 10.1080/02697450902827329

Cheshire, Jenny. 1978. Present tense verbs in reading English. In Peter Trudgill (ed.), *Sociolinguistic patterns in British English.* London: Edward Arnold, 52–68.

Cheshire, Jenny. 1987. Syntactic variation, the linguistic variable, and sociolinguistic theory. *Linguistics* 25: 257–82. doi: 10.1515/ling.1987.25.2.257

Cheshire, Jenny and Dieter Stein (eds.). 1997. *Taming the vernacular: From dialect to written standard language.* Harlow, UK: Longman. doi: 10.4324/9781315841410

Cresswell, Tim. 2006. *On the move: Mobility in the modern Western world.* London: Routledge. doi: 10.4324/9780203446713

Deumert, Ana. 2003. Describing language standardization: Models and methods. In K. Arneson (ed.), *Standardisering og variation i vestnordisk.* Reykjavik: Iceland University Press, 9–32.

Deumert, Ana. 2004. *Language standardization and language change: The dynamics of Cape Dutch.* Amsterdam: John Benjamins. doi: 10.1075/impact.19

Eckert, Penelope. 1989. *Jocks and burnouts: Social categories and identity in the high school.* New York: Teachers College Press.

Eckert, Penelope. 1997. Age as a sociolinguistic variable. In F. Coulmas (ed.), *The handbook of sociolinguistics.* Oxford: Blackwell, 151–67. doi: 10.1002/9781405166256.ch9

Fawcett, Liz. 2000. *Religion, ethnicity and social change.* London: Palgrave Macmillan. doi: 10.1057/9780333983270

Fernández de Molina Ortés, E. and J. M. Hernández-Campoy. 2018. Geographic varieties of Spanish. In K. Geeslin (ed.), *The Cambridge handbook of Hispanic linguistics*. Cambridge: Cambridge University Press, 496–528. doi: 10.1017/9781316779194.024

Harjus, Jannis. 2018. *Sociofonética andaluza y lingüística perceptive de la variación: El español hablado en Jerez de la Frontera*. Madrid: Iberoamericana-Vervuert.

Haugen, Einar. 1972. *The ecology of language*. Stanford, CA: Stanford University Press.

Hernández-Campoy, J. M. 2003. Exposure to contact and the geographical adoption of standard features: Two complementary approaches. *Language in Society* 32 (2): 227–55. https://www.jstor.org/stable/4169257

Hernández-Campoy, J. M. 2008. Sociolinguistic aspects of Murcian Spanish. *International Journal of the Sociology of Language* 193: 121–38. doi: 10.1515/IJSL.2008.051

Hernández-Campoy, J. M. 2010. Dialect contact and accommodation in a standard context. *Sociolinguistic Studies* 4: 201–25. doi: 10.1558/sols.v4i1.201

Hernández-Campoy, J. M. and J. M. Jiménez-Cano. 2003. Broadcasting standardisation: An analysis of the linguistic normalisation process in Murcian Spanish. *Journal of Sociolinguistics* 7 (3): 321–47. doi: 10.1111/1467-9481.00227

Hernández-Campoy, J. M. and Peter Trudgill. 2002. Functional compensation and Southern Peninsular Spanish /s/ Loss. *Folia Linguistica Historica* 23: 31–57. doi: 10.1515/flih.2002.23.1-2.31

Hernández-Campoy, J. M. and J. A. Villena-Ponsoda. 2009. Standardness and non-standardness in Spain: Dialect attrition and revitalization of regional dialects of Spanish. *International Journal of the Sociology of Language* 196/197: 181–214. https://doi.org/10.1515/IJSL.2009.021

Holmes, Janet. 1997. Women, language and identity. *Journal of Sociolinguistics* 1: 195–224. doi: 10.1111/1467-9481.00012

Jensen, Leif. 2018. Understanding rural social class in an era of global challenge. *Rural Sociology* 83 (2): 227–43. doi: 10.1111/ruso.12230

Jiménez-Cano, J. M. 2001. La enseñanza de la lengua española en contexto dialectal: Algunas sugerencias para el estudio del caso murciano. In M. I. Montoya-Ramírez (ed.), *La lengua española y su enseñanza*. Granada, Spain: Universidad de Granada, 27–53.

Johnstone, Barbara and Scott F. Kiesling. 2008. Indexicality and experience: Variation and identity in Pittsburgh. *Journal of Sociolinguistics* 12 (1): 5–33. doi: 10.1111/j.1467-9841.2008.00351.x

Kerswill, Paul and Ann Williams. 1999. Dialect levelling: Change and continuity in Milton Keynes, Reading and Hull. In P. Foulkes and G. Docherty (eds.), *Urban voices*. London: Edward Arnold, 141–62.

Kerswill, Paul and Ann Williams. 2000. Creating a new town koine: Children and language change in Milton Keynes. *Language in Society* 29: 65–115. doi: 10.1017/S0047404500001020

Labov, William. (1966) 2006. *The social stratification of English in New York City*. Washington, DC: C.A.L. doi: 10.1017/CBO9780511618208

Labov, William. 1973. The linguistic consequence of being a lame. *Language in Society* 2: 81–115. https://www.jstor.org/stable/4166708

Labov, William. 1994. *Principles of linguistic change I: Internal factors*. Oxford: Blackwell. doi: 10.1002/9781444327496

Lapesa, Rafael. (1942) 1988. *Historia de la lengua española*. Madrid: Gredos.

MacKenzie, L. 2014. Testing the predictions of usage-based models on language change across the lifespan. *Lingua* 124: 1–26.

Mendoza-Denton, Norma. 2008. *Homegirls: Language and cultural practice among Latina youth gangs*. Oxford: Wiley-Blackwell. doi: 10.1002/9780470693728

Merriman, Peter. 2012. *Mobility, space and culture*. London: Routledge. doi: 10.4324/9780203842102

Milroy, James. 2001. Language ideologies and the consequences of standardization. *Journal of Sociolinguistics* 5 (4): 530–55. doi: 10.1111/1467-9481.00163

Milroy, Lesley. 2002. Introduction: Mobility, contact and language change: Working with contemporary speech communities. *Journal of Sociolinguistics* 6 (1): 3–15. doi: 10.1111/1467-9481.00174

Milroy, Lesley and Carmen Llamas. 2013. Social Networks. In J. K. Chambers and N. Schilling (eds.), *The handbook of language variation and change*. Malden, MA: Wiley-Blackwell, 409–27. doi: 10.1002/9781118335598.ch19

Monroy-Casas, Rafael and J. M. Hernández-Campoy. 2015. Illustrations of the IPA: Murcian Spanish. *Journal of the International Phonetic Association* 45 (2): 229–40.

Nevalainen, Terttu and Helena Raumolin-Brunberg. (2003) 2017. *Historical sociolinguistics: Language change in Tudor and Stuart England.* London: Routledge. doi: 10.4324/9781315475172

Pérez, Hernán. 2003. Frecuencia de fonemas. *E-Rthabla. Revista Electrónica de Tecnología del Habla* 1. http://lorien.die.upm.es/~lapiz/e-rthabla/numero1.php

Penny, Ralph. 1991. *A history of the Spanish language.* Cambridge: Cambridge University Press. doi: 10.1017/CBO9780511992827

Penny, Ralph. 2000. *Variation and change in Spanish.* Cambridge: Cambridge University Press. doi: 10.1017/CBO9781139164566

Rampton, Ben. 1995. *Crossing: Language and ethnicity among adolescents.* London: Longman. doi: 10.4324/9781315205915

Rampton, Ben. 2006. *Language in late modernity: Interaction in an urban school.* Cambridge: Cambridge University Press. doi: 10.1017/CBO9780511486722

Rogers, Everett M. (1962) 1995. *Diffusion of innovations* (5th ed.). New York: Free Press.

Røyneland, Unn. 2011. Vertical convergence of linguistic varieties in a language space. In Alfred Lameli, Roland Kehrein and Stefan Rabanus (eds.), *Language and space. An international handbook of linguistic variation II: Language mapping.* Berlin: Mouton de Gruyter, 259–74.

Sankoff, G. and H. Blondeau. 2007. Language change across the lifespan: /r/ in Montreal French. *Language* 83 (3): 560–88. doi: 10.1353/lan.2007.0106

Siebenhaar, Beat. 2011. Horizontal convergence of linguistic varieties in a language space. In Alfred Lameli, Roland Kehrein, and Stefan Rabanus (eds.), *Language and space: An international handbook of linguistic variation II. Language mapping.* Berlin: Mouton de Gruyter, 241–58. doi: 10.1515/9783110220278.241

Taylor, David. 2003. Connectivity and movement. In P. Neal (ed.), *Urban villages and the making of communities.* London: Spon Press (Taylor & Francis Group), 149–74.

Trudgill, Peter. 1972. Sex, covert prestige and linguistic change in the Urban British English of Norwich. *Language in Society* 1: 179–95. doi: 10.1017/S0047404500000488

Trudgill, Peter. 1983. *On dialect: Social and geographical perspectives.* Oxford: Blackwell.

Trudgill, Peter. 1986. *Dialects in contact.* Oxford: Blackwell.

Urry, John. 2000. *Sociology beyond societies: Mobilities for the twenty-first century.* London: Routledge.

Urry, John. 2007. *Mobilities.* Cambridge: Polity.

Vandekerckhove, Reinhild. 2011. Urban and rural language. In Alfred Lameli, Roland Kehrein, and Stefan Rabanus (eds.), *Language and space. An international handbook of linguistic variation II: Language mapping.* Berlin: Mouton de Gruyter, 315–32.

Villena-Ponsoda, Juan. 2008. Sociolinguistic patterns of Andalusian Spanish. *International Journal of the Sociology of Language* 193/194: 139–60. doi: 10.1515/IJSL.2008.052

Wagner, S. E. and Isabelle Buchstaller (eds.). 2018. *Panel studies of variation and change.* New York: Routledge. doi: 10.4324/9781315696591

Zamora-Vicente, Alonso. (1960) 1989. *Dialectología española.* Madrid: Gredos.

Chapter 3

Da isch einfach eine Sehnsucht danach 'There is simply a longing for it': Indexicalities of Dialect Convergence and Renewal in Swabian

KAREN V. BEAMAN
University of Tübingen

THIS STUDY INVESTIGATES ATTRITION and renewal in Swabian, a dialect spoken in southwestern Germany, with the aim of uncovering the indexicalities of dialect convergence and maintenance. A panel study of 20 speakers recorded twice, 35 years apart, combined with a trend study of 40 speakers covering three generations, allows for a joint quantitative and qualitative analysis of language change in both real- and apparent-time. The findings reveal that with the inexorable advance of standard German, Swabian is in decline for speakers with higher levels of education and in the large urban center of Stuttgart. However, the dialect is alive and well among speakers with high levels of local orientation and interlocutor accommodation, particularly in the midsized town of Schwäbisch Gmünd. Unexpectedly, the results point to an emerging "Swabian Renaissance" among the younger, well-educated youth who consider Swabian to be "totally cool" and a variety they are "proud" to speak. One speaker describes the *Wechselspiel* 'interplay' in his mind and heart: he "knows" he should not use dialect in public because he fears he will not be taken seriously, yet he still "feels" a deep *Sehnsucht* 'longing' for it.

Introduction

Local dialects and nonstandard language varieties are obsolescing across the globe, leveling with standard languages or other dominant varieties in the region (e.g., Britain 2009; Dorian 1989; Schilling-Estes and Wolfram 1999; Smith and Durham 2011).[1] In deliberating the future of nonstandard varieties, on one side are those who claim that a widespread standardization process is taking place and that dialects across the world are rapidly receding under the encroachment of standard varieties (e.g., Auer 1998, 2018; Britain 2009). An opposing view considers dialect to be a vital and fundamental facet of culture and community, with speakers using a range of local dialect and standard language features to index social meaning and convey differing identities, styles, and stances (e.g., Coupland 2001; Eckert 2008; Moore and Carter 2015). A third, more balanced, viewpoint maintains that supraregionalized varieties are emerging, centered in major urban areas, which allow individuals to project both a unique personal identity and a sense of regional belonging (Britain 2010; Hickey 2003). A "New Regionalism" is developing, says Auer (2015, 17), which encompasses a "positive re-evaluation of identity," leading "speakers to deploy regionally indexed linguistic features in ways not systematically accounted for in traditional dialectology and variationism."

The linguistic dynamics of Swabian, a dialect spoken in southwestern Germany, reflect all three of these situations today: standard language convergence, a revalorization of the dialect, and the emergence of a supraregionalized variety. Prior research has documented substantial leveling of traditional Swabian features in the direction of the standard language (Beaman 2024; Spiekermann 2008; Svenstrup 2019), along with the birth of a "Swabian-accented" supraregionalized variety (Beaman 2024). This movement toward supraregionalization is accompanied by a revalorization of the dialect as young, urban speakers exploit specific linguistic features to index a Swabian identity (Beaman 2024) (cf. Benor's 2010 *linguistic repertoire*). A "Swabian Renaissance" is being reawakened through shared cultural heritage and intense regional pride, amidst a growing concern that the dialect is indeed being lost, as the following example from one Swabian speaker illustrates:

(1) Siegfried (57-year-old male, Schwäbisch Gmünd)

  i bin e stolzer Schwââbe, on i find s schade dass die Sprââch verlore gâht[2]
  'I am a proud Swabian, and I think it's a shame that the language is being lost'[3]
  [S021-17-I-1-00:25:36][4]

To investigate language change in this volatile and vibrant linguistic environment, this study addresses the following research questions:

1. How is the Swabian dialect changing, and how can we measure the change?
2. Which social factors are promoting or inhibiting dialect change in Swabian?
3. What does this change portend for the future of Swabian in particular, and perhaps for dialects in general?

To answer these questions, this study draws from two widely accepted sociolinguistic paradigms: social dialectology (e.g., Auer 2015; Cheshire and Britain 2003; Trudgill 1986) and quantitative variationist sociolinguistics (Labov 1963, 1966, 1994, 2001, 2011). The corpus consists of both a panel and trend study: 20 speakers recorded twice (1982 and 2017) comprise the panel component, and 40 speakers recorded once (2017) form the trend component, supporting a combined real- and apparent-time analysis. Dialect density indices measure speakers' levels of dialect use based on token-level analyses of different combinations of linguistic variables (Van Hofwegen and Wolfram 2010). Three composite measures probe the indexicalities of dialect use, drawing on methodological constructs adopted from social psychology and geography: *dialect identity* (e.g., Bucholtz and Hall 2005; Hoffman and Walker 2010; Le Page and Tabouret-Keller 1985; Tajfel 1978), *interlocutor accommodation* (e.g., Giles 1980; Milroy 1980; Sharma 2017), and *spatiality and mobility* (e.g., Auer 2007; Blommaert 2016; Britain 2013, 2016). The next section provides some background on these concepts and their relevance for the Swabian situation. The third section presents the data and methods used, and the fourth section reports the results. The fifth section discusses the implications of the findings, and the final section offers some conclusions and an outlook for the future.

Background

The situation in Swabia mirrors other dialect-standard language continua around the world, many of which are experiencing rampant dialect attrition under the relentless encroachment of standard or more dominant varieties, the inevitable byproduct of increasing globalization, immigration, mobility (both geographic and social), and education (e.g., Ammon 2001; Auer 1998, 2005, 2007, 2011, 2018; Britain 2009, 2013; Cheshire 1989; Schilling-Estes and Wolfram 1999; Trudgill 1986). While dialect attrition can occur for many reasons, this study focuses on three social factors that are particularly relevant for Swabia: *dialect identity*, *interlocutor accommodation*, and *geographic mobility*.

Dialect Identity

A copious body of research argues that *dialect identity* is a pivotal factor in dialect use (e.g., Dodsworth 2017; Moore and Carter 2015; Schilling-Estes 2004; Tabouret-Keller 1997). Tajfel (1978) defines identity as a speaker's concept of self that derives from their membership in social groups, encompassing the value and emotional attachment they have to the group(s). Along the same lines, Le Page and Tabouret-Keller (1985) use the term "acts of identity," suggesting that speakers create patterns of linguistic behavior that resemble those of groups they wish to be identified with and to differentiate themselves from groups they wish not to be associated with. Auer (2005, 28) affirms these views, suggesting that nonstandard language varieties allow "users to act out, in the appropriate contexts, an identity which could not be symbolized through the base dialects (which may have rural, backwardish or non-educated connotations) nor through the national standard (which may smack of formality and unnaturalness and/or be unable to express regional affiliation)."

Another interpretation of dialect identity is the notion of *local orientation*, which refers to whether speakers have "a strong attitudinal orientation" toward the group they want to associate with or dissociate from (Auer and Hinskens 2005, 356). This position combines both *etic* and *emic* perspectives to operationalize speakers' orientation to their local community and their personal dialect identity. Strong local orientation can compel speakers to exploit dialect variants in various ways to index group membership, and local belonging, as well as other personas (Eckert 2008; Moore and Carter 2015). This approach to identity measures speakers' *perception of differences* by both insiders and outsiders, the extent to which speakers *share qualities and values*, and the degree to which they *participate in shared activities* (Hoffman and Walker 2010). It is this view of *dialect identity* as *local orientation* that is operationalized in this research.

Interlocutor Accommodation

Another theoretical angle in explaining linguistic change in a dialect contact situation maintains that, when speakers of mutually intelligible dialects come into contact, they tend to accommodate, a process that is subtle and largely unconscious (Giles, Taylor and Bourhis 1973). Building on this research, Trudgill (1986) argues that repeated short-term speech accommodation in interaction leads to long-term accommodation and hence language change, maintaining that there is an "innate tendency to behavioral coordination" (Trudgill 2008, 252) and that "the mechanism which accounts for this is quasi-automatic accommodation in face-to-face interaction" (Trudgill 2008, 241). The degree to which speakers accommodate to the speech of their interlocutors affects their choice of linguistic variants and thus their subsequent convergence or divergence to the more dominant variety (Trudgill 1986, 1992).

Numerous studies have explored the role of the interlocutor (e.g., nature of the relationship, frequency of contact, power relations) and its impact on language variation and change, from Labov's (1963) discussion of contact between "Islanders" and "Mainlanders" and Gal's (1978) "Peasantness Index" to Milroy's (1987) "Network Strength Scale" and Sharma's (2017) "Ego Star Network," to name a few. Following this work, this study adopts a measure of speakers' choice to accommodate to different interlocutors by evaluating the statuses of speakers' regular social contacts with the view that people are indeed sensitive to the speech of their interlocutors and accommodate accordingly.

Spatiality and Mobility

In the study of dialects, traditional dialectologists—along with human geographers, sociologists, and cultural anthropologists—have been more interested in prototypical NORM (non-mobile, older, rural, male) speakers than in the speech of individuals who travel and move around (Chambers and Trudgill 1998). Britain (2016, 222) maintains that "a strong sedentarism prevails: mobility is either ignored, seen as peripheral to models of linguistic change, or positively shunned and treated as suspect." As a result, space and mobility have been undertheorized in variationist sociolinguistics, "treated as an empty stage on which sociolinguistic processes are enacted" (Britain 2013, 471). However, geographic mobility is integral to dialect contact and hence linguistic variation and change. Increasing mobility brings people into greater contact with more diverse groups of speakers (Auer 2007, 2015; Blommaert 2014; Britain 2013, 2016; Britain and Trudgill 1999), making it paramount to incorporate the concept of mobility into linguistic analyses of variation and change. The following section lays out the data and methods used to explore the effects of *local orientation*, *interlocutor accommodation*, and *geographic mobility* on dialect variation and change in Swabian.

Data and Methods

Swabian, or *Schwäbisch*, is an Upper German dialect belonging to the Alemannic family, spoken in southwestern Germany by approximately 800,000 people or 1 percent of the German population. The following subsections describe the corpus, the data collection and preparation process, and the dependent and independent variables.

Swabian Corpus

This investigation combines both a panel and a trend study: 20 speakers recorded in 1982 and again in 2017 comprise the real-time panel study; 40 comparable speakers from 2017, "social twins" (Blondeau 2001), were selected from a larger Swabian corpus to create a combined real- and apparent-time trend study (see figure 3.1). The "social twins" were selected for the "best match" with the panel speakers based on age, gender, education, and locality (Blondeau 2001). All speakers were of a similar socioeconomic status, namely, middle-class. While there were no problems in matching speakers with respect to location, age, and gender, finding speakers with comparable levels of education was difficult due to rising educational levels in Germany over the last 35 years (see the subsection on page 42). As a result, the trend study shows an 84% overall match with the panel speakers. The 16% unmatched portion is due to the fact that the German population overall is more highly educated today than 35 years ago.

Multistage corpora, such as the Swabian corpus—with a mixture of time dimensions based on speaker date of birth, age, and time of recording—provide the ability to discriminate between generational change and lifespan change, enabling the systematic comparison of community change and individual change linked directly

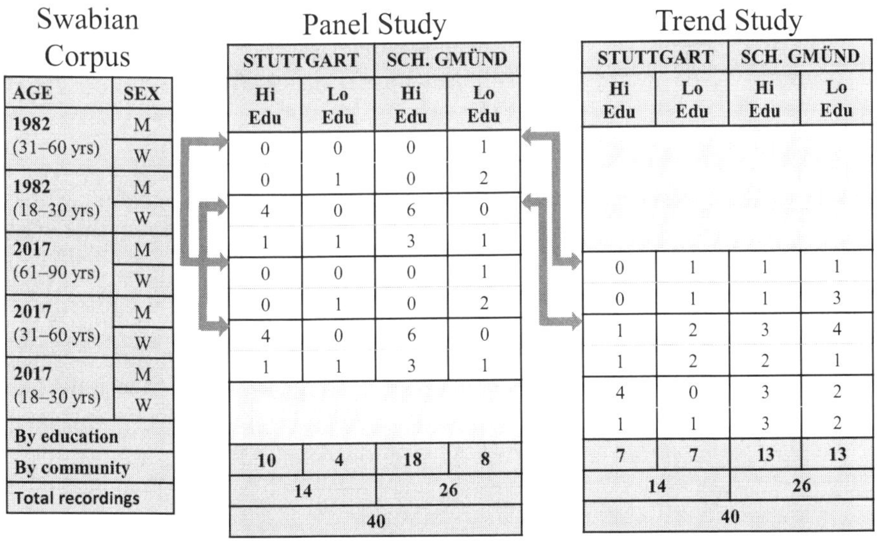

Swabian Corpus		Panel Study				Trend Study			
		STUTTGART		SCH. GMÜND		STUTTGART		SCH. GMÜND	
AGE	SEX	Hi Edu	Lo Edu	Hi Edu	Lo Edu	Hi Edu	Lo Edu	Hi Edu	Lo Edu
1982 (31–60 yrs)	M	0	0	0	1				
	W	0	1	0	2				
1982 (18–30 yrs)	M	4	0	6	0				
	W	1	1	3	1				
2017 (61–90 yrs)	M	0	0	0	1	0	1	1	1
	W	0	1	0	2	0	1	1	3
2017 (31–60 yrs)	M	4	0	6	0	1	2	3	4
	W	1	1	3	1	1	2	2	1
2017 (18–30 yrs)	M					4	0	3	2
	W					1	1	3	2
By education									
By community		10	4	18	8	7	7	13	13
Total recordings		14		26		14		26	
		40				40			

Figure 3.1. Swabian corpus*

to specific life stages, age ranges, and recording years, a factor that Fruehwald (2017) calls the *Zeitgeist* (spirit of time).

Data Collection and Preparation

The data were collected via semi-structured, sociolinguistic interviews, conducted by native Swabian speakers with me in attendance in the role of a friend of a friend. To increase compatibility across years, the same survey instrument and similar interviewing techniques were used in both 1982 and 2017. Transcriptions were done in ELAN (Wittenburg et al. 2006) by native German speakers, linguistics students at the University of Tübingen, following a strict orthography developed specifically for Swabian. Each transcript was reviewed and verified by an additional transcriber and myself to validate its accuracy and consistency. TextGrids were extracted from ELAN, and tokens were automatically annotated using a Python (version 3.10.6) script with variable tags for a binary distinction between dialect and standard based on a bespoke Swabian-German Lexicon (SGL) of over 12,000 lexemes. SGL was built manually from all lexemes in the corpus in which at least one of the 20 variables of interest occurred (see Beaman 2024 for details). Annotated, token-level extracts were loaded into R (version 4.1.3) (R Core Team 2014) for statistical analysis. Table 3.1 lists the 20 linguistic variables, token counts, and other relevant information for each variable (see Beaman 2024 for background on each variable).

Dependent Variables

Three dependent variables are analyzed in this study: one composite Dialect Density Index (with four permutations) and two individual variables to illustrate the importance of investigating the nature of the linguistic variable itself.

Dialect Density Index

The Dialect Density Index (DDI) is a token-based, aggregate measure of the proportion of dialectal variants from all existing variants (both standard and nonstandard) for a set of variables (Van Hofwegen and Wolfram 2010). Ten phonological and 10 morphosyntactic variables, typical of the Swabian dialect (see table 3.1), are included in the overall Dialect Density Index. Three additional permutations of dialect density are used to aggregate the 20 variables in different ways based on the nature of the linguistic variable—*variable family*, *variable salience*, and *variable stigma*, as described below.

Variable Family

Local and regional variables often take on different roles in the speech community and can portray deep-rooted levels of social meaning (Eckert 2008; Moore and Carter 2015). Two types of variables are considered in this study based on the variable's etymological origin: variables local to the Swabian family versus those that originate from other regional varieties, such as Alemannic or Frankish. Of the 20 linguistic variables investigated, 9 are unique to the Swabian family, while 11 are used throughout southern Germany, such as in Alemannic, Bavarian, and Swiss German. To examine the differences between these two types of variables, the Dialect Density Index is split into two: density of the 9 Swabian-only variables (Family = SWG, table 3.1) versus the 11 other regional variables.

Variable Salience

Speaker perceptions of linguistic variables (Trudgill 1986) have been shown to influence variant production. In this study, 9 of the 20 variables are considered high salience and 11 are low salience. Salience was subjectively evaluated based on speakers' responses when explicitly asked in the interview to comment on Swabian-specific features. To evaluate the impact of salience on speakers' variable usage, the Dialect Density Index was split into two: density of the 9 high-salience variables (Salience = HIGH, table 3.1) versus the 11 low-salience ones.

Variable Stigma

The level of stigma or prestige associated with a variable plays a major role in its variation and evolution (Sharma 2021). Five of the 20 variables in this study are considered high stigma (also subjectively evaluated based on comments made by the speakers), while the other 15 are classified as low stigma. Again, to assess the effect of stigma on variable use, the Dialect Density Index was split into two: density of the 5 high-stigma variables (Stigma = HIGH, table 3.1) versus the 15 low-stigma ones. For exemplary purposes, 2 of the 20 variables have been selected to demonstrate how individual features can respond differently based on their etymological origin and sociohistorical context.

(ai) Diphthong Shift (MHG /ei/)

The modern German (ai) diphthong evolved from the merger of two Middle High German (MHG) phonemes /ī/ and /ei/. This study focuses on lemmata originating from the MHG /ei/ diphthong, which is realized as [ɔɪ̯] in Swabian; thus, there is variation in words such as *glôi* [glɔɪ̯][5] in Swabian versus *klein* [klaɪ̯n] 'small' in standard German. This variable belongs etymologically to the Swabian family; it is highly salient and largely stigmatized (e.g., *von der Alb ra* 'from the mountains there') and thus widely considered to be a marker of low education (Beaman 2024).

(st) Coda Palatalization

Palatalization of coda (st) before an obstruent unless a morphological boundary intervenes is a common feature of the Alemannic dialects. Palatalization is frequent in second-person singular verbs, such as *weißch* [vɔɪʃ][6] in Swabian versus *weißt* [vaɪst] 'you know' in standard German; however, it also occurs in other word classes, such as *Fescht* [fɛʃt] in Swabian versus *Fest* [fɛst] 'party' in standard German. While this variable is highly salient, it is not stigmatized; rather, it serves as a positive, almost iconic, marker of regional identity.

Independent Variables

Seven independent variables are considered in this study: recording year, three demographic characteristics of the speaker (community, age, and education), and three socioindexical composite measures. While the sample was stratified for a binary

Table 3.1. Swabian linguistic variables

Variable Name	*n*	Family	Salience
PHONOLOGICAL VARIABLES			
(ai) Diphthong shift (MHG /ei/)	7,611	SWG	HIGH
(ai) Diphthong shift (MHG /iː/)	7,359	SWG	LOW
(an) Nasalization	5,146	SWG	HIGH
(ü) Front unrounded vowel	3,253	REG	LOW
(ö) Front unrounded vowel	1,407	REG	LOW
(eu) Unrounded diphthong	1,577	REG	LOW
(u) Diphthongization	3,941	REG	LOW
(e) Lower long vowel	3,616	REG	LOW
(-ig) Stop-fricative variation	1,288	REG	LOW
(-st) Coda palatalization	9,479	REG	HIGH
MORPHOSYNTACTIC VARIABLES			
Definite neuter article (*des*)	5,454	REG	HIGH
Negative marker (*ned*)	3,256	REG	HIGH
Periphrastic subjunctive (*dääd*)	293	SWG	LOW
Plural verb ending (*-ed*)	3,189	SWG	HIGH
Irregular verb *gehen*	556	SWG	HIGH
Irregular verb *stehen*	317	SWG	HIGH
Irregular verb *haben*	2,927	SWG	LOW
Swabian affix (*nåå*)	207	SWG	LOW
Diminutive suffix (*-le*)	807	REG	HIGH
Past participle prefix (*ge-*)	3,543	REG	LOW

Legend: Family = SWG (Swabian) or REG (regional); Salience = high or low; Stigma = high or low.

Stigma	Swabian ~ Std German	German/English
HIGH	[ɔɪ] ~ [aɪ] [glɔɪ] ~ [klaɪn]	*klein* 'small'
LOW	[əɪ] ~ [aɪ] [bləɪb] ~ [blaɪbə]	*bleibe* 'stay'
HIGH	[ã] ~ [an] [mã] ~ [ma]	*man* 'one'
LOW	[ɪə] ~ [ʏ:] [kɪəʃə] ~ [kʏːʃə]	*Küche* 'kitchen'
LOW	[e:] ~ [ø:] [be:s] ~ [bø:sə]	*böse* 'mean'
LOW	[əɪ] ~ [ɔʏ] [ləɪt] ~ [lɔʏtə]	*Leute* 'people'
LOW	[uə] ~ [u:] [guəd] ~ [guːt]	*gut* 'good'
LOW	[ɛ:] ~ [e:] [lɛːzə] ~ [le:zən]	*lesen* 'read'
LOW	[ɪk] ~ [ɪç] [ʀɪçtɪg] ~ [ʀɪçtɪç]	*richtig* 'correct'
LOW	[-ʃt] ~ [-st] [vɔɪʃ] ~ [vaist]	*weißt* 'know'
LOW	*des* ~ *das*	'the'
LOW	*et/net/nette* ~ *nicht*	'not'
LOW	*dääde* ~ *würde*	'would'
LOW	*mached* ~ *machen*	'do/make'
HIGH	*gange* ~ *gehen*	'go'
HIGH	*stande* ~ *stehen*	'stand'
LOW	*han/hen/khet* ~ *habe/haben/gehabt*	'have/had'
HIGH	[nɔ] ~ [hɪn] *nââstande* ~ *hinstehen*	'stand up'
LOW	[-lə] ~ [-çən] *Mädle* ~ *Mädchen*	'little girl'
LOW	[Ø] ~ [gə-] *kriegt* ~ *gekriegt*	'taken'

distinction based on speaker gender, none of the 20 variables showed any significant patterning based on gender in either the univariate or the multivariate analyses; thus, this common sociolinguistic factor is not reported further.

Recording Year

For the real-time component, the two recording years (1982 and 2017) allow the assessment of how dialect density has changed across the 35-year lifespans of the 20 panel speakers. As a result of pervasive dialect leveling in the region, lower levels of dialect are expected in the 2017 recordings than in the 1982 ones.

Community

Two speech communities are considered in this investigation: the large urban metropolis of Stuttgart and its neighboring suburbs with over 1 million inhabitants, and the midsized town of Schwäbisch Gmünd with its surrounding rural and semi-rural villages, which have over 60,000 inhabitants. This urbanity/rurality distinction provides the opportunity to explore dialect change in a large urban center versus a midsized, semi-rural community. As much sociolinguistic research has found (e.g., Beaman 2024; Britain 2013), lower levels of dialect are expected in the large urban center of Stuttgart and higher levels are anticipated in the semi-rural environment of Schwäbisch Gmünd.

Age

There are two age groups in the panel study and three in the trend study. Due to formidable challenges in relocating and reinterviewing speakers for a panel study after a 35-year time gap (Cukor-Avila and Bailey 2018; Wagner and Tagliamonte 2018), there are only 4 speakers in the older age group (31–60 years old in 1982 and over 60 in 2017) and 16 speakers in the younger age group (18–30 years old in 1982 and 31–60 in 2017). The larger age range in the trend study supports a three-way split: 8 speakers in the oldest age group (over 60 years old), 16 in the middle age group (31 to 60 years old), and 16 in the youngest age group (under 30 years old) (see figure 3.1). The three generations in the trend study provide a window into apparent-time change in Swabian. Due to extensive dialect attrition and expanding education, lower levels of dialect are expected by younger speakers.

Education

Labov (2001) considers education to be the single-best measure of a variable's social evaluation: generally, higher levels of education correlate with linguistic variants that have higher levels of prestige, such as those associated with the standard language, whereas lower levels usually correlate with greater use of nonstandard variants. Thus, in this study, education is used as a proxy for social class. Since Germany has a dual-educational system (Pritchard 1992), a common approach to assessing educational level is whether the individual has completed an *Abitur* 'German college preparatory examination.' This notable achievement is almost a "rite of passage" for a young adult and generally marks the entry to a professional, "white-collar" career. Historically, few people in Germany obtained an *Abitur* because it was not a requirement for most jobs. However, between the 1970s and 1990s, the German government promoted a process of *Bildungsexpansion* 'education expansion.' a large-scale expansion of upper secondary education. As a result, educational levels in Germany have been steadily increasing: individuals with an *Abitur* rose from 8% in 1970 to 24% in 2014 (OECD 2014). Germany now has one of the highest levels of secondary education in Europe, with 86% achieving an upper secondary degree (OECD 2014). Because the standard language is reinforced in school, lower levels of dialect use are expected for individuals with an *Abitur.*

Three composite indices are considered in this analysis to assess the differing socioindexicalities that speakers exploit in their choice of linguistic variants.

Local Orientation Index

The first composite variable is the Local Orientation Index (LOI), which is modeled on the work of Hoffman and Walker's (2010) "Ethnic Orientation" (EO). The Local Orientation Index is calculated based on the answers speakers provided to 12 questions asked during the interview related to the speakers' allegiance to Swabia and their attitudes toward and knowledge of the Swabian language and culture. Speakers' responses to each question were subjectively rated on a 5-point scale and then averaged to create an index from 1 for the lowest to 5 for the highest local orientation. The median LOI in the Swabian corpus is 4.00, with a range of 2.00 to 4.75.

Interlocutor Accommodation Index

The second composite variable, the Interlocutor Accommodation Index (IAI), is a subjective social network measure (Gal 1978; Milroy 1980; Sharma 2017) that considers the nature of the relationships of the people with whom speakers regularly interact with the expectation that people are sensitive to the speech of their interlocutors and thus accommodate. The IAI is calculated from informants' self-reported answers to questions about whether they "believe" they speak Swabian, standard German, or a combination of both with 13 different interlocutors, such as their family, friends, people in a train or bus, work colleagues, and so on. This creates a scale from 0, for those reporting they speak no Swabian to anyone, to 1, for those reporting they speak only Swabian with everyone. (No attempt was made to empirically validate the speakers' responses.) The median IAI in the current corpus is .74, ranging from .04 for someone who claims to speak Swabian only with their parents to 1 for someone who reports speaking Swabian with everyone.

Speaker Mobility Index

In response to Britain's (2013) call to operationalize and incorporate measures of mobility into our sociolinguistic analyses of variation, the third composite variable considered in this study is the Speaker Mobility Index (SMI). The SMI is a measure of a speaker's residential mobility in terms of *distance,* that is, how far they have moved from their birthplace, and *dispersion,* that is, how often they have moved, weighted by the number of years spent in each location and converted to logarithms to reduce skewness. This creates a scale from 0, for the least mobile, to 100, for the most mobile speaker. The median SMI in the current corpus is 34, and the range of speaker mobilities spreads from 0, for someone who still lives in the house in which they were born, to 84, for someone who has moved extensively around Swabia and even lived in northern Germany for a couple of years.

Results

The dynamic language situation in Swabia is undergoing dramatic change constrained by a complex web of social and linguistic factors (Beaman 2024). First, I present findings from the three composite social indices and document the change that is occurring in real- and apparent-time. Next, I discuss differences based on the nature of the linguistic variable. Finally, I bring the social and the linguistic together using multivariate analyses to uncover the interactions between these multifarious factors.

Social Indexicalities

The social indexicalities of Swabian can be observed in the relationship between dialect density (the aggregate of all 20 linguistic variables) and the three composite social indices: figures 3.2a–c for local orientation (LOI), figures 3.3a–c for interlocutor accommodation (IAI), and figures 3.4a–c for speaker mobility (SMI). In each figure, dialect density is plotted on the vertical axis and the composite index on the horizontal axis. Stuttgart speakers are represented by gray triangles, and Schwäbisch Gmünd speakers by black dots. The regression line is either solid and black, indicating a significant relationship, or dashed and pale gray, signaling no significant relationship.

Local Orientation

Figure 3.2 shows no significant relationship in 1982 between speakers' level of local orientation and the amount of dialect they speak upper plot. All Swabians exhibited higher dialect density 35 years ago. However, by 2017, both the 20 panel speakers (middle plot) and the 40 trend speakers (lower plot) show an increasing relationship between LOI and dialect use: speakers with high LOI use more dialect variants. Additionally, these charts reflect the effect of community, with the majority of Stuttgarters (gray triangles) appearing below the regression lines, signaling a lower level of dialect density in the large urban center than in the semi-rural environment of Schwäbisch Gmünd (black dots).

Interlocutor Choice

The plots in figure 3.3 illustrate the effect of interlocutor accommodation on dialect use. All subsamples echo a similar, significant pattern to that of local orientation, demonstrating that the role of interlocutor is a reliable factor in predicting the choice to speak Swabian or standard German: Swabians speak Swabian with other Swabians. Moreover, the charts for both local orientation (figure 3.2) and interlocutor accommodation (figure 3.3) show the speakers from Schwäbisch Gmünd clustered more tightly together in 1982 than in 2017, indicating that Schwäbisch Gmünd was a denser, more closely knit community with "strong ties" in 1982, which have loosened and become weaker by 2017 (Milroy 1980).

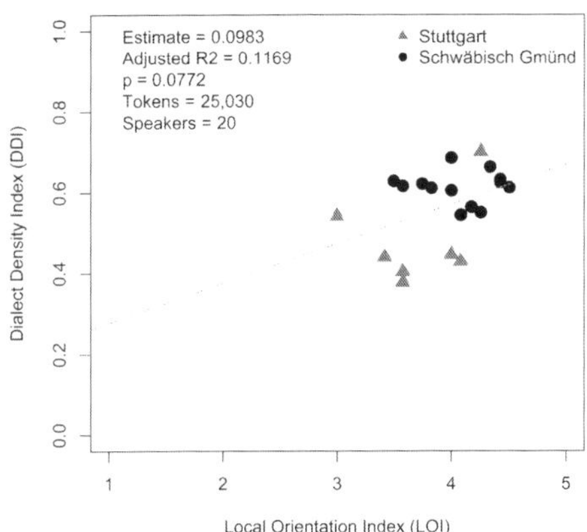

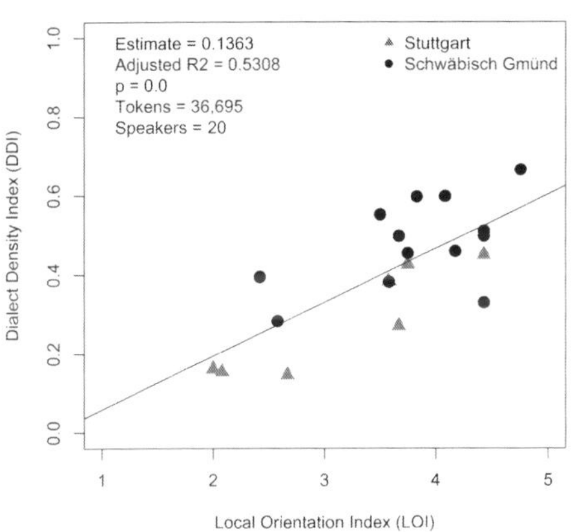

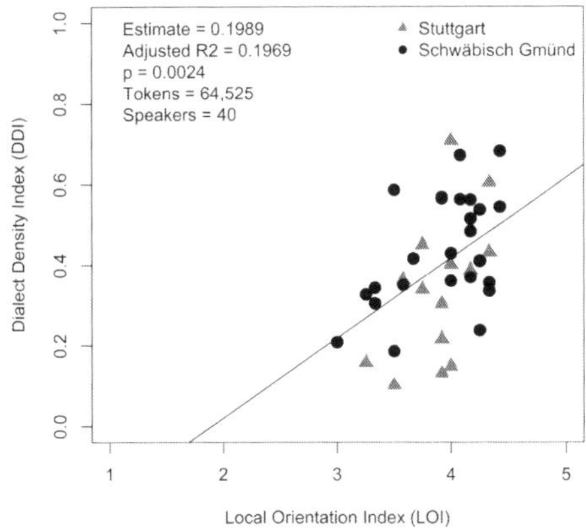

Figure 3.2. Dialect density and local orientation*

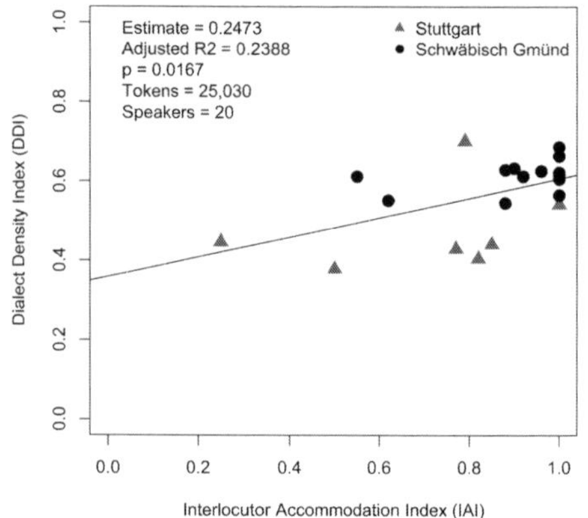

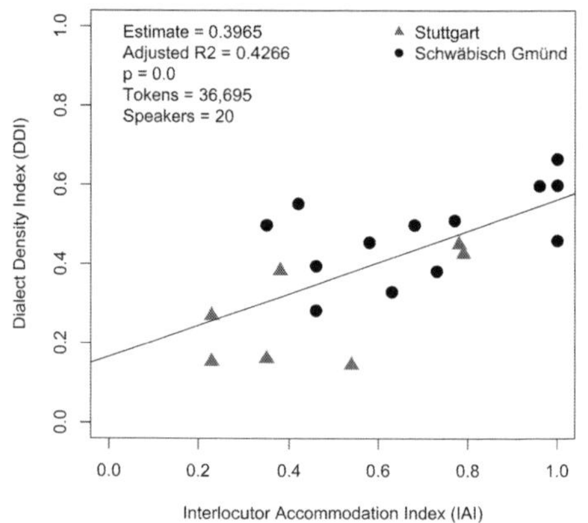

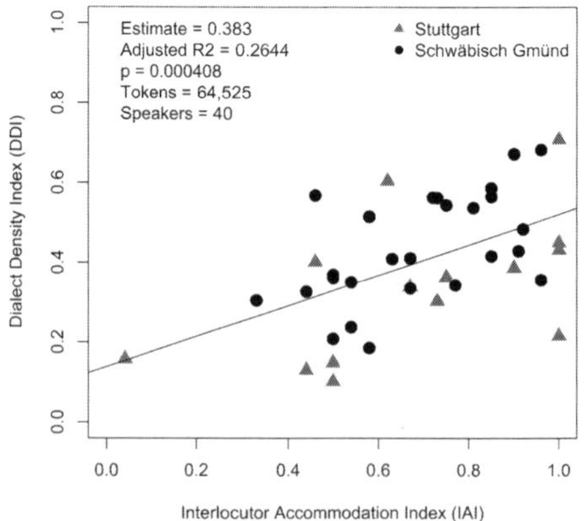

Figure 3.3. Dialect density and interlocutor accommodation*

Speaker Mobility
The plots in figure 3.4 depict the relationship between residential mobility (distance moved) and dialect density, revealing a significant influence only for the 1982 panel study participants. Even as older speakers became more mobile, both in real-time and apparent-time, their level of dialect use did not change. By 2017, mobility appears to have become a "way of life," demonstrating no direct influence on dialect use and signaling a world that has become "intrinsically and perpetually mobile" (Blommaert 2010). Residential dispersion (number of moves) indicated no significant relationship for any of the subcorpora, and thus those plots are not shown.

Not unexpectedly, these three composite measures are colinear; higher local orientation scores and more Swabian interlocutors promote greater dialect density, while higher geographic mobility deters dialect use. However, the effect sizes for each composite index are very different. Interlocutor accommodation is by far the strongest constraint for both the trend and panel studies, as shown by a random forest analysis (*cforest* function in the *party* R package, version 1.3-10). Effect sizes for mobility, as well as community and age, are minimal. Between the two extremes—i.e., high interlocutor accommodation and minimal speaker mobility—lies local orientation, but its effect differs between the two studies. Local orientation lags Swabian interlocutors by a modest 20% for the panel speakers (IAI = .005 vs. LOI = .004) but by 88% for the trend speakers (IAI = .008 vs. LOI = .001), demonstrating a retreat of local orientation and the rise of interlocutor accommodation as the most powerful factor constraining dialect use in Swabian. This finding is considered further in the discussion section.

Change in Real- and Apparent-Time

Figures 3.5, 3.6, and 3.7 depict linguistic change in Swabian in both real- and apparent-time, plotting two generations in the panel study and three in the trend study. Dialect density is denoted on the vertical axes and age group on the horizontal axes. The two left facets, Panel Study 1982 and Panel Study 2017, portray change in real-time across the 35 years. The rightmost facet, Trend Study 2017, reflects change in apparent-time across three generations of speakers.

Dialect Density
Figure 3.5 reports dialect density for all 20 linguistic variables. The panel study (left and middle panels) establishes that median dialect density has weakened across the lifespan, from 52.4% in 1982 to 39.1% in 2017, a 13.3% attrition. This overall pattern of decline holds true for all age groups. Similarly, the trend study (right panel) confirms a falling-off in apparent-time, from 47.7% for speakers over 60 years old to 32.7%, for speakers under 30 years old, a 15.0% reduction. The waning levels of dialect use demonstrate that people are malleable and can change their speech patterns across their lifespans, particularly in situations of wide-ranging societal change and massive dialect leveling as is occurring in Swabia.

(ai) Diphthong (MHG /ei/)
Figure 3.6 exhibits the real- and apparent-time trajectories for one exemplary variable, the (ai) diphthong (MHG /ei/), a traditional Swabian variable with low salience

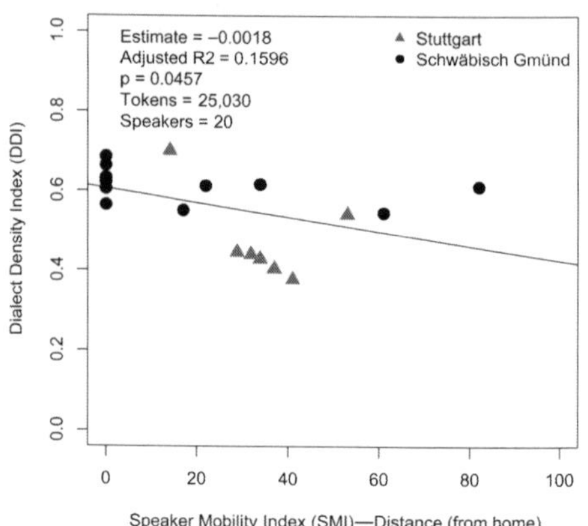

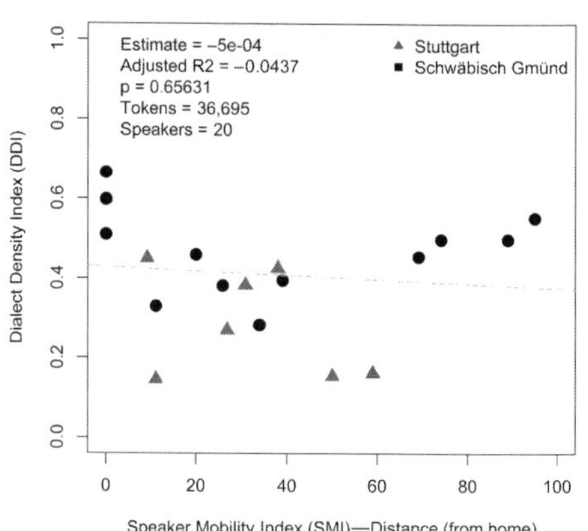

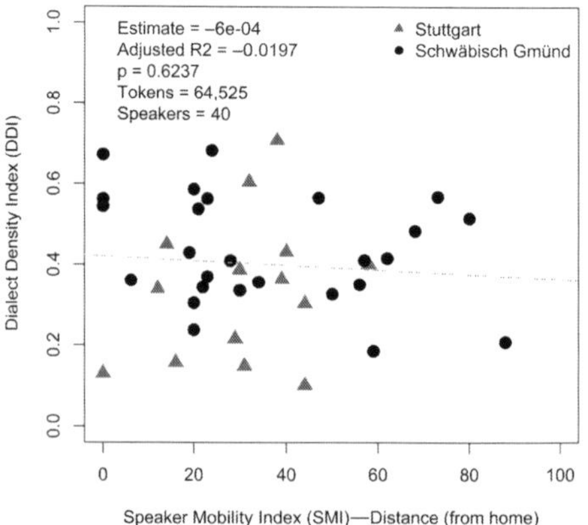

Figure 3.4. Dialect density and speaker mobility*

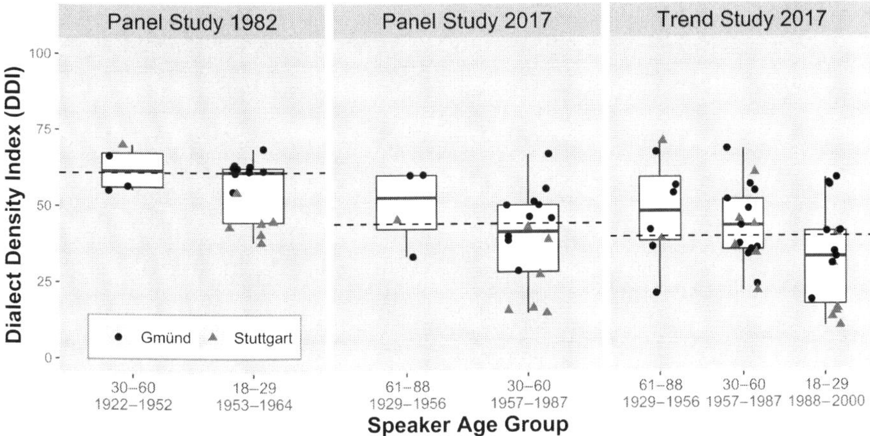

Figure 3.5. Change in dialect density in real- and apparent-time*

and high stigma. The evolution is clear: in 1982, speakers used the Swabian [ɔɪ] variant approximately 50% of the time (although considerably less for the younger Stuttgarters). In 2017, the youngest generation use the Swabian [ɔɪ] variant less than 20% of the time and many have eliminated this stigmatized form from their speech, shifting completely to the standard German [aɪ] variant. This finding points to the formidable effect that perceptions of dialect origin and stigma can play on the choice of linguistic variants.

(st) Coda Palatalization

Figure 3.7 presents a different picture for (st) coda palatalization, a variable that has been largely stable over the 35-year timespan. In real-time, the median frequency for

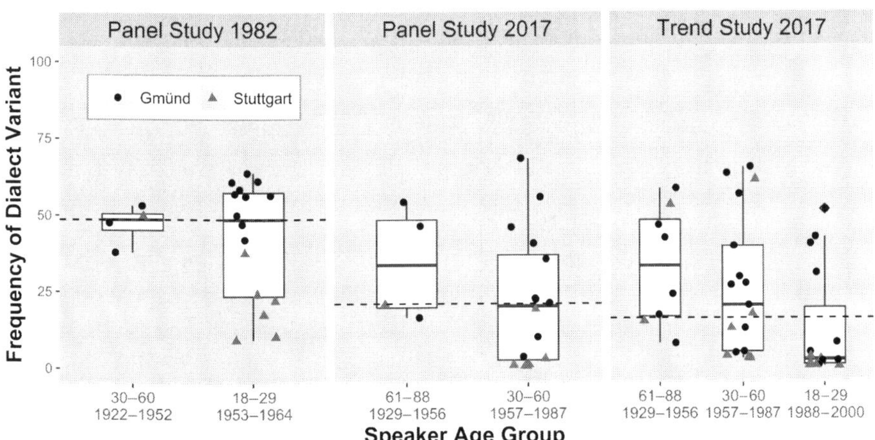

Figure 3.6. Change in (ai) diphthong (MHG /ei/) in real- and apparent-time*

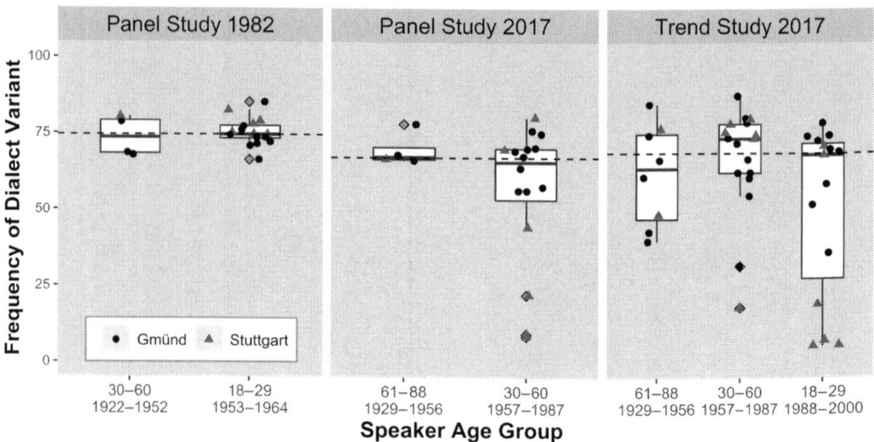

Figure 3.7. Change in (st) coda palatalization in real- and apparent-time*

the Swabian [ʃ] variant has changed little over the lifespan, from 68.9% in 1982 to 62.1% in 2017. In apparent-time, the Swabian variant ranges from 63.6% for the oldest speakers to 73.5% for the middle-aged group to 68.2% for the under 30-year-olds, differences that are not statistically significant. These findings reinforce the profound effect that variable type, salience, and stigma (or prestige) have on variable use. It is worth pointing out that the 2017 panel study exposes several outliers (gray diamonds) in the middle age group (30–60-year-olds), all from Stuttgart: Manni, an architect (9%), Helmut, a radio announcer (10%), and Ricarda, a school teacher (23%) all use considerably fewer Swabian variants than their cohorts, reflecting greater dialect leveling in the urban capital of Swabia.

Interaction between the Social and the Linguistic

To analyze the interactions between the social and linguistic factors, two mixed-effects regression models (*glmer* function from the R package *lme4*, version 1.1-21 [Bates et al. 2015]) were run to predict dialect density (all 20 linguistic variables) based on four social factors (recording year, community, orientation, and mobility)[7] and three linguistic factors (variable family, salience, and stigma). Figure 3.8 graphically depicts the estimated correlation coefficients showing the relative difference in weight between the predictors in the two models: one model for the panel study for real-time lifespan change (gray squares) and one model for the trend study for apparent-time generational change (black dots). Only significant effects ($p < .05$) are displayed on the plot. The effects are sorted by the estimated coefficient of the panel study, such that positive estimates favoring the Swabian variants are positioned to the top and to the right, while negative effects favoring the standard variants are sorted toward the bottom and to the left. For effects that are significant in one model but not in the other, the non-significant effect is plotted at the 0 point.

A comparison of the effect sizes indicates that recording year has the largest effect: the 2017 recordings disfavor dialect use relative to the 1982 recordings for the panel speakers (note the gray square at the bottom left), an effect that is obviously not applicable for the trend study (black dot plotted at the 0 point). The next strongest constraint concerns speaker mobility, dispersion (number of moves), and distance (kilometers moved). While neither of these are significant for the trend study, the panel study shows significant and opposing effects for these two constraints: in 1982, greater dispersion favored dialect use, while greater distance disfavored it. As we would expect, people who moved further away used less dialect than those who stayed close to home, while people who move around a lot within their home region used more dialect. However, over the 35 years of this study, this tendency has reversed. In 2017, speakers who move greater distances use more dialect variants, while those who move around a lot use fewer. This change highlights a profound change in Swabian society. Today, speakers who move far away tend to cling to their dialect more than speakers who simply move around a lot. Perhaps, as Vandekerckhove and Britain (2009, 5) comment, "People start cherishing what is perceived to have become rare." This assessment lends support to the notion that diasporas often unite to safeguard cultural and linguistic aspects of their homeland that they fear they may be losing through assimilation with the more prestigious community.

As with the previous figures, figure 3.8 reveals that younger speakers from Stuttgart disfavor dialect, a finding that is significant for the trend study but not for the panel study, a discrepancy that is likely the result of greater age distribution in the trend study sample. Also, as we saw earlier, higher local orientation favors greater dialect use, which holds true for both the panel and the trend study, an effect that is strongest in 1982 and for older speakers. Noteworthy is the role of higher education

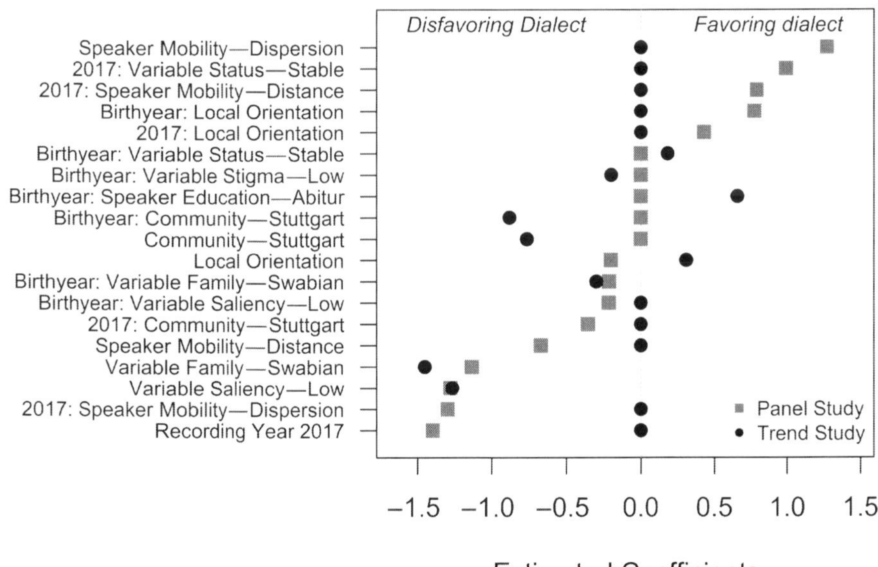

Figure 3.8. Significant effects from multivariate analyses*

on dialect use, an effect that is significant for the 2017 trend study speakers but not for the panel study speakers in either time period, underscoring the increasingly important role that higher education plays on language use today. Still, age usurps education, as older speakers, even those with higher education, use more dialect than younger speakers.

Nature of the Linguistic Variable

As discussed, the nature of the linguistic variable—its etymological origin and its social and historical context—plays a fundamental role in speakers' choice of variants. The graphs in figures 3.9–11 plot the partial effects (*plotLMER.fnc* from the R package *languageR*, version 1.5.0 [Baayen 2008]) for the three variable type predictors

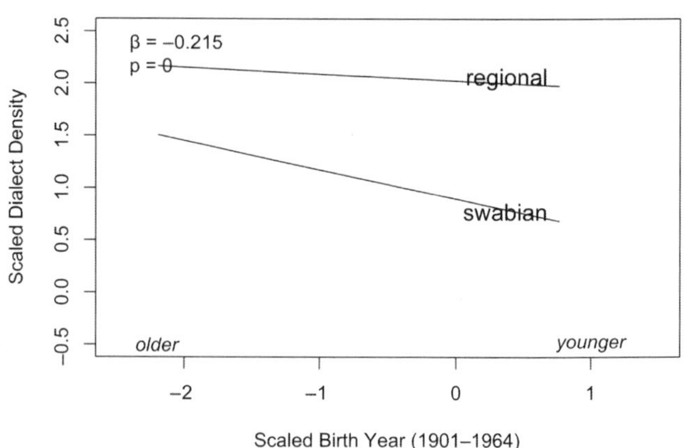

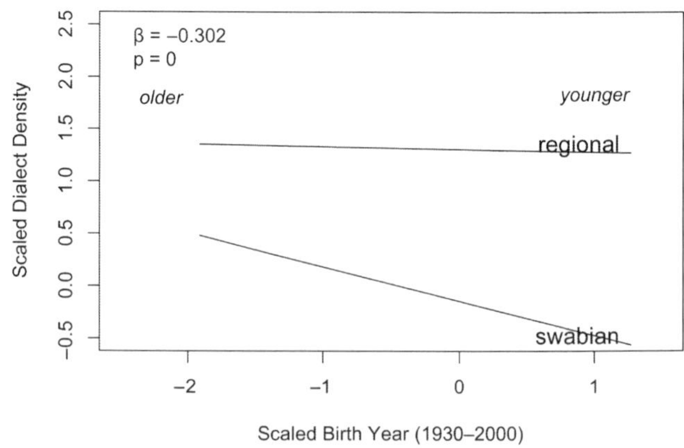

Figure 3.9. Indexicalities on the nature of the linguistic variable—family*

Variable Saliency—Panel Study

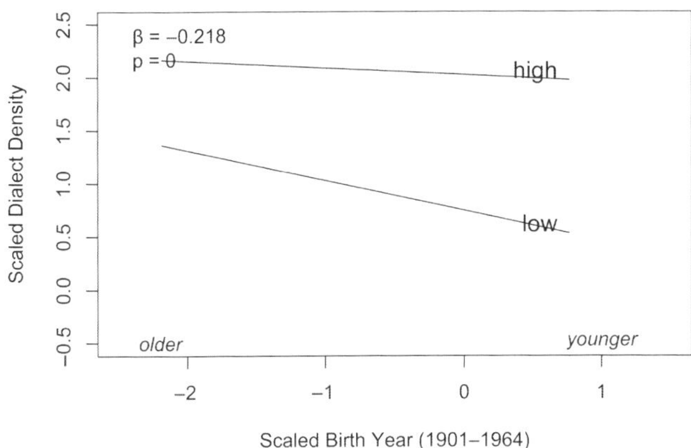

Variable Saliency—Trend Study

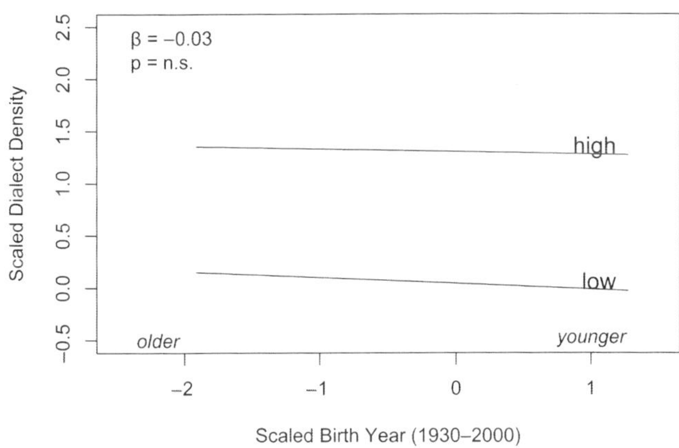

Figure 3.10. Indexicalities on the nature of the linguistic variable—saliency*

from the multivariate models discussed in the previous section. The vertical axes represent the correlation coefficient of dialect density (scaled), and the horizontal axes plot birth year (scaled). Note that negative numbers indicate lower dialect density and earlier birth years, i.e., older speakers. The lines plot three variations of dialect density based on the type of variable: *variable family* (figure 3.9), *variable salience* (figure 3.10), and *variable stigma* (figure 3.11) (see table 3.1 for the specific variables that comprise each type of variable).

Figure 3.9 demonstrates that *variable family* is a strong predictor of both dialect use and change in use over time: the 11 more widely used regional variables are largely stable, while the 9 Swabian-specific ones are in obvious decline in the panel study (upper plot), with even more blatant falloff in the trend study (lower plot). Figure 3.10

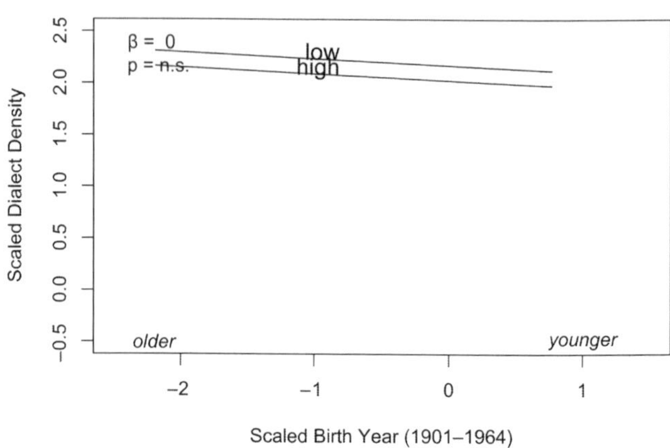

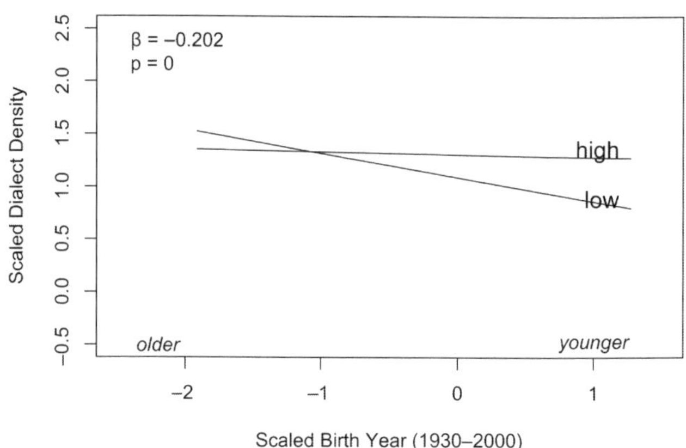

Figure 3.11. Indexicalities on the nature of the linguistic variable—stigma*

reveals that *variable salience* is an essential indicator of dialect use for the panel study speakers yet appears to be irrelevant for the trend study speakers. All speakers use more high salient dialect forms; however, salience is only relevant for change across the 35 years in the panel study in which low-salience variables are declining over the lifespan. It seems that people are consciously exploiting the Swabian dialect features, perhaps for identity reasons: "there's a longing for it," but they can only satisfy this longing via the salient variables they have access to; the lower-salience ones fly under the radar and are leveled out due to pressures from the standard language.[8]

In contrast to salience, figure 3.11 indicates that *variable stigma* does not play a role for the panel study speakers, yet it is a key factor for the trend study speakers, with low-stigma variables showing a greater decrease in dialect use. This finding may at first appear to be counter-intuitive; however, as elaborated in the following section, some of these "stigmatized" variables appear to be making a resurgence and kindling a "Swabian Renaissance," particularly among the younger generation. Many younger speakers report that they find the dialect to be "totally cool," "friendly," and "nice," and that they are "proud" to speak Swabian.

Discussion

The findings from this integrated panel and trend study of Swabian have profound implications for real- and apparent-time analyses with respect to the rate of change, the social indexicalities of the speakers, and the nature of the linguistic variables.

Rate of Change

Dialect use in Swabian shows stark attrition over the 35 years of this study, and this effect is seen in both real- and apparent-time. The findings validate the *Uniformitarian Principle* and Labov's "use of the present to explain the past" (Labov 1963, 275), demonstrating that apparent-time change can serve as an effective proxy for real-time change. The *apparent-time construct* relies on the critical assumption that speech patterns are largely "fixed" by early adulthood. Yet, the results from this real-time study indicate persistent and pervasive dialect leveling across the 35 years of the speakers' lifetimes, a type of linguistic change that Sankoff (2006) calls *lifespan change*, a situation in which both the community and the individual are changing together (Sankoff and Blondeau 2007; Wagner 2012). Speakers in Swabia have changed their speech patterns across their lifetimes, shifting in a predictable way with the community during a tumultuous time of extraordinary social change: expanding educational opportunities, increasing geographic mobility, and rising numbers of immigrants call for greater use of the standard language, allowing Swabians to effectively communicate with non-Swabians.

Crucially, the results reveal greater change across the lifespan than across the generations. Wagner (2012) points out that these differing rates of change are an expected consequence of lifespan change: speakers shifting in the direction of the community change over their lifespan (in real-time) has the effect of "flattening" the change curve (in apparent-time). Specifically, lifespan change means that the oldest speakers have changed their variable frequencies from when they were younger, thereby shifting the baseline. In Swabia, the oldest speakers have increased their use of standard variants over their lifespans, thus speeding up the apparent rate of change beyond the point that would have been expected in a typical apparent-time study. This finding underscores the value of combining real- and apparent-time studies in order to uncover the true rate of change.

Social Indexicalities

This study highlights the importance of considering the social indexicalities of the speakers. High indices of local orientation and interlocutor accommodation correlate with higher levels of dialect use, while high mobility promotes lower dialect use. Notably, the multivariate analyses reveal significant interaction effects across all indices and a conspicuous change in the relative weight of these constraints across time. Specifically, local orientation and interlocutor accommodation were not significant factors constraining dialect usage 35 years ago, while speaker mobility was a decisive indicator. Today, the effects of these factors have reversed, with interlocutor accommodation reigning paramount. While speakers continue to avow a positive orientation toward their homeland, evidence suggests they no longer use high levels of dialect density to convey these associations. Young, well-educated Swabian speakers today exhibit considerable dexterity with language. They are able to scale up or down their level of Swabian depending on their interlocutor and the image they want to portray (cf. Auer's 2005 "diaglossia").

The effects of education are also prominent in Swabia, confirming many other studies that speakers with higher levels of education use less dialect (Ammon 2001; Beaman 2024; Cheshire 1989). Moreover, all of these changes in frequency of dialect use are more pronounced in the larger urban center of Stuttgart, diffusing to the smaller community of Schwäbisch Gmünd, following the well-known effects of the *gravity/cascade model* (Labov 2003; Trudgill 1974). These findings reiterate our general understanding of the propagation of linguistic change by showing that smaller, peripheral communities—largely due to their denser social networks and stronger ties (Milroy 1980)—are more resistant to change.

Nature of the Linguistic Variable

Interacting with the social factors are the nature and social meaning of the linguistic variable, which are a potent constraint on the direction and degree of change. The significant differences uncovered between the Swabian-specific variables and the regionally dispersed ones emphasize the importance of considering the *variable family* and the sociohistorical and etymological background of each variable individually. The Swabian-only variables reflect what Milroy (2007) calls *under-the-counter* change: local variables carry socially indexical characteristics that are deeply embedded in speakers' mindsets and acutely reflect a sense of place and local belonging. The regional variables represent what Milroy (2007) calls *off-the-shelf*, or supralocal, change: such variables are usually the result of tenacious contact between speakers of different varieties and are often called upon as social and stylistic resources. The social meanings of these different types of variables provide speakers with the tools to index differing levels of belongingness, whether that be proclivity to the local community or connectedness to the wider, regional (perhaps global) community.

Low *variable salience* has an inhibiting effect on dialect variants in both studies, though only the panel speakers show a significant decrease in the use of low-salience variables over time. This finding runs contrary to Auer et al. (1998), who found that features perceived as salient retreat more readily than those perceived as less salient. These authors suggest that salience may be a necessary but insufficient condition for dialect attrition. The role of salience in language change remains unclear: empirical studies indicate that it can contribute both to the maintenance and to the loss of a feature (Erker 2017; Kerswill and Williams 2002), exposing the need for further research in this area.

Variable stigma is not a significant predictor of change in the panel study, yet highly significant in the trend study, implying that the stigmatization of Swabian-specific variables developed sometime between 1982 and 2017, concurrent with rising levels of education in Germany. An overarching motivation behind the leveling of the Swabian-only features may lie in speakers' associations of the dialect with *einfache Leute* 'simple people' (Helmut), *der letschte Bauer* 'the last farmer' (Michaela), or *Bauersäcke* 'simple-minded lazy bums' (Marius). While the stigmatized variants are in decline, the more broadly accepted regional variables are relatively stable, suggesting that a "refocusing" or "reallocation" of Swabian may be underway (Britain and Trudgill 1999).

Supraregionalization

Through increased contact, many studies suggest that local dialects are giving way to supralocal and supraregional varieties or "compromise dialects" (Britain 2009), a process that occurs when "linguistic variants with a wider socio-spatial currency become more widely adopted at the expense of more locally specific forms" (Britain 2010, 193; see also Hickey 2003). The dialect leveling in Swabia indicates that the dialect is taking on the characteristics of a supraregionalized variety. As one speaker explains, modern Swabian is *net ultra-schwäbisch* 'not ultra-Swabian', but "something in the middle":

(2) Markus (57-year-old male, Schwäbisch Gmünd)

> *ich hab dann wirklich so ene Art Schwäbischvermeidungsschwäbisch gehabt, also so ene Sprache, die dann sowohl im Schwäbischen . . . net doof äheert, und sich im Hochdeutschen au net als ultra-schwäbisch outet, so etwas in der Mitte was fe beide geht.*
>
> '[at that time] I really had a kind of Swabian-avoidance-Swabian, a sort of language that then both in Swabian . . . doesn't sound stupid, and as well as in standard German doesn't sound ultra-Swabian, so something in the middle that works for both.'
> [S014-17-I-1-00:46:14]

Another speaker points to the growing diversity across Germany, the result of increasing internal migration as well as immigration, which, in her view, makes it more important than ever to speak more standardly so that others can understand:

(3) Belinda (66-year-old female, Schwäbisch Gmünd)

> *sind ja au so viele andere Kinder ge aus andere Gegende da [Grundschul] oder die ganze Flüchtlinge jetzt, vielleicht muss ma scho, e bissle hochdeutscher spreche.*
>
> 'there are also so many other kids yeah from other regions there [elementary school] or all the immigrants now, probably you already have to speak a little more standard German.'
> [S053-17-I-1-00:39:48]

Concomitantly, in response to the persistent and insidious forces of supraregionalization, speakers express concern over the internal conflict to not give up Swabian completely and convert whole-heartedly to standard German:

(4) Willard (58-year-old male, Schwäbisch Gmünd)

> *Hochdeutsch . . . desch kein Bauch dabêi, des isch nur Kopf, kôine Seele drin*
> 'standard German . . . there's no belly in it, it's only a head, no soul inside'
> [S066-17-I-1-00:47:13]

The apparent-time results for the Swabian variables (see figure 3.4) divulge that some younger, well-educated speakers with high local orientation favor the use of traditional Swabian features, suggesting that a "Swabian Renaissance" may be emerging—a subliminal pride in speaking Swabian, as the following examples from Fabian and Patrizia illustrate:

(5) Fabian (24-year-old male, Stuttgart)

> *also gewisserweise isch mã da scho e bissle Stolz drauf ã . . . also des isch scho*
> *ganz cool*
> 'so in a certain way you're really kinda proud of it . . . so that's actually totally
> cool'
> [S119-17-I-1-00:37:16]

(6) Patrizia (22-year-old female, Schwäbisch Gmünd)

> *ich find Schwabe immer sympathisch . . . ich hab au viele Komplimente scho*
> *für ds Schwäbische [ge]kriegt . . . des würd sich total niedlich anhöre und total*
> *sympathisch genau*
> 'I always find Swabians congenial . . . I have also gotten many compliments
> already on my Swabian . . . it would sound totally cute and totally friendly
> yeah'
> [S120-17-I-1-00:43:21]

In sum, young Swabians today combine local, regional, and standard language variants to index a supralocal identity, one that simultaneously expresses a worldly, well-educated, and accomplished persona, along with regional pride, local consciousness, and community belonging.

Conclusion

The discussion section addressed answers to the first two research questions posed at the beginning of this paper: traditional Swabian features are in attrition in both real- and apparent-time, measured by changing levels of dialect density and frequencies of use over time; and, these changes are constrained by the speakers' community, educational level, local orientation, and choice of interlocutor, in combination with aspects of the nature of the variable, specifically, its etymological origin and its degree of social salience and stigma.

The answer to the third research question—what these changes herald for the future of Swabian, in particular, and for dialects in general—can be found in the indexicalities of social meaning for different speakers. With the interminable and intractable advance of the standard language, Swabian (like other dialects across the globe) is in precipitous decline for speakers with higher levels of education and in large urban centers. Nevertheless, the dialect is alive and well among speakers with strong local orientation, such as in the midsized town of Schwäbisch Gmünd, exposing the index-icality of urbanity versus rurality. The urban-rural divide in Germany is ever present and will likely remain a crucial factor in constraining linguistic choice.

A second powerful indexical factor—locality versus regionality—is also essential in determining speakers' choice of dialect or standard variants. There appears to be refocusing of the dialect toward more broadly used regional features to index identity and regional belonging and, at the same time, to ensure effective communication in the diverse and mutable sociodemographic landscape of modern German society. Use of dialect features, imbued with deep social meaning, index an ardent supralo-cal identity, one that simultaneously projects a worldly, well-educated persona, along with regional pride and community belonging. Helmut explains the personal mêlée well:

(7) Helmut (57-year-old male, Stuttgart)

. . . ist dieses Wechselspiel ganz deutlich geworden, auf der einen Seite dieses Gefühl in der Öffentlichkeit, du darfst nicht Mundart sprechen, weil du gleich dann nicht ernst genommen wirst, auf der anderen Seite halt man merkt, dass da einfach eine Sehnsucht danach ist.
'. . . this interplay has become quite clear, on one hand this feeling in public you shouldn't speak dialect, because right away you'll not be taken seriously, on the other hand, like you notice that there is simply a longing for it.'
[S036-17-I-1-01:25:16]

The personal and societal dialect-dualism that Swabian speakers feel appears likely to persist into future generations.

Notes

*Some figures in this chapter are available on the publisher's website (press.georgetown.edu) to make it easier to view the data.

1. This research has been funded by the Tübingen Universität Schwäbische Forschungsstipendium (TUSFS-2016-20). I wish to thank R. Harald Baayen at the University of Tübingen for his professional, administrative, and personal support, which made this study possible. Deep, heartfelt thanks go espe-cially to Jenny Cheshire and Devyani Sharma for their inspiration and painstakingly detailed review of prior versions of this work. I would also like to thank two anonymous reviewers and the editors of this volume, Víctor Fernández-Mallat and Jennifer Nycz, for their insightful and thought-provoking com-ments, which helped improve this work. Of course, any deficiencies remaining are my own.

2. All transcriptions follow a strict orthography developed specifically for Swabian (see Beaman 2024 for details).

3. All translations are my own. I have opted for more English-like translations over literal translations, as the intention of these citations is to illustrate opinions, beliefs, and experiences, rather than to demon-strate any particular linguistic structure.

4. All speakers have been assigned pseudonyms and numbers to protect the confidentiality of their identities. Each recording is referenced by the format [Snnn-yy-I-1-hh:mm:ss], where *nnn* is a unique speaker number, *yy* is the year of the recording (82 or 17), and *hh:mm:ss* is the starting point for the quoted citation.

5. Swabian exhibits lenition of stops [p, b, k] to [b, d, g] (Frey 1975, 27–28; Spiekermann 2008, 70).

6. This word *weißt* 'you know' actually has two variables of interest: (ai) diphthong [ɔi ~ ai] and (st) coda palatalization [ʃ ~ st]. Thus, it would be counted twice, one for each variable.

7. Interlocutor accommodation was removed from the model due to its high collinearity with local orientation.

8. Many thanks to Jennifer Nycz for pointing out this observation.

References

Ammon, Ulrich. 2001. Dialect as an educational and social challenge. In Eneko Barrutia (ed.), *Euskalkia Eta Hezkuntza*. Bilbao: Mendebalde Kultura Elkartea, 201–25.

Auer, Peter. 1998. Dialect levelling and the standard varieties in Europe. *Folia Linguistica* 32 (1–2): 1–9. doi: 10.1515/flin.1998.32.1-2.1

Auer, Peter. 2005. Europe's sociolinguistic unity, or: A typology of European dialect/standard constellations. In Nicole Delbecque, Johan van der Auwera and Dirk Geeraerts (eds.), *Perspectives on variation: Sociolinguistic, historical, comparative*. Berlin: Mouton de Gruyter, 7–42. doi: 10.1515/9783110909579.7

Auer, Peter. 2007. Mobility, contact and accommodation. In Carmen Llamas, Louise Mullany and Peter Stockwell (eds.), *The Routledge companion to sociolinguistics*. London: Routledge, 109–15. doi: 10.4324/9780203441497

Auer, Peter. 2011. Dialect vs. standard: A typology of scenarios in Europe. In Bernd Kortmann and Johan van der Auwera (eds.), *The languages and linguistics of Europe: A comprehensive guide*. Berlin: De Gruyter Mouton, 485–500. doi: 10.1515/9783110220261.485

Auer, Peter. 2015. The geography of language: Steps toward a new approach. *Freiberger Arbeitspapiere zur Germanistischen Linguistik (FRAGL16)* (16): 1–39.

Auer, Peter. 2018. Dialect change in Europe: Leveling and convergence. In Charles Boberg, John Nerbonne and Dominic Watt (eds.), *The handbook of dialectology*. Oxford: Wiley-Blackwell, 159–76. doi: 10.1002/9781118827628.ch9

Auer, Peter and Frans Hinskens. 2005. The role of interpersonal accommodation in a theory of language change. In Peter Auer, Frans Hinskens and Paul Kerswill (eds.), *Dialect change: Convergence and divergence in European languages*. Cambridge: Cambridge University Press, 335–57. doi: 10.1017/CBO9780511486623.015

Baayen, R. Harald. 2008. *Analyzing linguistic data: A practical introduction to statistics using R* (2nd ed.). Cambridge: Cambridge University Press. doi: 10.1017/CBO9780511801686

Bates, Douglas, Martin Mächler, Ben Bolker and Steve Walker. 2015. Fitting linear mixed-effects models using Lme4. *Journal of Statistical Software* 67 (1): 1–48. doi: 10.18637/jss.v067.i01

Beaman, Karen V. 2024. *Language Change in real- and apparent-time: Coherence in the individual and the community*. New York/London: Routledge.

Benor, Sarah Bunin. 2010. Ethnolinguistic repertoire: Shifting the analytic focus in language and ethnicity. *Journal of Sociolinguistics* 14 (2): 159–83. doi: 10.1111/j.1467-9841.2010.00440.x

Blommaert, Jan. 2010. *The sociolinguistics of globalization* (Kindle ed.). Cambridge: Cambridge University Press. doi: 10.1017/CBO9780511845307

Blommaert, Jan. 2016. From mobility to complexity in sociolinguistic theory and method. In N. Coupland, (ed.), *Sociolinguistics: Theoretical debates*. Cambridge University Press 2016, 242–60.

Blondeau, Hélène. 2001. Real-time changes in the paradigm of personal pronouns in Montreal French. *Journal of Sociolinguistics* 5 (4): 453–74. doi: 10.1111/1467-9481.00160

Britain, David. 2009. One foot in the grave? Dialect death, dialect contact, and dialect birth in England. *International Journal of the Sociology of Language* (196–197): 121–55. doi: 10.1515/IJSL.2009.019

Britain, David. 2010. Supralocal regional dialect levelling. In Carmen Llamas and Dominic Watt (eds.), *Language and Identities*. Edinburgh: Edinburgh University Press, 193–204. doi: 10.1515/9780748635788-021

Britain, David. 2013. Space, diffusion and mobility. In J. K. Chambers and Natalie Schilling (eds.), *The handbook of language variation and change*. Malden, MA: Wiley-Blackwell, 489–519. doi: 10.1002/9781118335598.ch22

Britain, David. 2016. Sedentarism and nomadism in the sociolinguistics of dialect. In Nikolas Coupland (ed.), *Sociolinguistics: Theoretical debates*. Cambridge: Cambridge University Press, 217–41. doi: 10.1017/CBO9781107449787.011

Britain, David and Peter Trudgill. 1999. Migration, new-dialect formation and sociolinguistic refunctionalisation: Reallocation as an outcome of dialect contact. *Transactions of the Philological Society* 97 (2): 245–56. doi: 10.1111/1467-968X.00050

Bucholtz, Mary and Kira Hall. 2005. Identity and interaction: A sociocultural linguistic approach. *Discourse Studies* 7(4–5): 585–614. doi: 10.1177/1461445605054407

Chambers, J. K. and Peter Trudgill. 1998. *Dialectology* (1st ed.). Cambridge: Cambridge University Press. doi: 10.1017/CBO9780511805103

Cheshire, Jenny. 1989. Dialect and education in Europe: A general perspective. In Jenny Cheshire, Viv Edwards, Henk Munstermann, and Bert Weltens (eds.), *Dialect and education: Some European perspectives*, eds. Clevedon, UK: Multilingual Matters Ltd, 1–10.

Cheshire, Jenny and David Britain. 2003. *Social dialectology: In honour of Peter Trudgill*. Amsterdam: John Benjamins.

Coupland, Nikolas. 2001. Dialect stylization in radio talk. *Language in Society* 30 (3): 345–75. https://www.jstor.org/stable/4169120

Cukor-Avila, Patricia and Guy Bailey. 2018. The effect of small Ns and gaps in contact on panel survey data. In Suzanne Evans Wagner and Isabelle Buchstaller (eds.). *Panel Studies of Variation and Change*. New York: Routledge, 181–212.

Dodsworth, Robin. 2017. Migration and dialect contact. *Annual Review of Linguistics* 3: 331–46.

Dorian, Nancy C. 1989. *Investigating obsolescence: Studies in language contraction and death* (Kindle ed.). Cambridge: Cambridge University Press. doi: 10.1017/CBO9780511620997

Eckert, Penelope. 2008. Variation and the indexical field. *Journal of Sociolinguistics* 12 (4): 453–76. doi: 10.1111/j.1467-9841.2008.00374.x

Erker, Daniel. 2017. Contact, covariation, and sociolinguistic salience: What Mister Rogers knows about language change. *University of Pennsylvania Working Papers in Linguistics (Selected Papers from NWAV45)* 23 (2): 1–13. https://repository.upenn.edu/pwpl/vol23/iss2/9

Frey, Eberhard. 1975. *Stuttgarter Schwäbisch: Laut- und Formenlehre eines Stuttgarter Idiolekts*. Marburg, Germany: N. G. Elwert Verlag.

Fruehwald, Josef. 2017. Generations, lifespans, and the Zeitgeist. *Language Variation and Change* 29 (1): 1–27. doi: 10.1017/S0954394517000060

Gal, Susan. 1978. Peasant men can't get wives: Language change and sex roles in a bilingual community. *Language in Society* 7 (1): 1–16.

Giles, Howard. 1980. Accommodation theory: Some new directions. In M. W. S. De Silva (ed.), *Aspects of linguistic behavior*. York: York University Press, 105–36.

Giles, Howard, Donald M. Taylor and Richard Y. Bourhis. 1973. Towards a theory of interpersonal accommodation through language: Some Canadian data. *Language in Society* 2 (2): 177–92. https://www.jstor.org/stable/4166723

Hickey, Raymond. 2003. How and why supraregional varieties arise. In Marina Dossena and Charles Jones (eds.), *Insights into Late Modern English*. Frankfurt: Peter Lang GmbH, 351–73.

Hoffman, Michol F. and James A. Walker. 2010. Ethnolects and the city: Ethnic orientation and linguistic variation in Toronto English. *Language Variation and Change* 22 (1): 37–67. doi: 10.1017/S0954394509990238

Kerswill, Paul and Ann Williams. 2002. "Salience" as an explanatory factor in language change: Evidence from dialect levelling in urban England. In Mari C. Jones and Edith Esch (eds.), *Language change:*

The interplay of internal, external and extra-linguistic factors. Berlin: Walter de Gruyter, 81–110. doi: 10.1515/9783110892598.81

Labov, William. 1963. The social motivation of a sound change. *Word* 19 (3): 273–309. doi: 10.1080/00437956.1963.11659799

Labov, William. 1966. *The social stratification of English in New York City*. Washington, DC: The Center for Applied Linguistics. doi: 10.1017/CBO9780511618208

Labov, William. 1994. *Principles of linguistic change. Internal factors* (vol. I). Oxford: Wiley-Blackwell.

Labov, William. 2001. *Principles of linguistic change. Social factors* (vol. II). Malden, MA: Blackwell Publishing.

Labov, William. 2003. Pursuing the cascade model. In David Britain and Jenny Cheshire (eds.), *Social dialectology: In honour of Peter Trudgill*. Amsterdam: John Benjamins Publishing Company, 9–22. doi: 10.1075/impact.16.03lab

Labov, William. 2011. *Principles of linguistic change. Cognitive and cultural factors* (vol. III). Oxford: Blackwell Publishing.

Le Page, Robert B. and Andrée Tabouret-Keller. 1985. *Acts of identity: Creole-based approaches to ethnicity and language*. Cambridge: Cambridge University Press.

Milroy, Lesley. 1980. *Language and social networks*. Oxford: Basil-Blackwell.

Milroy, Lesley. 1987. *Language and social networks* (2nd ed.). Oxford: Basil-Blackwell.

Milroy, Lesley. 2007. Off the shelf or under the counter? On the social dynamics of sound changes. In C. Cain and G. Russom (eds.), *Studies in the history of the English language*. Berlin: De Gruyter Mouton, 149–72. doi: 10.1515/9783110198515.3.149

Moore, Emma and Paul Carter. 2015. Dialect contact and distinctiveness: The social meaning of language variation in an island community. *Journal of Sociolinguistics* 19 (1): 3–36. doi: 10.1111/josl.12107

OECD. 2014. Education at a glance 2014: Country note—Germany. *Organisation for Economic Co-operation and Development* 2012: 1–14.

Pritchard, Rosalind M. O. 1992. The German dual system: Educational utopia? *Comparative Education* 28 (2): 131–43. https://www.jstor.org/stable/3099427

R Core Team. 2014. (R Foundation for Statistical Computing) *R: A language and environment for statistical computing*. Vienna.

Sankoff, Gillian. 2006. Age: Apparent time and real time. In Keith Brown (ed.), *Encyclopedia of language and linguistics* (2nd ed.). Amsterdam: Elsevier Science Ltd., 110–16.

Sankoff, Gillian and Hélène Blondeau. 2007. Language change across the lifespan: /R/ in Montreal French. *Language* 83 (3): 560–88. https://www.jstor.org/stable/40070902

Schilling-Estes, Natalie. 2004. Constructing ethnicity in interaction. *Journal of Sociolinguistics* 8 (2): 163–95.

Schilling-Estes, Natalie and Walt Wolfram. 1999. Alternative models of dialect death: Dissipation vs. concentration. *Language* 75 (3): 486–521. doi: 10.2307/417058

Sharma, Devyani. 2017. Scalar effects of social networks on language variation. *Language Variation and Change* 29 (3): 393–418. doi: 10.1017/S0954394517000205

Sharma, Devyani. 2021. Prestige factors in contact-induced grammatical change. In Karen V. Beaman, Isabelle Buchstaller, Sue Fox and James A. Walker (eds.), *Advancing socio-grammatical variation and change: In honour of Jenny Cheshire*. New York: Routledge, 55–72. doi: 10.4324/9780429282720

Smith, Jennifer and Mercedes Durham. 2011. A tipping point in dialect obsolescence? *Journal of Sociolinguistics* 15 (2): 197–225. doi: 10.1111/j.1467-9841.2011.00479.x

Spiekermann, Helmut. 2008. *Sprache in Baden-Württemberg: Merkmale des regionalen Standards*. Tübingen: Max Niemeyer Verlag. doi: 10.1515/9783484971028

Svenstrup, Christoph Hare. 2019. *"Weil de Zukunft in Hochdeutsch Liegt…" "Because the Hochdeutsch is the future…": Language attitudes amongst adolescents from the Stuttgart*. Unpublished PhD Dissertation, University of Copenhagen.

Tabouret-Keller, Andrée. 1997. Language and identity. In Florian Coulmas (ed.), *The handbook of sociolinguistics*. Oxford: Blackwell Publishing, 315–26.

Tajfel, Henri. 1978. The achievement of inter-group differentiation. In Henri Tajfel (ed.), *Differentiation between social groups*. London: Academic Press, 77–100.

Trudgill, Peter. 1974. Linguistic change and diffusion: Description and explanation in sociolinguistic dialect geography. *Language in Society* 3 (2): 215–46. https://www.jstor.org/stable/4166764

Trudgill, Peter. 1986. *Dialects in contact*. Oxford: Blackwell Publishing. doi: 10.1017/S0022226700011671

Trudgill, Peter. 1992. Dialect contact, dialectology and sociolinguistics. In Kingsley Bolton and Helen Kwok (eds.), *Sociolinguistics today: International perspectives*. London: Routledge, 71–79.

Trudgill, Peter. 2008. Colonial dialect contact in the history of European languages: On the irrelevance of identity to new-dialect formation. *Language in Society* 37 (2): 241–54. https://www.jstor.org/stable/20108124

Van Hofwegen, Janneke and Walt Wolfram. 2010. Coming of age in African American English: A longitudinal study. *Journal of Sociolinguistics* 14 (4): 427–55. doi: 10.1111/j.1467-9841.2010.00452.x

Vandekerckhove, Reinhild and David Britain. 2009. Dialects in Western Europe: A balanced picture of language death, innovation, and change. *International Journal of the Sociology of Language* 196–197: 1–6. doi: 10.1515/IJSL.2009.014

Wagner, Suzanne Evans. 2012. Age grading in sociolinguistic theory: Age grading in sociolinguistic theory. *Language and Linguistics Compass* 6 (6): 371–82. doi: 10.1002/lnc3.343

Wagner, Suzanne Evans and Sali A. Tagliamonte. 2018. What makes a panel study work? Research and participant in real time. In Suzanne Evans Wagner and Isabelle Buchstaller (eds.), *Panel studies of variation and change*. New York: Routledge, 213–32.

Wittenburg, Peter et al. 2006. ELAN: A professional framework for multimodality research. *Proceedings of the Fifth International Conference on Language Resources and Evaluation (LREC)*. Nijmegen: Max Planck Institute for Psycholinguistics, The Language Archive. 1556–59.

Chapter 4

Focusing and Feature Complexity in Amman Arabic

ENAM AL-WER
University of Essex, UK

AREEJ AL-HAWAMDEH
Jerash University, Jordan

Introduction

The formation of new dialects as a result of contact between speakers of mutually intelligible varieties involves six basic processes according to Trudgill (2006, 84–89). These are: mixing, leveling, unmarking, interdialect development, reallocation, and focusing. Trudgill refers to the first five processes collectively as "koineisation."[1]

As a linguistic process, focusing involves reduction in a mixture of linguistic elements from different dialectal stock, and hence reduction in intra-speaker and inter-speaker variability. What characterizes focusing and distinguishes it from leveling, which also involves reduction, is that it leads to stability in the usage of emergent linguistic forms and to the development of "societally shared norms" (Trudgill 2006, 89). Kerswill (2013, 525) further elaborates that focusing sets stable adult norms that future generations converge on.[2]

Focusing can take place at any stage in the formation of new dialects. This is because different linguistic features can show differential rates of development in dialect contact situations, often depending on the relative linguistic complexity of the feature involved. For instance, in his data from the Fens, a dialect transition zone in eastern England, Britain (2010) shows that while the realization of /ai/ along a Canadian-Raising pattern focused rather quickly, the intermediate form [ɤ], in words of the STRUT lexical set, was only beginning to focus 300 years after dialect contact had commenced.[3] He cites several factors to explain the delay in this case, both social and linguistic, including the phonological unpredictability of the original /u/ split that gave rise to the STRUT lexical set.

Social, or sociopsychological, factors alone can be the cause of delay in adopting certain features and ultimately focusing them. For instance, Trudgill (1986) points out that strong social stereotyping of linguistic features can delay or even prohibit linguistic accommodation, citing several such examples from contact situations between speakers of British and American varieties, and speakers of southern and northern English varieties. In our data from Amman, associations with local and national identity are major factors in the survival of the local Jordanian variant [g] in opposition to the pan-Levantine [ʔ] in the new dialect (see Al-Wer and Herin 2011).

In this chapter, we discuss the focusing of a complex morphological feature from the newly formed Arabic dialect of Amman, which emerged primarily as a result of contact, beginning from the 1920s, between Jordanian and Palestinian varieties. The feature in question concerns the imperfect conjugation of the two glottal-initial verbs *ʔakal* 'to eat' and *ʔaxað* 'to take.' This feature is only just beginning to stabilize in the new dialect, while several other features were focused much earlier. We propose that the delay in this case is primarily due to the relatively large number of different forms that went into the original mix.

We begin with a brief sketch of the history of Amman and population growth (the sections "Brief History of Amman" and "Demographics"). In the "Research" section, we summarize our research on the formation of the Amman dialect from inception to stabilization. The next section, "The Imperfect of *ʔakal* 'to eat' and *ʔaxað* 'to take,'" provides a description of the feature under investigation. "Historical Development of *ʔakal* and *ʔaxað* and Distribution in Arabic Dialects" presents some historical and distributional details. The data, range of variation, and results are presented in the sections "Range of Variation in the Amman Data," and "Results and Discussion," followed by the concluding section.

Brief History of Amman

Amman is the capital city of Jordan and home to approximately 3 million people, which constitutes one-third of the country's population. Although Amman is one of the oldest inhabited sites in the region, with a history going back to the twelfth century BC, and despite falling under Arab rule as early as the seventh century AD, it is fairly new as an Arabic-speaking community.

Amman derives its current name from Rabbath Ammon (the main city of the Ammonites), a Semitic civilization whose kingdom is dated to 1300–300 B.C. During the Hellenic Period (332 B.C.–AD 63), it was renamed "Philadelphia" after Philadelphus, Ptolemy II. The Romans (AD 63–636) kept the name Philadelphia and declared it as one of the Decapolis, a federation of 10 cities that they established in the region.

Upon their arrival in the seventh century, the Arab Umayyad dynasty restored the Semitic name of the city, and it has since then been known as "Amman." The Umayyad Arabs however ruled from Damascus and largely neglected Amman, which led to a period of decline that lasted until the early twentieth century.

The first settled community in the modern era came in the form of refugees from the Caucasus, commonly known as the "Circassians," speakers of several varieties of north Caucasian. The Circassians were allies of the Ottomans, the then rulers of the region. Waves of Caucasian refugees started to arrive in 1876 and lasted until the first decade of the twentieth century. Upon arrival and for quite some time thereafter, the Circassians did not speak Arabic. The successive generations acquired vernacular Arabic through contact with the locals. Their native language therefore did not have any influence on the Arabic dialect that emerged later.

Following the defeat and end of the Ottoman empire in the aftermath of World War I, a central Arab government was established in Jordan in 1921, and Amman, then a little village, was chosen as the capital and seat of government. It thus attracted migrants from other parts of the country, as well as from neighboring Syria, Lebanon, and Palestine, which were still under colonial rule. Amman therefore has no traditional Arabic dialect, simply because until relatively recently it had no indigenous and stable community.

Demographics

By the 1930s, the population of Amman had grown to 10,000, half of whom were Circassian, and by 1946 to 65,000. The vast majority of these early Arabic-speaking migrants came from two particular locations, namely the city of Salt (20 kilometers northwest of Amman) and the Palestinian city of Nablus (110 kilometers away). For all intents and purposes, these two groups can be considered "the founding population," in the sense of Mufwene (1996), whose vernaculars constitute the most significant input to the making of the new dialect. As explained in Al-Wer (2007), all of the competing features in the formation of the new dialect can be broadly described as "local Jordanian," as represented by characteristics of the traditional dialect of Salt, and "urban Palestinian," as represented by the dialect of Nablus. Both dialects belong to the southern branch of the Levantine dialect group. They are mutually intelligible and share a large number of linguistic features at all levels; at the same time, they are distinguished by several features, mainly phonological.

The largest increase in Amman's population happened because of the two major wars in the region: the 1948 war, which resulted in the establishment of the state of Israel in parts of historical Palestine, and the 1967 war, which led to the occupation of the remaining part, commonly known as the West Bank. These events caused an upheaval in the region as a whole and the displacement of well over 3 million Palestinians during the years. The successive arrival of speakers of Palestinian varieties in Amman further consolidated the influence of Palestinian dialects in the formation of the new dialect.

Amman's population grew at a rate of 500% during this period to reach just under 600,000 by 1974. There was relative stability in the population figures during the following two decades, rising at a rate of 30% to reach nearly 900,000 in 1994. It started to rise again in the 1990s as a result of the arrival of approximately 400,000 Palestinians from Kuwait. More refugees arrived later from Iraq and Syria because of the political turmoil in these countries. The emergence of a focused and distinctive dialect in the city happened most probably during a period of less dramatic population growth, namely, 1974–94, which coincides broadly with the third-generation descendants of the founder population.

Against this demographic background, it is important to bear the following points in mind. First, there is no geographically neutral variety of spoken Jordanian

Arabic. All speakers therefore use some form of local dialect, regardless of social class. Second, whereas in neighboring countries (Syria, Egypt, Lebanon, Palestine), the dialect of the capital acts as a standard prestigious norm, Jordan never had a linguistic center of its own. Third, Jordanians and Palestinians generally identify themselves with the area in which their forebears lived, rather than the locality in which they were born and bred. However, recently a growing number of inhabitants of Amman (particularly among the third and fourth generations of the earliest inhabitants) have begun to identify themselves as "Ammanis," by which they imply that they are native to the city (see Al-Wer 2020).

The emergence of a distinctive and focused dialect in Amman, in tandem with the emerging Ammani identity, represents a radical shift in the sociolinguistic patterns from a plethora of local varieties to a situation similar to that described above for neighboring states.

Research

The data presented in this chapter come from large-scale research in the city, which was conducted in stages and completed in 2020.[4] In the first stage, the research focused on three generations of families who moved into the city from Salt and Nablus during the 1920s and 1930s (39 speakers). The second stage focused on 20 additional speakers from the third generation. The third and final stage expanded the number of speakers interviewed, their social makeup, and place of residence to include all major areas in the city. Additionally, 30 young children from the fourth generation were included in the final stage. A total of 170 speakers were interviewed, following a standard sociolinguistic interview format. The interviews consisted of casual conversations. The topics raised varied depending on speakers' age, interests, professions, etc. The aim throughout was to record a style of speech that resembled the speakers' vernacular as closely as possible. Each speaker's biography and that of their families were recorded carefully. Individual interviews lasted for an average of 40 minutes; group interviews lasted an average of two hours.

The sociolinguistic profiles of the first three generations are summarized below.

First Generation

The first generation arrived in the city as adults. They speak the original dialects characteristic of their hometowns, while leveling out most localized features. Trudgill (2006: 89) refers to leveling at this early stage as "rudimentary levelling." Examples of this type of development include the following:

- Affrication of /k/ to [ʧ] in the vicinity of front vowels is one of the most salient and stigmatized features in Jordanian Arabic as a whole. While this feature occurs in the Salt dialect, first-generation speakers of this dialect in Amman do not affricate, using [k] instead in all environments; thus the Salt forms [ʧaːn] 'if', [ʧɛːf] 'how', [ʔuxtiʧ] 'your (f) sister', occur as [kaːn], [kɛːf], [ʔuxtik], respectively.

- Another development in this generation is the leveling out of the feminine forms of the second- and third-plural pronouns and suffixes such that gender distinction is neutralized in favor of the masculine forms; thus, /ʔintin/ 'you (f)', /btoːklin/ 'you (f) eat'; /hinne/ 'they (f)', /boːklin/ 'they (f) eat', are realized using the (originally) masculine forms /ʔintu/, /btoːklu/, /humme/, /boːklu/, respectively.

- In the speech of the first-generation immigrants from the Palestinian city of Nablus, lowering of /aː/ in words such as /mbeːriħ/ > /mbaːriħ/ 'yesterday', /seːʕə/ > /saːʕa/ 'hour' is very common. The raised variant is a stereotypical feature of Palestinian varieties in general, which is often used to mimic these varieties in Jordan.

Second Generation

This generation is represented by those who arrived in Amman as children or were born there, roughly during 1935–50. We find in their speech extreme inter-speaker and intra-speaker variability, typical of a diffuse linguistic situation (see Le Page and Tabouret-Keller 1985). In this generation, "gender" emerges as a major organizing factor, with women leading men in the use of forms that become focused in the third generation.[5] All of our speakers from this generation, however, used a mixture of Jordanian and Palestinian forms in the following features: pronominal suffixes -ku ~ -kon, -hum ~ -hon; both variants of (q): [g], [ʔ]; both variants of (dʒ): [dʒ], [ʒ]; both interdental and stop variants of the interdental fricatives [θ], [t]; [ð], [d], or [z]; [ðˤ], [dˤ], or [zˤ].

Third Generation

Members of this generation were all born in the city. In their speech, there is a clear divergence from the heritage dialects, and the mixture and variability present in the second generation are much reduced. Instead, we find orderly linguistic behavior, stable usage of several features, and the use of intermediate fudged forms as well as totally new features—none of these items present in the input varieties. In this generation the new dialect is identified as "Ammani," and there is intuitive agreement among its speakers on its characteristics.

An example of a fudged feature that was used by third-generation speakers consistently is the realization of the feminine ending -ah in pausal position. This morpheme is either realized as /a/ or raised under certain conditions to /e/ in most dialects in the region as a whole. In Amman, the input dialects differ from each other in two respects: (1) the phonological environment that prompts raising, and (2) degree of raising (phonetics). Input dialects from the Jordanian side use a low variant [a], except after coronal sounds, where the vowel is raised to [ɛ] (i.e., [a] is the default variant, which is raised to cardinal vowel 3 after coronal sounds). The following examples illustrate this rule:

ħilwa 'pretty', *biʃʕa* 'ugly', but *sanɛ* 'year', *farʃɛ* 'mattress'

On the other hand, input from urban Palestinian varieties raises the ending /a/ to [e], or [i], everywhere except after velarized, emphatic, and pharyngeal sounds (i.e., [e] is the default variant, which is lowered under certain conditions). Thus, we get:

ħilwe 'pretty', *mixtilfe* 'different', but *ʒaːmʕa* 'university', *ruxsˤa* 'license'

Third-generation speakers use a fudged form that consists of urban Palestinian phonology and Jordanian phonetics. They raise the ending /a/ everywhere, except after velarized, emphatic, and pharyngeal sounds, and the phonetic property of the raised vowel is [ɛ], cardinal vowel 3.[6]

All of the features that have been analyzed so far, 15 in total, show stable usage and clear structure in their correlation with the linguistic and social factors.[7] One feature that stands out as continuing to show characteristics of a diffuse status is the conjugation of the imperfect of the two verbs dealt with in this chapter.

The Imperfect of *ʔakal* 'to eat' and *ʔaxað* 'to take'

The pool of data for this feature was primarily obtained through elicitation. This is because not all forms occurred in the interviews. The tokens that were obtained through free speech were unevenly distributed; most of them were first-person singular and plural forms, with some third-person forms but very few second-person forms. The forms that occurred in free speech confirmed the existence of variability within the speech of the same speaker as well as across speakers.

To obtain the full paradigm of conjugations for each verb, a subset of the sample of speakers were prompted to provide the required forms at the end of the interview. A third verb, *liʕib* 'to play', which has one invariable form of conjugation, was used first, to get the speakers acquainted with the task and to divert their attention as much as possible from the precise aspect of variation being elicited. In total, we were able to obtain the full paradigms from 105 speakers for EAT, of whom 88 are third and fourth generation; and 83 speakers for TAKE, of whom 72 are third and fourth generation.[8]

Currently two basic paradigms for the conjugation of imperfect EAT and TAKE are used in Amman:

- Paradigm I, conjugation with /aː/ in the first syllable
- Paradigm II, conjugation with /oː/ in the first syllable

Examples 1 and 2 below illustrate these paradigms. Note that the imperfect forms of all verbs in Levantine dialects, including Jordanian and Palestinian, begin with the prefix *b-*, which denotes present indicative mood.

1. *b-taːkol* 'she eats' or 'you(SM) eat'
2. *b-toːkil ~ b-toːkol* 'she eats' or 'you(SM) eat'

Input from the Jordanian side has only the /o:/ forms in the first syllable and /i/ in the second syllable, i.e., *bto:kil* (see further below). This form is invariably used in all traditional Jordanian dialects and has been so for at least 100 years. Evidence can be found in Bergsträsser's atlas of 1915, which shows that all Jordanian dialects conjugate with /o:/ only. This is confirmed in contemporary research in various parts of Jordan (see Herin and Al-Wer forthcoming). Bergstrasser's atlas shows that urban and rural Palestinian dialects, including the dialect of Nablus, also have /o:/ forms for the most part. The exceptions, according to Bergstrasser's atlas, are the dialects of Jerusalem, Hebron, and Gaza—all of which are marked in this atlas as having /a:/ in the conjugation of these verbs, i.e., Paradigm I (for Palestinian dialects, see also Geva-Kleinberger and Behnstedt 2019; Seeger 2013). Our research in Amman contains interviews with speakers whose families hail from these cities. The data we have corroborate the atlas data regarding Gaza and Hebron but not Jerusalem; several older speakers who moved to Amman from Jerusalem during the late 1940s and 1950s use /o:/ variably with /a:/ in our data. It is possible that what Bergstrasser's atlas captured in 1915 is variation and possibly change in the direction of /a:/ in Jerusalem. In any case, based on the atlas data and interviews with early immigrants from various Palestinian cities, we can confirm that the Palestinian dialects that were transplanted in Amman were already variable with respect to this feature. In summary, input to the formation of the Amman dialect from the Jordanian side manifests only /o:/ in the first syllable, while input from the Palestinian side includes both possibilities, /o:/ and /a:/.

In addition to variation in the realization of the vowel in the first syllable of the imperfect forms of these verbs, the input dialects differ in the realization of the vowel in the second syllable. As mentioned above, the traditional Jordanian dialects have /i/ only, while the Palestinian dialects have /o/ in the second syllable in the forms for 2SM, 3SF, and 1P, as illustrated in table 4.1.

A further difference between the input dialects concerns the conjugations of 3SM and 3P forms. Input from Jordanian has no *Yod*, /j/, as illustrated in table 4.2. The Yod in these forms is present in the imperfect 3SM and 3P stem of all verbs, which functions as a subjunctive form; thus, *yiktib* 'he write', *ya:kul* 'he eat', *ya:xuð* 'he take.' Broadly speaking, the indicative is formed by adding the prefix *b-*, with elision of /j/ in certain phonological environments, depending on the dialect. Traditional Jordanian dialects omit /j/ in the indicative for all verbs; whereas urban Palestinian dialects typically only omit /j/ in open syllables, except in the two verbs *ya:kul* 'eat' and *ya:xuð* 'take' (on this feature, see Al-Wer 2014).

Table 4.1. Second-syllable differences between Jordanian and urban Palestinian dialects

	Jordanian	Urban Palestinian	
2SM/3SF	*b-to:kil*	*b-to:kol* or *b-ta:kol* 'you eat'	'she eats'
1P	*b-no:kil*	*b-no:kol* or *b-na:kol*	'we eat'

Table 4.2. Yod-realization differences between Jordanian and urban Palestinian dialects

	Jordanian	Urban Palestinian
3SM	*b-oːkil*	*b-yoːkol* or *b-yaːkol*
3P	*b-oːklu*	*b-yoːklu* or *b-yaːklu*

Table 4.3. Summary of differences between Jordanian and urban Palestinian dialects

Typical forms in the input varieties	**Jordanian**	**Urban Palestinian**
Paradigm I, conjugation with /aː/ in first syllable		✓
Paradigm II, conjugation with /oː/ in first syllable	✓	✓
/i/ in second syllable	✓	
/o/ in second syllable		✓
Yod in 3SM and 3P		✓

To recap, upon transplantation in Amman, the input varieties to the formation of the new dialect differed in three aspects:

(1)　The paradigm of conjugation they used. While input from Jordanian follows Paradigm II invariably, i.e., conjugation with a rounded vowel /oː/, input from the Palestinian side contains both paradigms, i.e., variably /aː/ or /oː/.

(2)　The quality of the vowel in the second syllable, /i/ in Jordanian versus /o/ in Palestinian.

(3)　Presence or absence of Yod, /j/, in 3SM and 3P.

These points are summarized in table 4.3.

In the contact situation in Amman, these differences have produced six different forms for the 3SM conjugation alone, and 19 different morphological forms for each verb altogether, instead of the six or seven forms for each of the verbs in the input dialects, as will be explained later. The sheer number of options available in the social environment in Amman is a major aspect of complexity in the case of these verbs, which is likely to be the primary cause of the delay found in the focusing of this feature (see "Range of Variation in the Amman Data").

Historical Development of *ʔakal* and *ʔaxað* and Distribution in Arabic Dialects

Paradigm I, conjugation with /aː/, is the one found in the vast majority of Arabic varieties, including Classical Arabic. The historical development of this form is straightforward. It is assumed to be as follows: the imperfect stems /jaʔkul/ 'he eats', /jaʔxuð/ 'he takes', first lost the glottal stop, followed by compensatory lengthening of the preceding vowel, yielding /jaːkul/, /jaːxuð/. Paradigm I is thus derived from these stems.

In contrast, the derivation of Paradigm II is peculiar, in both its historical development and its geographical distribution. Based on the descriptions of Arabic varieties available so far, conjugation with /oː/ in these verbs is only found in the following locations: three peripheral areas in Arabia—namely, Marib and Dathina in Yemen (Behnstedt 1985; Landberg 1901, cited in Behnstedt 1985) and Khabura in Oman (Brockett 1985)—and in Jordanian and Palestinian dialects (Southern Levantine dialects).

There is as yet no satisfactory account for the historical development of this paradigm, nor for its geographical distribution.[9] For the purposes of this chapter, it is sufficient to note that Paradigm II is quite unusual and rare in Arabic dialects. It is also important to point out that none of the major and dominant city dialects in either Syria or Lebanon has this form. At the regional level, it can be described as a localized feature. As pointed out in Al-Wer (2007, 2020), the formation of the Amman dialect is also influenced by pan-Levantine koine forms. In the case of the verbs under discussion in this chapter, the koine forms would be Paradigm I. The sum of the factors outlined in this section would render Paradigm II particularly susceptible to leveling out in contact situations, as seems to be happening in Amman, albeit at a slow rate.

Range of Variation in the Amman Data

To understand the range of variation found in the data from Amman in relation to the input dialects, we shall first list the paradigms of conjugation of these verbs in the input dialects. The morphological patterns in each input variety are the same for both verbs, and therefore only the conjugations of the verb 'to eat' are listed below in table 4.4.

Table 4.4. Conjugation of the verb 'to eat' in the Jordanian and Palestinian input dialects

	Jordanian input	Palestinian input
1S	boːkil	baːkol
2SM	btoːkil	btoːkol, btaːkol
2SF	btoːkli	btoːkli, btaːkli
3SM	boːkil	byoːkol, byaːkol
3SF	btoːkil	btoːkol, btaːkol
1P	bnoːkil	bnoːkol, bnaːkol[a]
2P	btoːklu	btoːklu, btaːklu
3P	boːklu	byoːklu, byaːklu

[a] The prefix *b-* assimilates to [m] in the first-person plural derivations; hence these forms are realized as *mnoːkil, mnoːkol, mnaːkol* 'we eat'.

Table 4.5. Range of variation of EAT and TAKE in Amman

EAT

1S I eat	2SM You eat	2SF You eat	3SM He eats	3SF She eats	1P We eat	2P You eat	3P They eat
boːkil baːkol	btoːkil btoːkol btaːkol	btoːkli btaːkli	baːkul boːkil boːkol byoːkol byoːkil baːkol byaːkol	btoːkil btoːkol btaːkol	bnoːkil bnoːkol bnaːkol	btoːklu btaːklu	boːklu byoːklu baːklu byaːklu

TAKE

1S I take	2SM You take	2SF You eat	3SM He takes	3SF She takes	1P We take	2P You take	3P They take
boːxid baːxod	btoːxid btoːxod btaːxod	btoːxdi btaːxdi	boːxid boːxod byoːxod byoːxid baːxod byaːxod	btoːxid btoːxod btaːxod	bnoːxid bnoːxod bnaːxod	btoːxdu btaːxdu	boːxdu byoːxdu baːxdu byaːxdu

Input from Jordanian includes six different morphological forms, as there is no person distinction in 1S and 3SM; similarly, 2SM and 3SF are identical forms. Input from the Palestinian dialects is a variable system with 13 different forms; 2SM and 3SF are identical forms.

The Jordanian form for 1S, *boːkil*, is morphologically unusual since for all other verbs Jordanian dialects follow the regular template with /a/ in 1S derivation, e.g., *baktub* 'I write'; *baʕmal* 'I do.' As we will see later, the 1S conjugation *boːkil* is the most susceptible form to leveling out in the Amman data.

We turn now to the range of variation found in Amman regarding the conjugation of these verbs, which is displayed in table 4.5.[10]

The first observation about these data is the number of forms used. There are 21 different morphological forms, instead of the 19 forms inherited from the input dialects. One of the new derivations is 3SM *byoːkil* 'he eats.' This new form contains the Yod typical of Palestinian dialects but also /i/ in the second syllable, which is characteristic of Jordanian dialects. This form is thus morphologically 'fudged' (see Trudgill 1986). Interestingly, we do not get fudged forms of the type /aː/ in the first syllable and /i/ in the second, e.g., **b-yaːkil*. The indicative form *yaːkil*, without *b*-prefix, does occur in Jordanian Arabic but only in the dialects of the non-Levantine type, namely, those that are collectively referred to in Arabic dialectology as Bedouin dialects. Such dialects are spoken in all regions throughout Jordan, but they have virtually no influence in the making of the Amman dialect. Crucially, as non-urban dialects, they tend to be stigmatized in urban contexts like Amman. It is possible that the absence of such forms, i.e., a combination of /a:/ in the first syllable and /i/ in the second syllable, relates to the social stigmatization of Bedouin dialects of which this form is a stereotype.

Another new derivation is 3P form *ba:klu* 'they eat.' The emergence of this form is most likely connected with developments in the singular form *ba:kol*. In the input from Palestinian dialects this form indicated only 1S, but in Amman it is also used as an option for 3SM; thus, *ba:kol* can now mean 'he eats' as well as 'I eat.' The new 3P form *ba:klu* 'they eat' is morphologically the plural form of this innovative 3SM use of *ba:kol* 'he eats.' The process involved in this development is a type of regularization by analogy (see Trudgill 2006). In the input we get singular *bo:kol* 'he eats' and plural *bo:klu* 'they eat'; by analogy, the form *ba:klu* 'they eat' emerges as the plural form of innovative *ba:kul* 'he eats.'

Turning now to the innovative use of *ba:kul* as a 3SM form in place of or in addition to *bya:kol* 'he eats', we notice two developments. Firstly, Yod is dropped from the original 3SM form *bya:kol*, yielding *ba:kol*. This development is analogous to the dropping of Yod in third-person forms in other verbs, which is common in Amman, e.g., *byilʕab > bilʕab* 'he plays'; *byikitbu > bikitbu* 'they write' (see Al-Wer 2014). The outcome of the dropping of Yod in *bya:kol* is a merger with the 1S form *ba:kol*.[11] Second, the function of *ba:kol* is expanded: in addition to this form's original assignment to 1S, it is now assigned to both 1S and 3SM. We suggest that this development is a form of reallocation on the basis that the form *ba:kol* has been refunctionalized.[12]

Results and Discussion

Earlier we pointed out that the input dialects differ in the realization of vowels in both syllables of these verbs in the imperfect conjugations, namely /o:/ versus /o:/ or /a:/ in the first syllable, and /i/ versus /o/ in the second syllable. It has also been pointed out that 3SM and 3P have variants with or without /j/. In this chapter we present the results of the analysis of variation in the first syllable and in relation to two factors only, generation and heritage dialect.

Figures 4.1a and 4.1b show the percentage use of /a:/ versus /o:/ in the whole sample.

We notice in these figures a clear trend toward a transition from conjugation along Paradigm II (with /o:/) to Paradigm I (with /a:/). The transition however is not uniform but seems to happen piecemeal: the most advanced transition is in 1S for both verbs, showing almost categorical usage of the forms *ba:kul* 'I eat' and *ba:xod* 'I take.' Recall that /o:/ in 1S conjugation occurs only in the Jordanian input. It is an absolute minority form and as such is also extremely salient, which explains its high susceptibility to change (see Britain 2010; Trudgill 1986). In the rest of the paradigm, the rate of occurrence of the incoming variant /a:/ is fairly advanced, hovering around 70% for 'eat' and 75% for 'take.' However, for 'eat', the 3SM and 3P forms lag behind at rates of 65% and 68%, respectively. This is likely to be connected with the

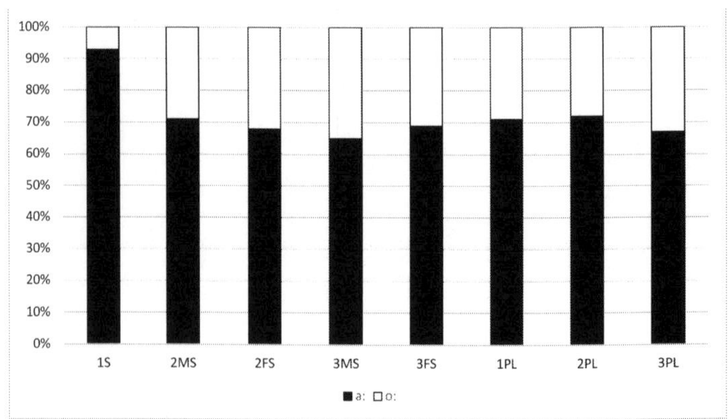

Figure 4.1a. AKAL (*ʔakal*): Percentage of paradigms a: and o: across the sample*

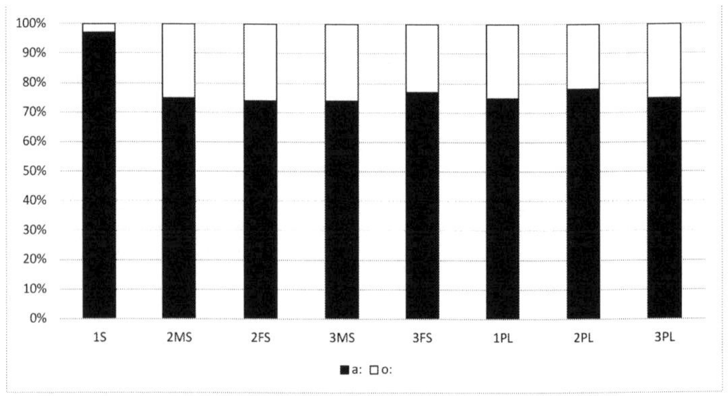

Figure 4.1b. AXAD (*ʔaxað*): Percentage of paradigms a: and o: across the sample*

number of options available. Recall that 3SM and 3P have more forms available in the original mix, with or without /j/, in addition to /oː/ versus /aː/ (see "Range of Variation in the Amman Data"). The rate of occurrence of Paradigm I is higher for the verb 'to take'; the transition is almost complete for 1S, and 74%–78% for the rest of the forms. Here too we notice that the rates for 3SM and 3P are slightly lower than the average. While focusing in TAKE is faster than EAT, both verbs show a similar pattern across the paradigm as a whole, which is an indication that the speakers treat the developments in both verbs as one feature.

The Role of Generation and Dialectal Heritage

One of the interesting aspects in the process of dialect formation in Amman is the layering of the social correlates across the generations, as well as the emergence of

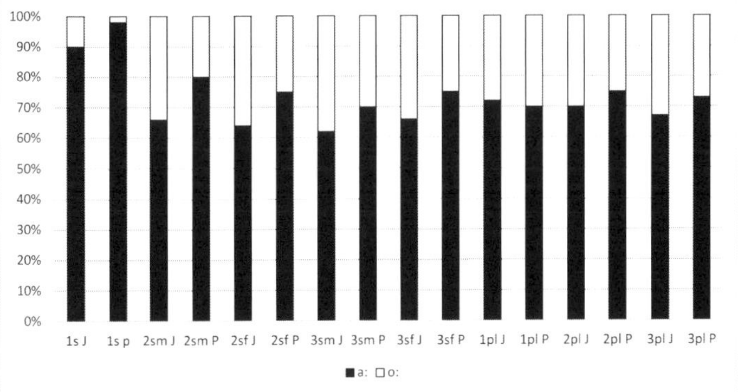

Figure 4.2a. AKAL (*ʔakal*): Percentage of paradigm a: for all speakers by heritage*

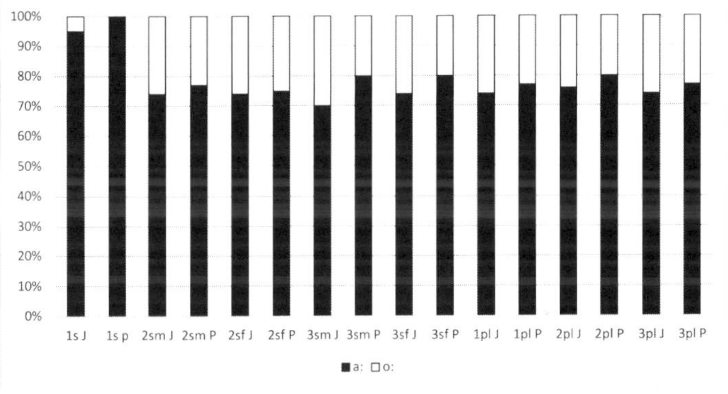

Figure 4.2b. AXAD (*ʔaxað*): Percentage of paradigm a: for all speakers by heritage*

new social variables. For instance, the variable (q) has two competing variants: local Jordanian [g] and urban Palestinian [ʔ]. In the first generation, dialectal background is the strongest predictor of the occurrence of (q) variants. In the second generation, gender emerges as a major factor that interacts with dialect heritage in constraining speakers' linguistic behavior. In the third generation, style and type of profession emerge as additional factors, and dialectal heritage is relegated to an even lower ranking among the social correlates (for details, see Al-Wer and Herin 2011). In another variable, namely, the 2P pronominal suffix -*kum*, dialectal heritage plays no role at all in the behavior of the third generation (for details see Al-Wer 2003).

Figures 4.2a and 4.2b show a breakdown of the results for the two verb paradigms by dialectal heritage, combining all generations.

As can be seen, the speakers who have a Palestinian dialectal heritage are overall ahead of the speakers with Jordanian heritage in using the incoming feature /aː/ for

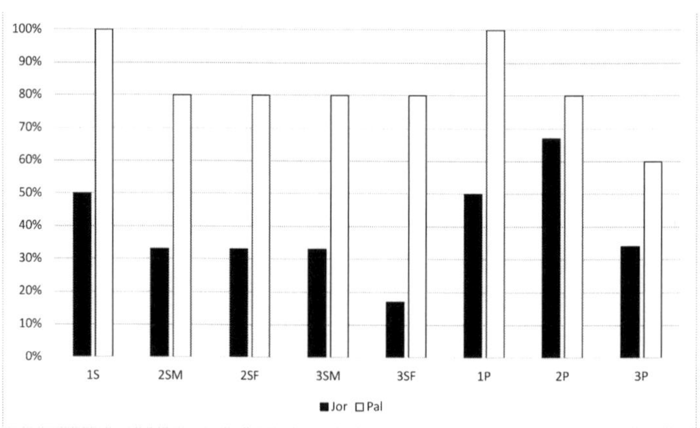

Figure 4.3. AKAL (*ʔakal*): Percentage of paradigm a: by heritage in the second generation*

both verbs. This group's lowest score is 70%, while in the case of Jordanian heritage it is 62%. Notice that, in EAT, the lowest score overall is that of 3SM, i.e., the conjugation with more options in the input varieties.

To see the effect of heritage across generations, let us first consider figure 4.3, which shows the results for EAT in the second generation by heritage. As mentioned earlier, the sample of speakers that supplied the full paradigm of EAT and TAKE are predominantly from the third and fourth generations. The sample, however, also includes 11 speakers from the second generation, 6 of whom are of Jordanian heritage.

Bearing in mind the much smaller sample, these results clearly show that the heritage dialect has a considerable effect in this generation. The incoming variant, conjugation with /a:/, is used considerably less by the second generation, who have a Jordanian dialectal heritage, and the trend toward this paradigm is led by the speakers with Palestinian heritage for all conjugations. Recall that /a:/ forms had been available in the Palestinian environment prior to immigration to Amman. We also notice that the use of the unusual Jordanian derivation 1S *bo:kol* is already reduced by half in the speech of those who would have inherited it from their parents (Jordanian heritage), while it is not used at all by the other group (Palestinian heritage).

Let us now look at the younger generations. Figures 4.4a and 4.4b display the results of the third and fourth generations by heritage dialect.

This figure shows that the gap between the two groups is considerably narrower compared with the second generation. For 1S, the unique Jordanian form *bo:kil* is almost completely leveled out. A plausible reason is that the Jordanian group changes their behavior in the direction of the koine form *ba:kul*. For the Palestinian group, which never had the *bo:kil* 'I eat' variant, it is simply a case of maintenance of a heritage form, which happens to be identical to the pan-Levantine form. The rest of the forms, however, tell a rather different story. For the Jordanian group, we

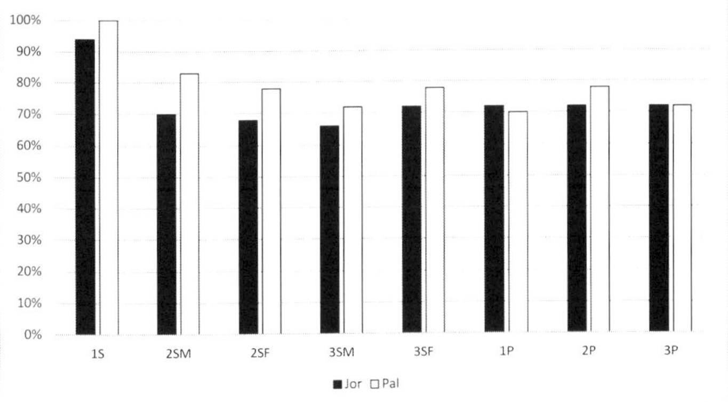

Figure 4.4a. AKAL (*ʔaxað*): Percentage of paradigm a: by heritage for generations 3 and 4*

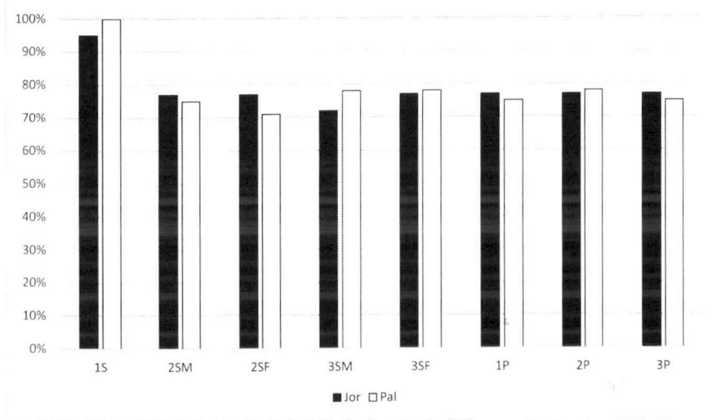

Figure 4.4b. AXAD (*ʔaxað*): Percentage of paradigm a: by heritage for generations 3 and 4*

see an increase in the use of /aː/ forms, but not to the same extent as for 1S. This is consistent with the general trajectory of change. However, for the Palestinian group, the younger speakers actually reduce the amount of /aː/ in comparison to the older speakers, moving in the opposite direction of the general trajectory. In doing so, they reduce the heritage gap seen in the previous generation, aligning their linguistic behavior with their Jordanian counterparts. The difference between these forms and 1S can be attributed to the fact that both /aː/ and /oː/ variants were available in the input dialect from Palestinian. Although the end result is a fairly homogeneous pattern, the effect of dialect heritage is still discernible from the existence of variation except for the disparity between the 1S form, exclusively with /aː/, and the rest of the paradigm, maintaining variation between /aː/ and /oː/.

The remaining important question that emerges from this investigation concerns the nature of the variation between the /aː/ and /oː/ forms in the younger generations, since dialectal heritage is no longer a significant factor. In ongoing research we investigate the possible effects of factors such as gender, type of education, and place of residence. However, this is a complex issue that we cannot resolve here. The results for individual speakers often reveal disparities between different parts of the paradigm, which do not appear to form a coherent pattern, e.g., /aː/ in 3SF and /oː/ in 3SM or vice versa. Moreover, the elicitation method obscures the potential for intra-speaker variation. Indeed, evidence from free speech indicates that some speakers are inconsistent in their use of /aː/ and /oː/ variants for the same element of the paradigm (also with respect to other features such as presence or absence of /j/ and the quality of the vowel in the second syllable). For instance, several speakers use more than one variant of 'he eats': *boːkil, boːkol, byoːkil, byoːkol, byaːkol, baːkul.*

Conclusion

The developments with respect to the verbs discussed in this chapter can be construed in the following ways. First, from the perspective of the traditional Jordanian dialects, these developments can be seen as a complication in the sense that there is now more than one possible form for the conjugation of the first, second, and third person; altogether there are now 21 different forms, instead of the 6 forms used in the traditional dialects outside Amman. At the same time, the split of 1S and 3SM leads to regularization of person representation: each person is assigned a unique form; 3SM form *boːkil* is maintained and assigned exclusively to 3SM; and the form *baːkul,* which emerged as a result of the contact situation, is assigned exclusively to 1S. Hence there is a reduction in meaning-form assignments.

Second, from the perspective of the Palestinian dialects, the mixed pattern that was transplanted in Amman has become more complex (as a result of contact, more forms are available in the environment). The net result of these developments is a high degree of dialect leveling in which Jordanian versus Palestinian heritage is no longer a determining factor. At the same time, the continued variation between /aː/ and /oː/ forms, roughly 3:1, clearly indicates that the younger generations have not yet settled on a fixed set of forms for the paradigms of these two verbs. While some aspects of this variation remain perplexing, as observed at the end of the previous section, their very existence underlines the hypothesis that the variation in the paradigms of these two verbs is still in a state of flux a century after the initial cohabitation of the two heritage communities.

Notes

*Some figures in this chapter are available on the publisher's website (press.georgetown.edu) to make it easier to view the data.

1. On koineization, see also Neteland (2017), Siegel (1985), and Tuten (2001).

2. Le Page (1980) distinguishes between a focused linguistic situation—where the norms are clear, stable, and shared—and a diffuse situation, where extreme heterogeneity and multiple systems prevail (see also Le Page and Tabouret-Keller 1985).

3. In Canadian Raising, the first element of the diphthongs /ai/ and /au/ is centralized before voiceless consonants but maintains an open quality elsewhere.

4. This research was funded by a Leverhulme Major Research Fellowship (MRF-2016-075) awarded to Enam Al-Wer.

5. We do not discuss "gender" as a variable further in this chapter. For details and discussion about the emergence of gender as a variable, see Al-Wer and Herin (2011).

6. It is worth noting that the urban Palestinian phonological pattern is identical to the pattern found in all city dialects in the Levant region. It is therefore possible to consider the development found in Amman as an example of regional koineization. The choice of a Jordanian-type of raising, to [ɛ], can be explained by the fact that it is a majority feature in Jordan as a whole. At the same time, extreme raising is a marked feature. For detailed analysis of the feminine ending and other developments in the third generation, see Al-Wer (2003, 2007, 2020).

7. These include the interdental phonemes, /dʒ/, negative polarity items, and pronominal suffixes.

8. The disparity in the figures for the two verbs is due to samples that were discarded because of misunderstanding on the part of participants or gaps in their responses.

9. From a historical perspective, the /oː/ forms cannot be accounted for through assuming derivation from the classical root *yaʔkul*. A possible alternative, suggested to us by the late Peter Behnstedt and Manfred Woidich, for which we are grateful, is derivation from an obsolete root, something like *yawkul > yoːkul*. This, however, does not account for its peculiar geographical distribution. In particular, it does not account for the concentration in a particular part of the Levant and in a particular subtype, Southern Levantine. The concentration in Southern Levantine may be attributed to substratal influence. Uri Horesh, personal communication, suggested that one possible substrate is Canaanite. In the only surviving descendent of Canaanite, namely, Hebrew, the verb 'to eat' does indeed have a back rounded vowel, historically /oː/, which is shortened in modern Hebrew *yoxal* 'he will eat.' We thank Uri Horesh for this suggestion, which we intend to explore further.

10. [d] is a variant of /ð/ in Amman Arabic. We use this variant in the spelling of all derivations for convenience, irrespective of which variant the speakers used.

11. Based on earlier stages of the research in Amman, Al-Wer (2014) maintains that dropping of Yod was least likely in EAT and TAKE precisely because it led to the merger of 1S and 3SM. Therefore, the occurrence of forms without Yod in these verbs in the current data is an indication that this constraint has been broken.

12. Reallocation normally refers to cases where more than one variant survive the koineization process and are redistributed and/or refunctionalized in the new system (see Britain and Trudgill 2005, 184; Kerswill 2003). Also see Al-Wer and Herin (2011) on reallocation of variants of /q/ in Amman.

References

Al-Wer, Enam. 2003. New dialect formation: The focusing of–*kum* in Amman. In D. Britain and J. Cheshire (eds.), *Social dialectology: In honour of Peter Trudgill*. Amsterdam: Benjamins, 59–67. https://doi.org/10.1075/impact.16.06alw

Al-Wer, Enam. 2007. The formation of the dialect of Amman. In C. Miller, E. Al-Wer, D. Caubet and J. C. Watson (eds.), *Arabic in the city*. New York: Routledge, 55–76.

Al-Wer, Enam. 2014. Yod-dropping in *b-imperfect* verb forms in Amman. In R. Khamis-Dakwar and K. Khamis-Dakwar (eds.), *Perspectives on Arabic linguistics*. Amsterdam: Benjamins, 29–44.

Al-Wer, Enam. 2020. New dialect formation: The Amman dialect. In C. Lucas and S. Manfredi (eds.), *Arabic and contact-induced language change: A handbook*. Berlin: Language Science Press, 551–66. doi: 10.5281/zenodo.3744549

Al-Wer, Enam and Bruno Herin. 2011. The lifecycle of *Qaf* in Jordan. *Langage et Société* 138: 59–76.

Behnstedt, Peter. 1985. *Die norjeminitischen Dialekte, Teil 1, Atlas*. Wiesbaden, Germany: Reichert.

Bergsträsser, G. 1915. *Sprachatlas von Syrien und Palästina*. Leipzig: Hinrichs.

Britain, David. 2010. Dialect contact, focusing and phonological rule complexity: The Koineisation of Fenland English. In M. Meyerhoff and E. Schleef (eds.), *The Routledge Sociolinguistic Reader*. Oxford: UK, 231–47. https://repository.upenn.edu/pwpl/vol4/iss1/10

Britain, David and Trudgill, Peter. 2005. New dialect formation and contact-induced reallocation: Three case studies from the English Fens. *International Journal of English Studies* 5 (1): 183–209. doi: 10.6018/ijes.5.1.47951

Brockett, Adrian A. 1985. The spoken Arabic of Khābūra on the Bātina of Oman. *Journal of Semitic Studies*. Monograph 7. https://www.jstor.org/stable/617766

Geva-Kleinberger, Aharon and Behnstedt, Peter. 2019. *Atlas of the Arabic dialects of Galilee (Israel)*. Leiden: Brill. doi: 10.1163/9789004411395

Herin, Bruno and Al-Wer, Enam. Forthcoming. *Grammar of a central Jordanian dialect*. Cambridge: Cambridge Semitic Languages and Cultures.

Kerswill, Paul. 2013. Koineization. In J. K. Chambers and N. Schilling (eds.), *The handbook of language variation and change*. Oxford: Wiley-Blackwell, 519–36. doi: 10.1002/9781118335598

Landberg, Comte De. 1901. *Ḥaḍramôut*. Leiden, Netherlands: Brill.

Le Page, R. B. 1980. Projection, focusing, diffusion, or, steps towards a sociolinguistic theory of language, illustrated from the Sociolinguistic Survey of Multilingual Communities. *York Papers in Linguistics* (Department of Language and Linguistic Science, University of York) 9: 9–32.

Le Page, Robert B and Andrée Tabouret-Keller. 1985. *Acts of identity*. Cambridge: Cambridge University Press.

Mufwene, Salikoko. 1996. The founder Principle in Creole genesis. *Diachronica* 13 (1): 83–134. doi: 10.1075/dia.13.1.05muf

Neteland, Randi. 2017. Koine formation in context. *Journal of Historical Sociolinguistics* 3 (1): 37–54. doi: 10.1515/jhsl-2017-0002

Seeger, Ulrich. 2013. *Der arabische Dialekt der Dörfer um Ramallah, Teil 3, Grammatik*. Wiesbaden: Harrassowitz.

Siegel, Jeff. 1985. Koines and Koineization. *Language in Society* 14 (3): 357–78. https://www.jstor.org/stable/4167665

Trudgill, Peter. 1986. *Dialects in contact*. Oxford: Blackwell.

Trudgill, Peter. 2006. *New-dialect formation: The inevitability of Colonial Englishes*. Edinburgh: Edinburgh University Press.

Tuten, Donald. 2001. Modeling Koineization. In Laurel J. Brinton (ed.), *Historical linguistics 1999: Selected papers from the 14th international conference on historical linguistics*. Amsterdam: John Benjamins, 325–36. doi: 10.1075/cilt.215.22tut

Chapter 5

● Unwitting Convergence: Kolokwa and Liberian Settler English

ALLISON SHAPP
New York University

MICHAEL MARINACCIO
L-Università ta' Malta

JOHN VICTOR SINGLER
New York University

Introduction

Dialect contact occurs when speakers of different but mutually intelligible varieties of a language interact regularly, and its results can be seen in borrowings of linguistic features between the two dialects or, put another way, the two varieties converging toward each other.[1] The extent to which this happens, and in which direction, is tied to both linguistic and social factors. In this chapter we focus on one such case, the contact of two Englishes in Liberia, and consider the convergence we see in the vowel systems of the two in terms of linguistic/phonological patterns of change, as well as its place within the specific sociocultural history of the region.

There are two non-standard Englishes in Liberia (Singler 1997), and the distinction between them embodies a fundamental ethnic and political separateness. Kolokwa is the modern Liberian descendant of the West African Pidgin English that developed widely along coastal eighteenth-century West Africa. Liberian Settler English (LSE) is the language of the descendants of the 16,000 African Americans who immigrated to Liberia in the nineteenth century. Throughout their history in Liberia, the Settlers have seen their separateness as necessary to the survival of their identity as a group. Accordingly, they have sought to maintain linguistic distinctiveness and, they would argue, superiority. Certainly, there have been borrowings in each direction, but more often and more centrally features have gone from LSE to Kolokwa (Singler 2012). In this chapter we examine the vowel systems of both dialects and consider how being in contact has affected them. We show that Kolokwa's vowel system reflects the vowel systems of the Niger-Congo languages spoken in and around Monrovia. We then argue that despite the Settlers' intentional separateness and maintained sense of superiority, the vowel system of LSE has moved toward that of Kolokwa.

In sociolinguistics, changes in progress can be categorized as a "change from above" or a "change from below," which refers to whether the linguistic variable in question is above or below the level of consciousness for speakers participating in the change (Labov [1996] 2006). Because they often line up, these same terms are often also used to refer to whether a new form is being adopted from a more prestigious group or standard variety of the language, i.e., "from above" in that sense, or from a less prestigious group within the speech community, i.e., "from below" (Labov 1994).

Another way to categorize "level of consciousness" of a linguistic variable for its speakers is *salience*. Salience is a continuous measure of the degree to which speakers are aware of a certain feature, rather than the binary notion of above or below. Previous studies focusing on salience have shown vowels to be on the low end of salience for speakers (Kang 2022), that is, speakers are not very aware of their vowel systems or changes to them.

The present case is a change from below in both ways, as well as likely low in salience. More notably, and in focus here, is that the change involves a more prestigious group assimilating its vowel system toward that of a group that they deem to be lower in status (hence, "unwitting convergence").

In what follows, we begin with an overview of English-lexifier varieties in Liberia (the "History" section). We then describe a corpus of Kolokwa speech in the following section. The Kolokwa speakers whose speech we examine all had a local Niger-Congo language as a co-first language (co-L1). We present the Kolokwa speakers' vowel system and argue for the influence of speakers' Niger-Congo languages on it. In the "Settler English" section, we describe a Settler English corpus. We argue for Kolokwa influence on the Settlers' vowel system. We consider the comparative status of Settlers and Kolokwa speakers and examine Settler attitudes toward Kolokwa speakers (the "Attitudes" section). Finally, in a concluding section, "Discussion," we return to the original discussion of dialect contact and locate the interaction between Kolokwa and LSE relative to that discussion.

History

The presence of an English-lexifier variety in Liberia is frequently pinned to the arrival in 1822 of the first of the African American immigrants. In fact, more than a century earlier, an English-lexifier trade language had begun to develop all along the West African coast. Along what was to become the Liberian portion of the coast, the earliest references to local individuals speaking English come from 1702 (Snoek, in Bosman 1705, 484) and 1726 (Smith [1744] 1967, 107). In the course of the eighteenth century, the trade language evolved into West African Pidgin English. Attestations to its presence in Liberia at the time of the Settlers' arrival come from Jehudi Ashmun, a white American missionary, the agent of the American Colonization Society, who governed the Settlers' colony initially:[2]

> . . . very many in all the maritime tribes, speak a corruption of the English language. (*African Repository* 1827, 263)
>   A . . . facility which few pagan tribes [elsewhere] offer to the American Missionary, is to be found in the circumstance, that every head man around us, and hundreds of their people speak, and can be made to understand our language without an interpreter. (qtd. in Gurley 1835, app. 30)

Upon establishing themselves in Liberia, the Settlers quickly took command. Those who immigrated to Liberia in the nineteenth century and their descendants have never constituted more than 3–5% of the population, yet, once they had established their primacy, they maintained political, economic, and social control absolutely until a 1980 military coup toppled the Settler government.

From the outset, the Settlers grounded their right to rule in their Christianity, their exposure to Western culture, and—especially—their command of English, as articulated in Alexander Crummell's 1860 Independence Day oration in the Liberian city of Harper:

> Here, on this coast . . . is an organized community, republican in form and name, a people possessed of Christian institutions and civilized habits, with this one marked peculiarity, that is, that in color, race, and origin, they are identical with the masses around them; and yet speak the refined and cultivated English language . . .
>   [T]he exile of our fathers from their African homes to America, [has] given us, their children, at least one item of compensation, namely, the possession of the Anglo-Saxon tongue; that this language put us in a position which none other on the globe could give us: and that it was impossible to estimate too highly, the prerogatives and the elevation the Almighty has bestowed upon us, in our having as our own, the speech of Chaucer and Shakespeare, of Milton and Wordsworth, or Bacon and Burke, of Franklin and Webster. (Crummell 1862, 9, qtd. in Singler 1977, 73)

Even after the 1980 military coup and continuing to the present day, the Settlers have maintained cultural hegemony, continuing to exert their narrative regarding Settler-indigene relations, culture, and command of English. It is worth noting, however, that the immigrants to Liberia came overwhelmingly from the American South. In the period from 1822 to the start of the American Civil War in 1861, the period when most of the Settlers came to Liberia, a majority of them were enslaved, with immigration to Liberia a condition for their manumission. Thus, the language that they brought with them was not standard English but was instead (nineteenth-century) African American English vernacular.

For the focus of the present study, it is crucial to look at the vowel system that the Settlers, reinforced by missionary educators, would have introduced to Liberia. This system, which we adapt from the mid-nineteenth-century African American English

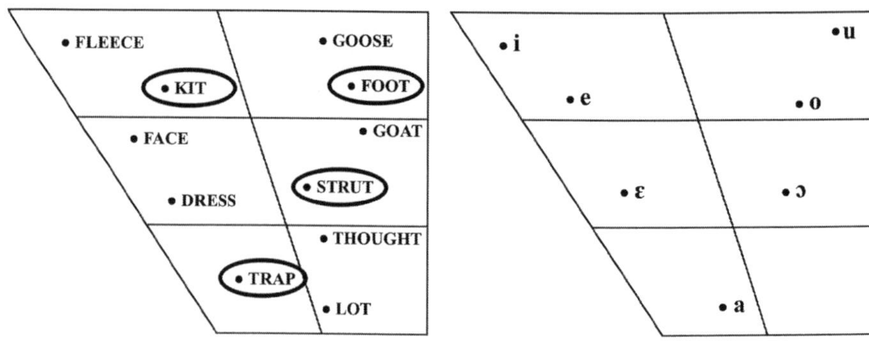

Figure 5.1. The Niger-Congo vowel chart (right) lacks the TRAP, STRUT, KIT, and FOOT vowels present in the mid-nineteenth-century African American English vowel chart (left), adapted from Bailey and Thomas (1998)

vowel charts included in Bailey and Thomas (1998), is presented in figure 5.1, left. We use the lexical sets proposed by Wells (1982) to map the vowels. We have not included the NURSE vowel on this chart and do not include it in the discussion that follows. We are still investigating the nature of this vowel and will be reporting on it subsequently.

A further point with regard to Liberia's Englishes involves terminology. Singler (1997) reports that in Liberia all English-lexifier speech—whether descended from International English, West African Pidgin English, or Settler English—is called "English." In the present century, the term "Kolokwa" (< *colloquial*) has emerged for the Liberian instantiation of West African Pidgin English. In what follows, we use, anachronistically, the term "Kolokwa" for data collected in the late 1980s.[3] In Liberia, when Settler English is singled out, it is most often designated "Congo English," "Congo" being a term for Settlers (cf. Singler 2022a, forthcoming).

Kolokwa

Our data comprise two corpora, one Kolokwa, and the other Settler English, both collected in 1988–89, just prior to the civil war and subsequent turmoil that devastated Liberia in the years from 1989 to 2003. We first present the Lakpazee Kolokwa Corpus and then set forth the methodology that we used to assess speakers' vowel systems. The speakers represented in this corpus all had a Niger-Congo language as a co-L1 with Kolokwa. The influence of these languages on the Kolokwa vowel system stands as an instance of change arising from language contact.

The Lakpazee Kolokwa Corpus

The Kolokwa data consists of 24 sociolinguistic interviews carried out in the ethnically mixed Monrovia neighborhood of Lakpazee. John Mason, the interviewer, was a stevedore in his early 30s with a junior high school education. He had lived in

Lakpazee for six years at the time of the interviews. Like Mason, 12 of the people he spoke with were ethnically Bassa, the largest of Monrovia's original ethnic groups. The Bassa language is from the Kru branch of Niger-Congo. The other 12 speakers were from ethnolinguistic groups whose homeland is in the Liberian interior—Kpelle, Lɔma, Mano (Maa), and Dan (Gio). These four languages come from the Mande branch of Niger-Congo. All 24 of the speakers presented themselves as Monrovia born. They were selected so as to fit into three groups on the basis of age and amount of western education: the Elders, who were born in the 1930s and early 1940s and had little or no western education; the Marketers, who were born in the 1960s and had limited western education; and the Book People, who were born in the 1960s and had some secondary schooling. Each group had equal numbers of Bassa and Mande speakers and equal numbers of men and women.

Singler (2022b) illustrates differences between the three cohorts in number marking, specifically in the overt marking of semantically plural regular nouns. There are two markers of plural number, the English *-z* and the creole postposed marker *dem* (< 3PL.OBJ.PRO). Examining the 12 Bassa speakers, Singler shows that overt marking was far more frequent among the two younger cohorts (Book People, 49%; Marketers, 45%) than among the Elders (16%). The two younger cohorts then differ from each other as to the frequency with which they use each number marker. Of the times when they mark number, the Book People use *-z* by itself 82% of the time and *dem* by itself 10% of the time, while for the Marketers the frequency for *-z* is 67% and *dem* 27%. While the move toward *-z* is in the direction not only of LSE but also standard English, various nonstandard features of LSE (and ultimately African American English) have entered Kolokwa as well, indicating a direction of diffusion from LSE to Kolokwa. Among these features are the use of *ain't* in place of *didn't*, stressed *bin*, the semi-auxiliary *come*, and auxiliary *steady* (see Singler 2007). Rather than the division of the Lakpazee speakers by age and amount of education that obtains for number marking, there is a difference by ethnicity in the use of the imperfective AUX *də*, a feature that in Liberia has a Settler provenance (Singler 2015; see also Gullah *də*). In the sociolinguistic interviews that comprise the Lakpazee Kolokwa corpus, 11 of the 12 ethnolinguistically Bassa speakers use *də* while only 4 of the 12 speakers from Mande ethnolinguistic groups do so. The difference reflects an ongoing difference in the amount of contact that the coastal Bassa had historically with the Settlers when compared with the amount that interior-based Mande groups had.

An example of Kolokwa speech is given in (1). The speaker is Kathryn, an Elder whose other L1 is the Mande language Kpelle.[4]

(1) bɔ des tã aɪ o na, hi kæ̃ lʊk aʔ ma feʔ bəkɔ aɪ oʔ
    but this time I old now. he can't look at my face, because I old.
    bɔ də tã aɪ wə ɲɔŋ, wɛ̃ aɪ go dɛ, hi we lʊk aʔ ma feʔ.
    but the time I was young. when I go there, he will look at my face.
    'But now I'm old and he ignores me because I'm old. But when I was young, when I went there [to his office], he paid attention to me.'

The example in (1) also illustrates a prominent feature of Kolokwa, the frequency with which underlying syllable-final consonants are left unpronounced. Expressed in

Optimality-Theoretic terms, Kolokwa speakers assign a high ranking to the *CODA constraint.

Liberia's Niger-Congo Languages

The languages spoken in and around Monrovia historically all have the seven-vowel system, represented by the vowel chart on the right in figure 5.1; this is true regardless of their affiliation within Niger-Congo.

The languages in question include Bassa and Dewoin (Kru branch), Vai (Mande), and Gola (Atlantic).[5] This characterization also applies to Kpelle, Lɔma, and Mano (Maa)—three of the four "interior" Mande languages spoken by members of the Lakpazee set. The remaining Mande language, Gio (Dan), has a 10-vowel system that diverges sharply from that of the other languages under discussion: it has 3 front vowels, 4 central vowels, and 3 back vowels. We return to Gio below.[6]

If we assume that the 11-vowel system, presented on the left of figure 5.1, is the model for English in Liberia, then we can see that four of these vowels have no analogue in the Niger-Congo 7-vowel system, shown on the right of the figure. As comparing the two vowel charts in figure 5.1 shows, there is no equivalent to TRAP, STRUT, FOOT, and KIT.

Methodology

Each of the interviews in the Lakpazee Kolokwa Corpus was annotated in Praat and run through Dartmouth Linguistic Automation (DARLA) (Reddy and Stanford 2015) for alignment and vowel extraction. The application of DARLA to a variety that was not standard American English required us to make certain adjustments (see Chevalier 2016; MacKenzie and Turton 2020). Normalization was performed at the time of vowel extraction using the Lobanov method.

Subsequently, the data were processed using R (R Core Team 2023), and several types of tokens were removed from the analysis. The first five minutes of each interview were removed, along with a list of stop words. Vowels in specific phonological environments were thrown out: when they were preceded by a nasal, glide, or /l/, as well as when they were followed by a nasal, liquid, glide, another vowel, or /g/ (Wong 2015, 192). Finally, all unstressed vowels were removed from the dataset. This process resulted in a Lakpazee Corpus of 13,955 vowel tokens across 24 speakers and 11 vowel categories.

Analyzing Vowel Overlap

To analyze speakers' vowel systems, we used Bhattacharyya's Affinity (BA), a statistical measure of affinity (overlap) between two populations, in the present case to ascertain degree of vowel merger (Bhattacharyya 1943; Johnson 2015; Marinaccio, Shapp, and Singler 2021; Stanley and Sneller 2021). BA scores range from 0 (completely distinct sets of data points) to 1 (completely overlapping sets of data points). Adapting from Strelluf (2018), we used a benchmark of ≥.8 to represent two vowels with a high overlap, i.e., a vowel merger, and <.6 to identify the two vowels as distinct. Vowel pairs whose BA score was intermediate between the two benchmarks of .6 and .8 were seen as displaying partial overlap but were not considered to be merged.

Kolokwa Results

Figure 5.2 plots the vowels of Kathryn, the speaker cited above. The label of each vowel is located at the mean formant values for that vowel for the speaker, and the ellipses represent one standard deviation from the mean. Plotting the vowel data like this offers a visual representation of vowel overlap, which we quantify by calculating BA scores for each pair of vowels for each speaker.

In Kathryn's speech, the four vowels not found in Liberia's Niger-Congo languages (see figure 5.1) have all undergone mergers with existing vowels: TRAP has merged with LOT (BA = .839), STRUT with THOUGHT (BA = .867), FOOT with GOAT (BA = .908), and KIT with FACE (BA = .843). These mergers point to a seven-vowel Kolokwa system. In fact, the three-way merger of high-front vowels (Kathryn's BA score for KIT-FLEECE is .895 and for FACE-FLEECE is .831) shows Kathryn to have a six-vowel system.

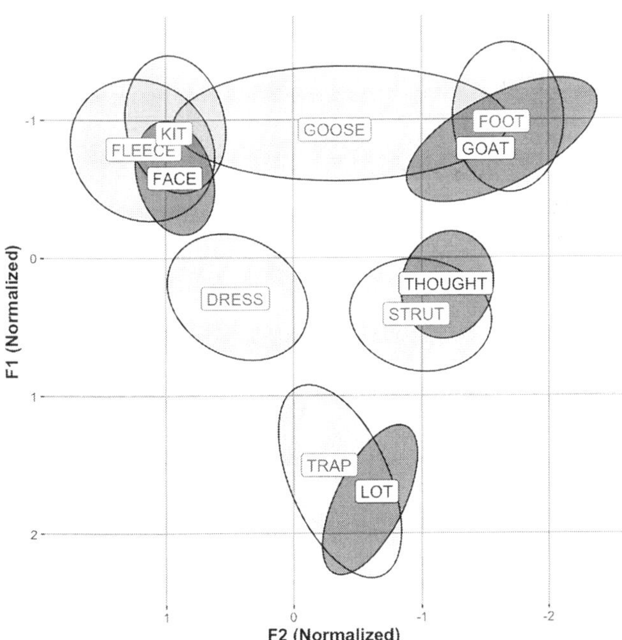

Figure 5.2. Kolokwa speaker Kathryn's vowel plot, showing six vowel pairs that overlap to the extent of merger (BA Score ≥ .8): TRAP-LOT (BA = .839), STRUT-THOUGHT (BA = .867), FOOT-GOAT (BA = .908), KIT-FACE (BA = .843), KIT-FLEECE (BA = .895), and FACE-FLEECE (BA = .831)

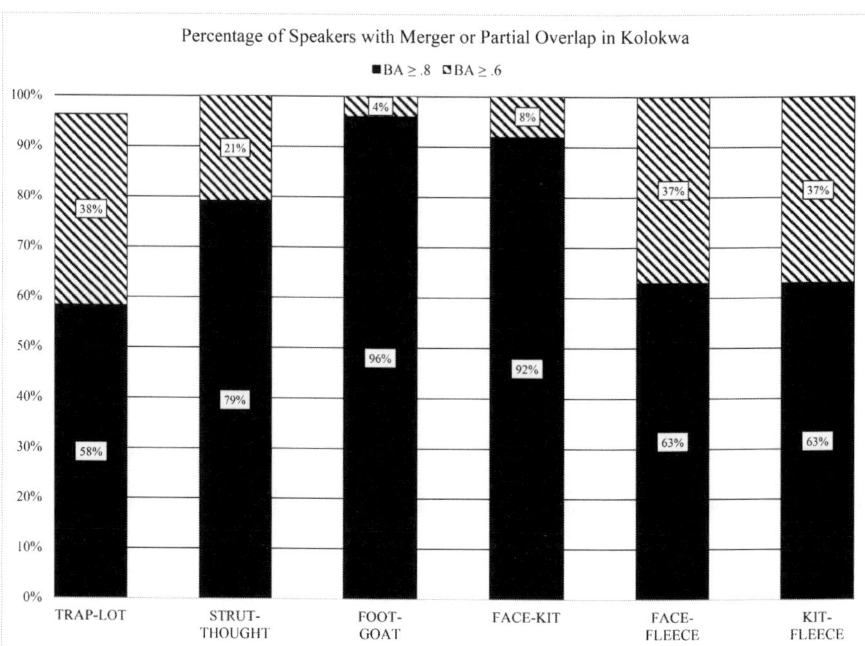

Figure 5.3. The percentage of Kolokwa speakers ($n = 24$) who have mergers (solid color) for a given vowel pair; the graph also shows the percentage of speakers ($n = 24$) who, while not having a merger, show partial overlap (striped); the BA scores for mergers are ≥ .8 and for partial overlap $.8 > x > .6$*

As figure 5.3 demonstrates, Kathryn's six-vowel system is representative of the Lakpazee Kolokwa speakers more generally. A majority of the 24 speakers show values that surpass the .8 BA threshold for each of the six pairs.

In sum, apart from the additional conflation of high front vowels, the Kolokwa vowel system parallels the vowel system that obtains generally in the region's Niger-Congo languages.[7]

Unlike the morphosyntactic features mentioned earlier that displayed sensitivity to such social features as age/formal schooling and speaker's co-L1, the vowel system in the Lakpazee Kolokwa Corpus does not show any correlation with speaker's social attributes. This may indicate that the current state of the Kolokwa vowel system is a long-standing one.

As noted earlier, Gio (Dan) constitutes an exception to the local Niger-Congo pattern, most significantly in its having four central vowels. Thus, Gio would seem to have a vowel that corresponds rather directly to the English vowel STRUT. Of the 12 Lakpazee Kolokwa speakers with a Mande co-L1, 4 have Gio as this language. This sets up the possibility that the Kolokwa vowel system for these 4 speakers would be different from the other speakers, whether the other 8 speakers with a Mande co-L1 or all 20 of the other Lakpazee Kolokwa speakers. In fact, this does not obtain (see table 5.1).

Table 5.1. Mean BA scores by speakers' co-L1

Ethnolinguistic group	Number of speakers	TRAP-LOT	STRUT-THOUGHT	GOAT-FOOT	FACE-KIT
Gio	4	.795	.831	.868	.897
Other Mande	8	.790	.827	.894	.839
Bassa	12	.809	.858	.873	.878

The explanation for the lack of a difference between the speakers with a Gio co-L1 and the others lies in the historical progression of Kolokwa acquisition. Within Liberia, Kolokwa developed along the coast in the eighteenth century. Those in the interior did not acquire Kolokwa until the twentieth century. Thus, the ethnolinguistically Gio—like the Kpelle, the Loma, and the Mano—acquired Kolokwa through contact with existing Kolokwa speakers on the coast, speakers who, we argue, had already transformed the vowel system (see Singler 2000).

Settler English

The language of the communities of African American emigrants—and, now, their descendants—is Settler English. Among other things, these communities vary in the American provenance of the original settlers and in the degree and character over time of the interaction with indigenous Liberians. The focus of the present research is on elderly Settlers in Sinoe County, 150 miles down the coast from Monrovia. Unlike Settlers elsewhere—who came primarily from the mid-Atlantic states of Virginia, Maryland, and North Carolina—the original Sinoe Settlers came overwhelmingly from a five-state swath of the Lower South, from South Carolina across to Louisiana (Singler 1989). Additionally, Settler-indigene relations were especially fraught in Sinoe.

The Sinoe Settler Corpus

The Settler data consist of sociolinguistic interviews carried out with 15 Sinoe Settlers. Some of the interviews took place in the county capital, Greenville (plus Farmersville, which Greenville has now absorbed), while the rest took place with residents of three agricultural settlements up the Sinoe River from Greenville—Lexington, Louisiana, and Bluntsville. The interviewer in most instances was Hosea Ellis, a teacher and seminary student from the settlement of Louisiana. With two exceptions, the interviews took place in 1988–89, the same time period when the Lakpazee Kolokwa Corpus was being compiled in Monrovia.[8]

Table 5.2 presents the 15 Sinoe Settlers, arranged in order from least amount of formal education to greatest.

The range extends from Absalom and Ishmael, who had no formal schooling whatsoever, to Jemima, a high school graduate. A study of number marking (Singler

Table 5.2. The demographic information of the participants
in the Sinoe Settler Corpus

Settler name	Home settlement	Highest grade	Birth year
Absalom	Bluntsville	0	1916
Ishmael	Bluntsville	0	1919
Ezekiel	Louisiana	1st	1910
Dolly	Greenville	4th	1927
Keziah	Lexington	4th	1919
Claudius	Louisiana	5th	1910
Hamilton	Bluntsville	5th	1927
Nancy	Lexington	5th	1927
Etmonia	Greenville	6th	1923
Wilmot	Louisiana	6th	1910
Carolina	Farmersville	8th	1910
Rosabella	Lexington	9th	1906
Florence	Lexington	10th	1910
Cephas	Greenville	11th	1914
Jemima	Greenville	12th	1917

1994) shows a three-way occupational distinction to have a greater correlation
with linguistic features than does education: those who held a government job as
a teacher, those who held some other government job, and those who did not hold
a government job. That same study shows a correlation with the speaker's home
settlement (speakers who had grown up in the county capital Greenville showed
greater frequency of overt marking than did those from settlements up the Sinoe
River from the coast) and number of trips to Monrovia (with greater frequency
of travel *disfavoring* overt marking) but does not show a correlation with speaker
sex or age (all of the speakers were elderly) or whether Singler was present at the
interview or not. Another example of a job-related difference involves possessive 's.
Teachers use it a bit less than 25% of the time, but non-teachers do not use it at all
(Singler 2015, 122n).

An example of Settler speech is given in (2). The speaker is Wilmot, a retired
justice of the peace who was born in 1910 and had a sixth-grade education.

> (2) aɪ we bed ə pəteto be ɛ̃ kɔt wʊd, ɔ do kan ə tɛ̃ dɛ
>   I will build a potato bay and cut wood, all those kind of thing there
>   ef aɪ kɛ̃ bed ə pəteto be gut, dɛ̃ aɪ we gɛ dæ gɛ.
>   if I can build a potato bay good, then I will get that girl.
>   dæ haʊ wi justə kɔt ɔ wumɛ̃.
>   that how we used-to court our women.

Settler Results

The same methodology was employed for the Sinoe Settlers as had been used for the Kolokwa speakers, resulting in a Sinoe Settler Corpus of 10,508 vowel tokens across 15 speakers and 11 vowel categories.

Figure 5.4 plots the vowels of Wilmot, the Settler speaker cited above. Again using .8 as the threshold for merger, we see that there are three mergers (unlike the six that Kathryn and the Kolokwa speakers more generally displayed): STRUT-THOUGHT (BA = .813), FOOT-GOAT (BA = .894), and KIT-FACE (BA = .938).[9] While the other three pairs—TRAP-LOT (BA = .681), KIT-FLEECE (BA = .631), and FACE-FLEECE (BA = .605)—display partial overlap, they clearly do not display the merger of any of these pairs.

Figure 5.5 compares the distribution of mergers between Kolokwa speakers (solid black bars, near mergers striped black bars) and Settlers (solid dark-gray bars, near mergers striped dark-gray bars). A majority of the Settlers display the three mergers outlined above. We ran linear models in R to test for effects of social factors on the BA scores of each relevant vowel pair for the Settlers. There were no significant results

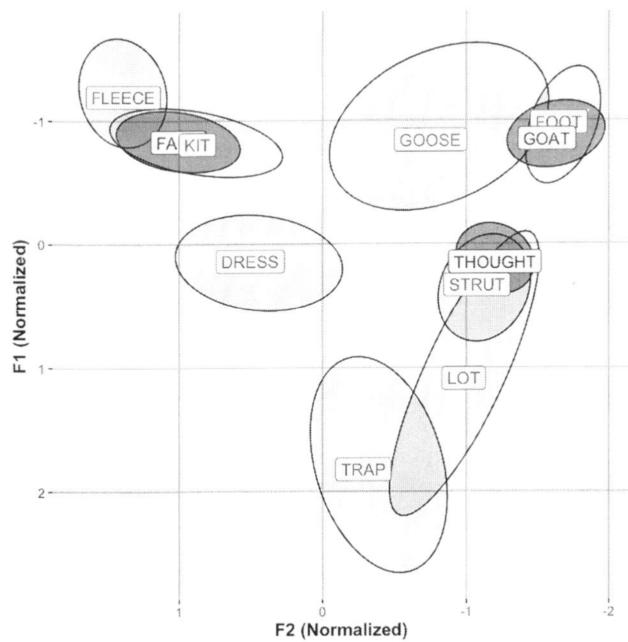

Figure 5.4. Settler English speaker Wilmot's vowel plot, showing three vowel pairs that overlap to the extent of merger (BA Score ≥ .8): STRUT-THOUGHT (BA = .813), FOOT-GOAT (BA = .894), and KIT-FACE (BA = .938); three other vowel pairs display partial overlap (BA Score .8 > x > .6): TRAP-LOT (BA = .681), KIT-FLEECE (BA = .631), and FACE-FLEECE (BA = .605); in the top left of the graph, the mean formant value for FACE is partially obscured by the mean formant value for KIT

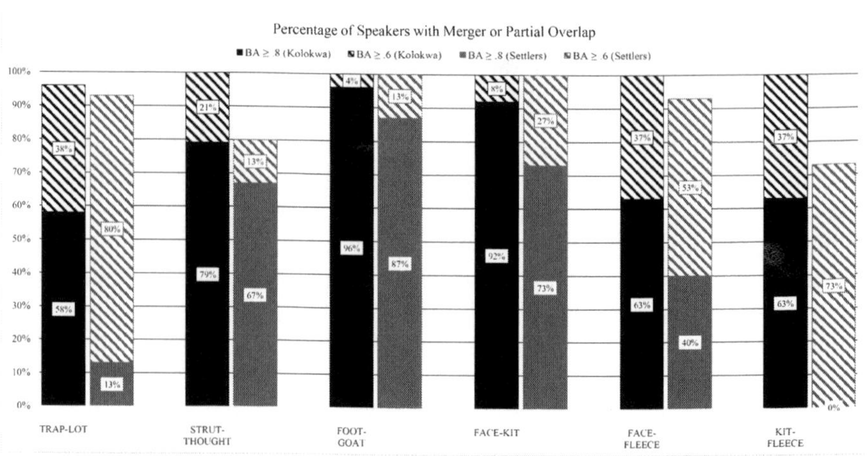

Figure 5.5. The percentage of Kolokwa speakers (*n* = 24) and Settler English speakers (*n* = 15) who have mergers (solid color) for a given vowel pair; the graph also shows the percentage of speakers (Kolokwa, *n* = 24; Settlers, *n* = 15) who, while not having a merger, show partial overlap (striped); the BA scores for mergers are ≥ .8 and for partial overlap .8 > *x* > .6*

for models containing year of birth, sex, amount of education, job type, and settlement where childhood was spent as predictors of BA scores for KIT-FACE ($p = .22$), STRUT-THOUGHT ($p = .77$), or FOOT-GOAT ($p = .35$).

Attitudes

We contend that the vowel system that the Settlers brought with them from America (as shown in figure 5.1) has now undergone three vowel mergers as a consequence of contact with Kolokwa. The Sinoe Settlers would have been in daily contact with Kolokwa speakers; thus, the Kolokwa model was present for them. However, there is the question of Settler attitudes about indigenous Liberians, i.e., Kolokwa speakers. As noted above, from the outset the Settlers have seen themselves as culturally superior, continually disparaging indigenous culture. In 1835, the Settler newspaper, *Liberia Herald*, characterized the indigenous people around them as "these half cannibals" (qtd. in *African Repository* 1835, 11:338). A century later, Richard Strong, leader of the Harvard African Exhibition to Liberia in 1926–27, observed: "A number of Americo-Liberians [i.e., Settlers] . . . maintain an attitude of high superiority" toward Liberia's indigenous population (1930, 36). The attitude continues to be entrenched. As noted, while the 1980 military coup d'état ended the Settlers' political control, their cultural hegemony persists. This attitude has been lexicalized, specifically with the use of "civilized" to refer to Settlers: "But the Kru people now they sing when they be dancing. But we civilized people we go by the music, that's all." It is noteworthy that the speaker is Absalom, a Settler with no formal education.[10]

The Sinoe Settler Claudius in an interview says, "I think that what I can remember well, they had war two time." Singler asks, "With who?" and Claudius answers, "With the bush. With the heathen. You know, the heathen people." When he said this, those present laughed. Singler sensed that the laughter was nervous, that the others felt that "heathen" was not a term to be used around outsiders. Further inquiry has shown the term to be one that Settlers, especially elderly Settlers, continue to use in in-group settings.

The persistence of the Settlers' attitude of superiority emerges in a 2019 interview with a Settler quiltmaker and quilting instructor in Greater Monrovia. The original Settlers brought the practice of quilt making to Liberia, a history that all modern quilters are aware of, including the indigenous women who now make quilts as well (Beck Cohen 2016, 29–30). The Settler quilt maker being interviewed is retired. She taught in an after-school program and reports that she liked teaching girls from indigenous backgrounds: "Because sometimes, the illiterate person will want to know this work quicker than the girls that we call civilized. They don't want to know it; they want to be up and down. But the illiterate girl will come and sit down. Because she don't know anything; she want to know something." For the retired quilting teacher, "illiterate" and "civilized" indicate ethnic affiliation.

Discussion

The mergers shown above of three vowel pairs in the speech of the Settlers is a contact-induced change, moving the vowel system of LSE closer to that of Kolokwa. Within LSE, we did not find the number of mergers exhibited by each speaker to be linked to social factors such as employment history, education, or home settlement (see the "Settler Results" section).

The fact that the LSE vowel mergers are not stratified by social factors is perhaps surprising in relation to the language ideology described in the previous section, with which the Settlers maintain a clear sense of superiority for their group, bolstered by their claim to a more Westernized version of English. So why would they let their vowels drift toward those of the "heathens"?

While this is a change to LSE that is from "below" in terms of the prestige of the social groups, it is also likely of low salience to the speakers and therefore, we argue, more easily available for acquisition by a higher-prestige group, even though the variety as a whole is stigmatized among those speakers.

Kang (2022, this volume), in a study of second dialect acquisition and long-term accommodation between varieties, analyzes the speech of two groups of Korean speakers who had moved to a new area where a different dialect of their same language was prominent. One group moved from Seoul, the home of the most prestigious dialect of Korean, to a rural area with a less-prestigious dialect, and the other group had done the opposite. Similar to the present results, Kang also found some adoption by the speakers from Seoul of features from the less-prestigious rural dialect.

Kang examined several factors that could offer explanation as to which features tended to be adopted by each group and which tended not to be adopted. A meaningful component was the salience of the linguistic variable undergoing change. Kang asked speakers to identify linguistic features that they were aware of and found that the ranking in terms of salience for the relevant features patterned identically for speakers of the higher- and lower-prestige dialects. She also found that changes in vowel quality were ranked low in terms of salience, often not rising to the level of conscious awareness at all. Further, she found that salience correlated with which features were more extensively adopted by each group. The features of the high-status dialect acquired by the speakers of the lower-status group were those that were more salient, while the converse was also true: the features of the stigmatized dialect most acquired by speakers of the higher-status variety were those that had the least salience.

Although the change in the vowel system under discussion does not appear to correlate with any social factors, other patterns of variation in LSE such as coda consonant deletion have been found to be more sensitive to variation along social lines (Singler, forthcoming), and these are the variables that are also more salient to speakers of LSE, and that are associated with Kolokwa, the more stigmatized variety. Examples of more salient features in English in Liberia are those that entail a change between input and output in the number of surface segments, e.g., deletion of /s/ in an onset obstruent cluster (Singler 2010, 2011), addition of a vowel after a word-final coda consonant (Singler 1991, 1996, 2000), and coda consonant deletion (Singler, forthcoming). While a certain degree of coda consonant deletion is seen in nineteenth-century African American English (Harrison [1884] 1975), all of these more salient features of LSE can be linked directly to the phonotactics of relevant Niger-Congo languages. This presumably causes Settlers (and speakers of Kolokwa as well) to stigmatize them, thereby making them more sensitive to stratification by social factors.

While most previous work on salience focuses on how more salient variables can be adopted or avoided intentionally by speakers (Erker 2022; Nycz 2011; Trudgill 1986), we draw on the opposite side of that coin, that variables low in salience are the ones that are available to be involved in a "change from below" in terms of prestige. The distinctiveness of vowel categories in a dialect's vowel system is low in terms of salience (Kang 2022), which we contend makes it more available to changes that go against conscious language ideology. Thus, in this instance in Settler English of a phenomenon that is low in salience and below the level of consciousness, we see a change that directly contradicts the Settlers' deeply held sociocultural ideology of separateness and superiority.

Notes

*Some figures in this chapter are available on the publisher's website (press.georgetown.edu) to make it easier to view the data.

1. We thank the Sinoe Settler elders and the Lakpazee residents for sharing their lives. We owe much to the late Hosea Ellis and the late John Mason for their skill at talking with people and their insights about language. The Sinoe Settler research was initially funded by a National Endowment for the Humanities Summer Stipend and then by NSF Grant 9011706, and the Lakpazee research by a Fulbright Senior

Research Scholarship, African Region. Both areas of research were subsequently funded by NSF Grant 1749459. We thank Jen Nycz and the GURT audience for helpful discussion of our topic.

2. In its efforts to attract free African Americans to its colony in Africa in the 1820s, the American Colonization Society was competing with a campaign to attract members of the same population to Haiti (Jackson 1976). Implicit in Ashmun's assertion that a form of English already obtained along the Liberian coast was a comparison with Haiti.

3. Like other modern varieties of West African Pidgin English, Kolokwa has, over time, undergone extensive expansion. In distinguishing between pidgins and creoles, Kouwenberg and Singler (2011, 286) state: "*Creole* designates a language which is either natively spoken, or functions as community language, or both." Kolokwa has native speakers, and it is definitely the community language. One cannot pinpoint exactly when it started to have a meaningful number of native speakers or to emerge, say, as the language of Monrovia and then of other cities, but by now this has been the situation for decades. Calling Kolokwa a creole both recognizes its history, specifically its evolution from a pidgin, and the presence of creole structures.

4. All speakers are designated by pseudonyms.

5. The references for the vowel systems of the Niger-Congo languages discussed in this section are the following: Bassa: Bertkau (1975), Dewoin: Welmers (1977), Gio (Dan): Welmers (1973), Gola: Sindlinger (1975), Grebo: Innes (1966), Klao: Singler (2008), Kpelle: Thach (1981), Lɔma: Sadler (1951), Mano (Maa): deZeeuw and Kruah (1981), and Vai: Welmers (1976).

6. The Kru languages in southeastern Liberia, including Klao and the Grebo languages along the coast, historically have had ATR vowel harmony and 9-vowel systems. In terms of vowel height, these systems are analogous to the 7-vowel systems presented here. Singler (2008) presents evidence that Klao is in the process of shifting from a 9-vowel system to a 7-vowel one and losing vowel harmony as a consequence, but this would seem to be a relatively recent development.

7. For each of the vowel pairs in figure 5.3, if the BA scores of a majority of speakers reach the level of merger, it follows that the BA scores of a minority of speakers do not. With the exception of one speaker's score for FACE-FLEECE, every Kolokwa speaker who fails to produce a full merger displays partial overlap, that is, a BA score greater than .6 but less than .8.

8. Singler carried out the interview with Carolina in 1980. The interview(s) with Nancy took place in 1994 in Monrovia. She had fled Sinoe during the war and was now staying with her daughter. Ellis interviewed her, and then on another occasion Singler and Ellis together interviewed her.

9. A reviewer questions whether or not, in the absence of longitudinal or apparent-time data, we can legitimately refer to the modern LSE vowel system as having undergone these mergers. We acknowledge the circumstantial nature of our claim: there is evidence (from Bailey and Thomas 1998) of an earlier system with a greater number of vowels, positing mergers then yields a system that looks very much like the Kolokwa system. The advanced age of the speakers in the Sinoe Settler Corpus suggests that this is an established rather than a recent change.

10. The designation "civilized" has entered Kolokwa as well. However, while the Settlers' use of the term is self-referential, regardless of the amount of education a Settler has, for Kolokwa speakers, it means "westernized" (see Singler 1990). Thus, it is probably the case that Absalom's statement would not offend indigenous people. On the other hand, the characterization by Cephas, another Settler, of the 1914 Sinoe war could well be objectionable to them: "They [the Settlers] subdued them. They ran them back. And God was with the Pioneers, and they ran them back." The term "Pioneers" evokes historical Settler privilege, and here Cephas endows it with divine endorsement.

References

African Repository [*Journal of the American Colonization Society*]. 1827, 1835. vols. 3, 11.

Bailey, Guy and Erik Thomas. 1998. Some aspects of African-American vernacular English phonology. In Salikoko S. Mufwene, John R. Rickford, Guy Bailey and John Baugh (eds.), *African American English: Structure, history and use*. London and New York: Routledge, 85–109.

Beck Cohen, Stephanie Elizabeth. 2016. *The visual nation: Exhibition, quilting, and cultural diplomacy in Liberia, 1847–2015*. Unpublished PhD Dissertation, Indiana University, Bloomington.

Bertkau, Jana. 1975. *A phonology of Bassa*. Monrovia, Liberia: U.S. Peace Corps and Liberian Ministry of Education, Department of Research and Planning.

Bhattacharyya, A. 1943. On a measure of divergence between two statistical populations defined by their population distributions. *Bulletin Calcutta Mathematical Society* 35: 99–10.9.

Bosman, Willem. 1705. *A new and accurate description of the Coast of Guinea, divided into the Gold, the Slave, and the Ivory Coasts . . . written originally in Dutch . . . and now faithfully done into English*. London: James Knapton.

Chevalier, Alida. 2016. *Globalisation versus internal development: The reverse short front vowel shift in South African English*. Unpublished PhD dissertation, University of Cape Town.

Crummell, Alexander 1862. *The English language in Liberia: The future of Africa*. New York: Scribner.

deZeeuw, Peter and Rexanna Kruah. 1981. *A learner directed approach to Mano*. East Lansing: Michigan State University, African Studies Center.

Erker, Daniel. 2022. How social salience can illuminate the outcomes of linguistic contact. In Karen Beaman and Gregory Guy (eds.), *The coherence of linguistic communities*. New York: Routledge, 145–62. doi: 10.4324/9781003134558

Gurley, Ralph Randolph. 1835. *Life of Jehudi Ashmun*. Washington: J.C. Dunn.

Harrison, J. A. (1884) 1975. Negro English. *Anglia* 7: 232–79. Reprinted in Joey L. Dillard (ed.), *Perspectives on Black English*. The Hague: Mouton, 143–95.

Innes, Gordon. 1966. *An introduction to Grebo*. London: School of Oriental and African Studies, University of London.

Jackson, James O'Dell, III. 1976. *The origin of Pan-African nationalism: Afro-American and Haytian relations, 1800–1863*. PhD dissertation, Northwestern University, Evanston, IL.

Johnson, Daniel. 2015. Quantifying overlap with Bhattacharyya's Affinity and other measures! NWAV44, Toronto. https://danielezrajohnson.shinyapps.io/nwav_44/

Kang, Yoojin. 2022. *Acquisition of new dialect features by Seoul and Kyungsang Korean speakers: Social and attitudinal factors influencing production*. Unpublished PhD dissertation, Georgetown University, Washington, DC.

Kouwenberg, Silvia and John Victor Singler. 2011. Pidgins and creoles. In Rajend Mesthrie (ed.), *The Cambridge handbook of sociolinguistics*. Cambridge: Cambridge University Press, 283–300.

Labov, William. (1966) 2006. *The social stratification of English in New York City*. Cambridge: Cambridge University Press. doi: 10.1017/CBO9780511618208

Labov, William. 1994. *Principles of linguistic change, Internal factors* (vol. I). Oxford: Blackwell.

MacKenzie, Laurel and Danielle Turton. 2020. Assessing the accuracy of existing forced alignment software on varieties of British English. *Linguistics Vanguard*, doi: 10.1515/lingvan-2018-0061

Marinaccio, Michael, Allison Shapp and John Victor Singler. 2021. Evaluating the efficacy of token exclusion based on high bandwidth in sociolinguistic data. NWAV49, conference. Austin, October.

Nycz, Jennifer. 2011. *Second dialect acquisition: Implications for theories of phonological representation*. Unpublished PhD dissertation, New York University.

R Core Team. 2023. R: A language and environment for statistical computing. Vienna: R Foundation for Statistical Computing. https://www.R-project.org/

Reddy, Sravana and James Stanford. 2015. A Web application for automated dialect analysis. *Proceedings of the 2015 Conference of the North American Chapter of the Association for Computational Linguistics: Demonstrations*. Denver, May 31–June 5, 71–75.

Sadler, Wesley. 1951 *Untangled Loma: A course of study of the Lɔɔma language of the Western Province, Liberia, West Africa*. Baltimore: Board of Foreign Missions for the United Lutheran Church in America.

Sindlinger, Daniel. 1975. A phonology of the Gola language and consideration towards a practical orthography. The Institute for Liberian Languages. Unpublished ms.

Singler, John Victor. 1977. Language in Liberia in the nineteenth century: The Settlers' perspective. *Liberian Studies Journal* 7: 73–85.

Singler, John Victor. 1989. Plural marking in Liberian Settler English, 1820–1980. *American Speech* 64: 40–64.

Singler, John Victor. 1990. Civilization and pleasure. Annual meeting of the Liberian Studies Association, Marlboro College, March.

Singler, John Victor. 1991. Phonology in the basilect: The fate of final consonants in Liberian English. *Studies in African Linguistics* 22: 1–44. doi: 10.32473/sal.v22i1.107429

Singler, John Victor. 1994. Plural marking in Sinoe Settler English. Joint meeting of the Society for Pidgin and Creole Linguistics and the Society for Caribbean Linguistics, University of Guyana, August.

Singler, John Victor. 1996. An OT account of pidgin phonology: Coda consonants in Vernacular Liberian English. In Jan Johnson, Matthew L. Juge and Jeri L. Moxley (eds.), *Proceedings of the twenty-second annual meeting of the Berkeley Linguistics Society*. Berkeley: Berkeley Linguistics Society. 375–86. doi: 10.3765/bls.v22i1.1320

Singler, John Victor. 1997. The configuration of Liberia's Englishes. *World Englishes* 16: 205–31. doi: 10.1111/1467-971X.00060

Singler, John Victor. 2000. Optimality Theory, the minimal-word constraint, and the historical sequencing of substrate influence in pidgin/creole genesis. In John H. McWhorter (ed.), *Current issues in pidgin and creole linguistics*. Amsterdam: John Benjamins, 336–51. doi: 10.1075/cll.21.12sin

Singler, John Victor. 2007. Samaná and Sinoe. Part I: Stalking the vernacular. *Journal of Pidgin and Creole Languages* 22: 123–48. doi: 10.1075/jpcl.22.1.09sin

Singler, John Victor. 2008. The restructuring of the Klao (Kru) vowel system and its morphophonemic consequences. Thirty-ninth Annual Conference of African Linguistics, University of Georgia, April.

Singler, John Victor. 2010. Keeping pace with space: The creation and negotiation of stigmatized linguistic elements. Keynote at the 2010 University of Chicago / University of Michigan Linguistic Anthropology Conference, University of Chicago, May.

Singler, John Victor. 2011. Stereotypes, stigma, and agency in Vernacular Liberian English. Society for Pidgin and Creole Linguistics, University of Ghana, August.

Singler, John Victor. 2012. Vernacular Liberian English [Kolokwa]. In Bernd Kortmann and Kerstin Lunkenheimer (eds.), *Mouton world atlas of variation in English*. Berlin, New York: Mouton de Gruyter, 369–81. doi: 10.1515/9783110280128.369

Singler, John Victor. 2015. African American English over yonder: The language of the Liberian Settler community. In Sonja Lanehart (ed.), *The Oxford handbook of African American language*. Oxford: Oxford University Press, 105–24.

Singler, John Victor. 2022a. Congo and Country, Settler English and Kolokwa: Liberians and their Englishes. English in Liberia: Language and Literature seminar, European Society for the Study of English, Johannes Gutenberg Universität, Mainz, Germany, August.

Singler, John Victor. 2022b. Number marking in Liberian Kolokwa. In Aloysius Ngefac, Hans-Georg Wolf and Thomas Hoffman (eds.), *World Englishes and creole languages today: The Bobdian thinking and beyond* (vol. II). Munich: LINCOM GmbH, 118–37.

Singler, John Victor. Forthcoming. Liberia. In Raymond Hickey (ed.), New Cambridge History of the English Language, *Africa, Asia, Australasia and the Pacific* (vol. VI). Cambridge: Cambridge University Press.

Smith, William. (1744) 1967. *A new voyage to Guinea*. London: John Nourse. Reprinted in *Travels and narratives*, Frank Cass, London, 22.

Stanley, Joseph A. and Betsy Sneller. 2021. Sample size matters when calculating Pillai scores. Poster presented at the 181st Meeting of the Acoustical Society of America (ASA), Seattle, November.

Strelluf, Christopher. 2018. *Speaking from the heartland: The Midland vowel system of Kansas City*. Durham, NC: Duke University Press.

Strong, Richard P. (ed.). 1930. *The African republic of Liberia and the Belgian Congo, based on the observations made and material collected during the Harvard African Expedition*. Cambridge: Harvard University Press.

Thach, Sharon V., with G. Shadrich Woah-tee and Moses G. T. Quimbeei. 1981. *A learner directed approach to Kpelle*. East Lansing: Michigan State University, African Studies Center.

Trudgill, Peter. 1986. *Dialects in contact*. New York: Basil Blackwell.

Wells, John L. 1982. *Accents of English: An introduction* (vol. I). Cambridge: Cambridge University Press.

Welmers, William E. 1973. *African language structures*. Berkeley: University of California Press.

Welmers, William E. 1976. *A grammar of Vai*. Berkeley: University of California Press.

Welmers, William E. 1977. Mood in Dewoin. In Paul F. A. Kotey and Haig der Houssikian (eds.), *Language and linguistic problems in Africa*, 344–50. Columbia, SC: Hornbeam.

Wong, Amy Wing-mei. 2015. *Diverse linguistic resources and multidimensional identities: A study of the linguistic and identity repertoires of second generation Chinese Americans in New York City*. Unpublished PhD dissertation, New York University.

The Relative Acquirability of Different Types of Dialect Features by Mobile Speakers of Korean

YOOJIN KANG
Cheongju University

Introduction

The study of second dialect acquisition (SDA) explores how people acquire a second dialect (D2) of what is perceived to be the same language. While studies of second *language* acquisition often focus on how new features are learned in the context of formal instruction, most variationist studies of SDA have examined more naturalistic contexts, in which features are acquired without any formal teaching. Such naturalistic SDA often occurs either when people who already speak a particular national dialect move to another country where a different national dialect is spoken—for example, speakers of Canadian English moving to New York (Nycz 2013) or speakers of American English moving to New Zealand (Bayard 1995; Starks and Bayard 2002)—or when people move to another region of the same country where a different regional dialect is spoken—for example, speakers of various American English dialects to the Philadelphia suburb of King of Prussia (Payne 1980).

Naturalistic SDA likely happens via accommodation, which starts out as a short-term process happening between specific adults but that over time, given enough interactions with consistent new dialect input, can result in long-term accommodation or SDA (Chambers 1992). The term *accommodation* has been used since its introduction into linguistics from social psychology (Giles and Powesland 1975) to characterize the act of adjusting one's linguistic production as a direct response to a particular interlocutor. There has been a debate regarding the primary motivation for phonetic accommodation. In some theories, convergence toward an interlocutor is uncontrolled and automatic, the result of the production and perception feedback loop that causes speakers to mimic the behavior of their interlocutors as a way of facilitating processing (Pickering and Garrod 2004; Trudgill 2008). However, other scholars (Giles and Coupland 1991) argue that phonetic accommodation is an intentional social act that occurs when speakers adjust their speech patterns to change the social distance between themselves and their interlocutors. Through convergent accommodative acts, speakers signal solidarity and similarity and a desire to maintain positive social identities and increase the prominence of in-group identity. The converse of accommodation is divergence, in which speakers increase the linguistic distance between themselves and an interlocutor to accentuate social differences or emphasize disapproval of the addressee and their communicative behaviors.

One way to assess these accounts—of accommodation as automatic, or agentive— is to examine how different dialect features, subject to differing levels of conscious awareness, are acquired (or not) by mobile speakers. If accommodation is automatic, we would expect speakers living in a new dialect region to show some level of adoption of most ambient features, regardless of how salient these features are, or the social meaning that attaches to them. If, instead, accommodation is an active choice by speakers, we would expect feature salience to have more influence on which new dialect features are accommodated to in the short term and ultimately acquired in the long term.

This study addresses the role of salience in SDA by examining the speech of 62 mobile Korean speakers: people who have moved as adults from Seoul to the rural area of the North Kyungsang Province, located approximately 200 kilometers away from Seoul, as well as people who have moved from the North Kyungsang Province to Seoul. Here I focus on two features that distinguish these two regions and also differ in their level of salience, /wɑ/ variation and use of tone. I find that these features are accommodated to quite differently by the two groups of speakers, in a way that suggests salience and related social-attitudinal factors such as prestige play a key role in motivating (or preventing) SDA.

This study also fills an empirical gap in SDA research more generally. While previous studies of SDA among adults have focused either on people who have moved internationally, or people who have moved within-nation from a rural region to a more urban region (Kerswill 1994), there is little research on within-nation reciprocal mobility between rural and urban regions.

Community and Dialect Background

Seoul

Seoul is the capital of South Korea, located in the northwest of the country (figure 6.1). The city has a population of approximately 9.8 million people as of 2021, which makes it the largest city in the country. More than 50% of the total population of the entire country is estimated to be concentrated in the Greater Seoul area (GSA), whose residents all share the Seoul dialect or the Kyunggi dialect. This is a remarkable concentration of population, considering the fact that the GSA represents just 11% of South Korea's total area of 100,210 km².

The concentration of people, wealth, and power in Seoul has been in place since the country's industrialization in the 1960s and 1970s, when under the Lee Myung-Bak and Park Geun-Hye administration, business and industry regulations on Seoul were loosened. Civilian social organizations have been calling on the government to come up with a policy for balancing the extensive development of Seoul against the

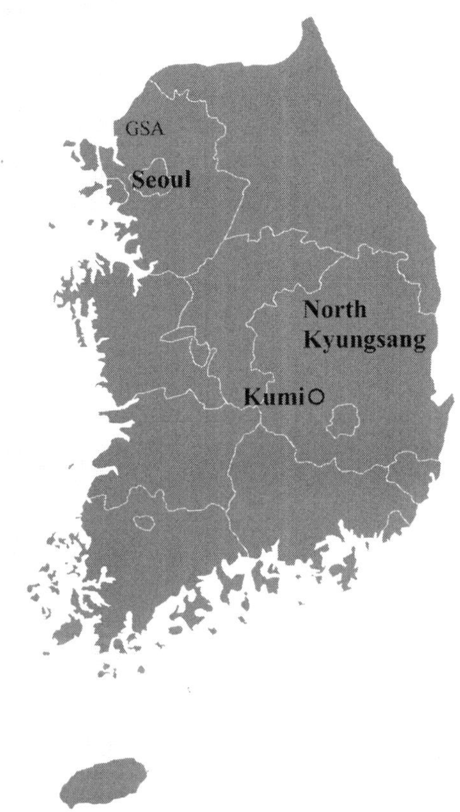

Figure 6.1. Map of South Korea (Map by FreeVectorMaps.com https://freevectormaps .com)

lack of advancement in the provinces, but the government has yet to come out with any vigorous balanced development plans. The increase in the population of Seoul is fueled by the growing inflow into Seoul for education and employment. Moreover, the majority of Korea's important socioeconomic, cultural, and political assets have also become concentrated in the GSA, whereas other regions outside the GSA have seen their assets shrink and their populations fall in recent years. As the population declines outside the GSA, universities are facing student shortages and financial difficulties, while businesses outside the GSA are also feeling a threat as the population of local towns declines.

With the poor social and cultural infrastructure and the low economic and educational opportunities in other areas of the country, it is inevitable for young people to flock to Seoul, which becomes part of a vicious cycle of destruction and decline in the provinces. The economic development of Seoul and the socioeconomic status of the people who live there also impact the evaluation of the dialect spoken in the region.

According to Chapter 1, Section 1 of the Korean Standard Language Act, "the standard Korean in principle is the modern speech of Seoul widely used by the well-cultivated" (Korean Standard Language Act 2017). Though not all features of Seoul Korean (SK) are considered standard, SK is generally perceived as standard Korean by the public (Jeon 2013; Long and Yim 2002). The Korean government's language policy has given standard Korean an absolute authority and a strong normative bias. The National Institute of the Korean Language has codified SK in such domains as government, education, and the mass media (Song 2012). The national curriculums both at the primary and secondary school level designate SK as the medium of instruction and explicitly state that regional dialects should be avoided. This absolute authority of SK in Korea may lead people to be inculcated with a positive attitude toward SK. In a study of perceptual dialectology in Korea, Long and Yim (2002) show that the speech of Seoul is considered linguistically attractive and appealing on an emotional level; the majority of respondents displayed tendencies to rate the speech of Seoul as being standard and most pleasant.

North Kyungsang Province

North Kyungsang Province is located in the southeastern part of South Korea. North Kyungsang has a population of approximately 2.4 million people. It has a relatively aging population, with the proportion of the elderly (aged 65 years and above) increasing steadily in recent years. In 2020, the proportion of the elderly in the province was 20.2%, which is higher than the national average of 15.7%.

In this study, the majority of participants who were originally from Seoul and later moved to North Kyungsang were sought in Kumi. Kumi is a city located in the southern part of North Kyungsang. Kumi has a population of approximately 410,000 people as of 2020 and is the second-most populous city in North Kyungsang. Kumi is an industrial center of South Korea with many companies, including Samsung and LG. However, the population of workers in Kumi has steadily decreased from 102,240 in 2015 to 78,942 in 2021 due to major companies' relocation from Kumi to the GSA. As in the Seoul sample, most of the participants in this sample moved from Seoul to Kumi for employment, which provides at least some level of control across groups regarding their motivations for mobility. The city also has a strong agricultural sector, with the production of rice, fruits, and vegetables.

In the past few years, South Korea has undergone a phenomenon called the "local university crisis," which describes the drop in enrollment and financial challenges faced by universities situated outside major cities such as Seoul. North Kyungsang is currently experiencing a similar crisis due to a variety of factors. Among them, the main reason is the dwindling population in the area, which has resulted in a decline in the number of high school graduates, thus reducing the potential pool of university students. Consequently, universities in North Kyungsang are facing difficulties in attracting and retaining students, because there are fewer people interested in pursuing higher education.

In previous studies of perceptual dialectology and language attitudes in Korea, North Kyungsang Korean (NKK) is commonly considered a non-standard dialect, especially because of its distinctive lexical pitch accent (Jeon 2013; Long and Yim 2002). In a previous study, my coauthor and I examined perceptions that NKK speakers have about the Korean language spoken in Korea (Kang and Kim 2015). The study showed that the vast majority of NKK speakers negatively rated NKK as non-standard, rural, ignorant, angry, and aggressive but positively rated SK as standard, urban, educated, attractive, and classy.

Lexical Tone and /wa/ in Seoul Korean and North Kyungsang Korean

SK and NKK share many basic phonetic features, but there are several key differences. For example, while speakers of SK make a distinction between the central unrounded high vowel /ɯ/ and the low-mid back unrounded vowel /ʌ/, NKK is characterized by an unconditioned merger of /ɯ/ and /ʌ/. Also, in NKK, certain lexical items with an initial lax stop have changed the initial consonant to tense. SK, in contrast, does not exhibit the word-initial tensification: all initial lax stops remain in the lax class (e.g., [k*upta ~ kupta] 'to bake', [t*arɯn ~ tarɯn] 'different').

This study focuses on two additional features, lexical tone and /wa/, which distinguish NKK from other Korean dialects (including that spoken in Seoul) and have been the focus of most dialectological research in Korea (Ahn 2010; Hong 2011).

NKK has preserved the lexical pitch accent from Middle Korean (fifteenth–sixteenth century), while SK lost its lexical pitch accent in the seventeenth century. In monosyllables, NKK contrasts High (H), Low (L), and Rising (R) (Lee 2000). In disyllables, NKK distinguishes HL, LH, LL, and RH, so it is possible to find minimal pairs such as *kájì* (HL) 'sort' and *kàjí* (LH) 'eggplant' (Lee 2000). In contrast, SK does not use contrastive tone patterns for cueing meaning differences. In her study of the phonetics and phonology of Korean prosody, Jun (1998) proposed that the accentual phrase (AP), the smallest unit in Seoul Korean, commonly has a final rising accent pattern (i.e., LH), which does not contrast with any other pattern. The NKK tones are highly salient features, and they are overtly stigmatized; they are very often ridiculed in the Korean media and on television and are often mentioned in jokes. Thus, the NKK tones are stereotypes of NKK, and they are subject to conscious awareness (Jeon 2013; Long and Yim 2002). I thus expect that Seoul-in-Kyungsang speakers in this study will not acquire the NKK tones and maintain their D1 prosody (i.e., final-rising accent pattern), while Kyungsang-in-Seoul speakers will acquire the SK prosody and lose their NKK tones.

Another difference between SK and NKK involves the realization of the diphthong /wa/. SK has eleven diphthongs—including /wa/, /we/, /wæ/, /wʌ/, /ja/, /je/, /jæ/, /jo/, /ju/, /ɯj/, and /jʌ/. All diphthongs, except /ɯj/, are made up of glides (either /w/ or /j/) preceding monophthongs. NKK shares this inventory but is characterized by unconditioned monophthongization of /wa/ to [a] (e.g. [sagwa ~ saga] 'apple', [busagwan ~ busagan] 'sergent', [gaŋbakgwannyeom ~ gaŋbakgannyeom] 'obsession'). Speakers of SK, in contrast, distinguish /wa/ and /a/. This feature, in contrast with lexical tone, is not subject to metalinguistic commentary. Because this feature is not salient, I expect neither group of speakers to accommodate toward the D2 form of this variable.

Of course, it is also important to consider the linguistic status of each of these features, and the task faced by each group of mobile speakers if they are to accurately reproduce the patterns of their new region. Chambers (1992) argues that the complexity of D2 features is one of the factors that determine the degree of D2 attainment, maintaining that simple rules are acquired faster and earlier than complex rules. He defines simple rules as "automatic processes that admit no exceptions" and complex rules as having "opaque outputs, that is, they have exceptions or variant forms" or having "in their output a new or additional phoneme" (682). Acquiring a new linguistic contrast—in this case, either new lexical tones or a new distinction between /wɑ/ and /ɑ/—is a complex change, because it requires a person to learn not only that there is a contrast but how the contrasting elements are distributed across lexical items. Neutralizing a contrast—no longer making a tonal distinction, or realizing all /wɑ/ as [ɑ]—is simple in comparison. Thus, in this data I expect it will be relatively harder for Seoul-in-Kyungsang speakers to acquire the NKK tones for linguistic reasons as well as social reasons but easier for the Seoul-in-Kyungsang speakers to acquire NKK-like /wɑ/ monophthongization. The Kyungsang-in-Seoul speakers, however, are not expected to acquire the SK-like /wɑ/ diphthongization.

Methods

Participants

Two groups of mobile speakers participated in this study, all of whom moved to their current region after the age of 18: 30 Seoul-in-Kyungsang speakers, who were born and raised in Seoul (and thus presumed to be first dialect [D1] SK speakers) and later moved to North Kyungsang Province (figure 6.2a), and 32 Kyungsang-in-Seoul speakers, who were born and raised in North Kyungsang province (D1 NKK speakers) and later moved to Seoul (figure 6.2b). The speakers in each region were stratified according to the length of stay in the D2 region and gender.

This study also collected control data from each field site to check assumptions about the features of SK that the Kyungsang-in-Seoul mobile speakers have been exposed to and the features of NKK that the Seoul-in-Kyungsang mobile speakers have been exposed to. The control group consisted of four lifelong SK speakers who were born and raised in Seoul and have never lived in other regions for more than six months (referred to as the Seoul control group), and four lifelong NKK speakers, again in the sense of having been born and raised there and having never lived in other regions for more than six months (referred to as the Kyungsang control group). Each control group consisted of two males and two females, matched in age to the average age of the main participants. For the Kyungsang-in-Seoul participants, the mean age was 30, and for the Seoul-in-Kyungsang participants, the mean age was also 30.

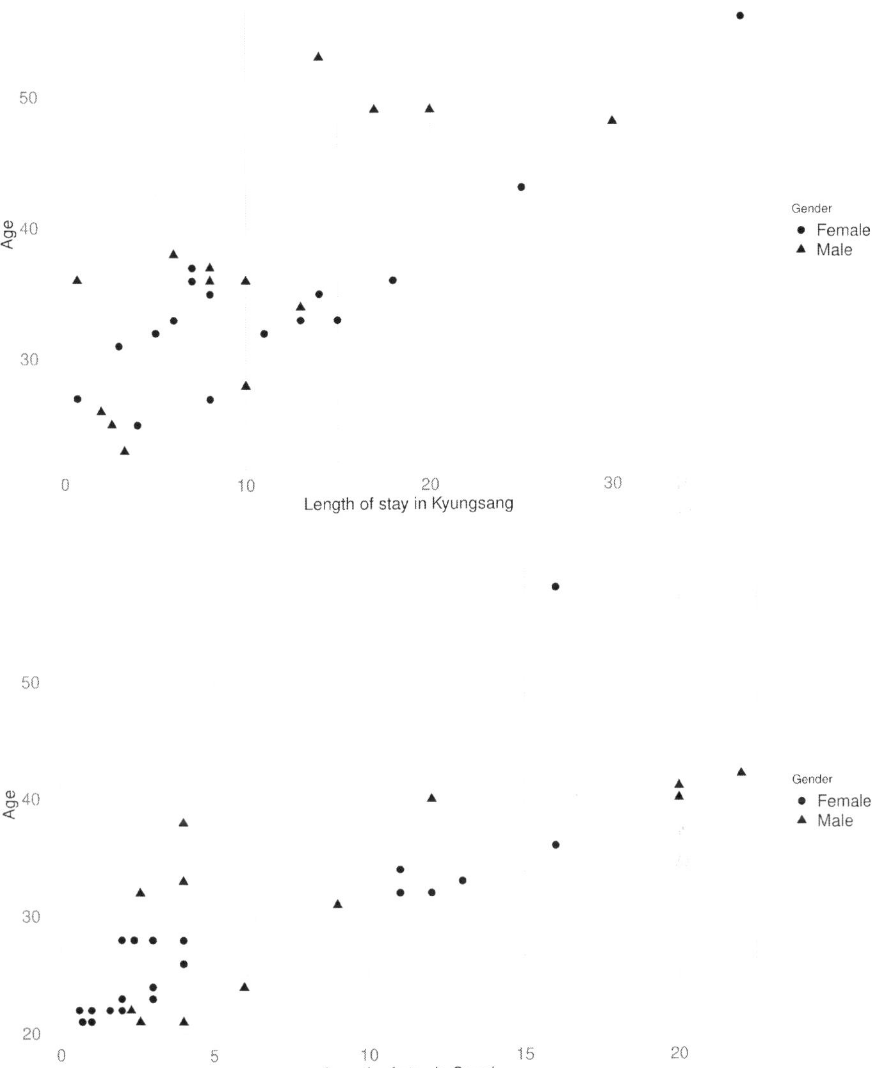

Figure 6.2a and b. Scatter plots showing the Seoul-in-Kyungsang speakers (top) and the Kyungsang-in-Seoul speakers (bottom) according to gender, length of stay in the D2 region, and age*

Instruments and Analysis

Reading Passage

Speakers were asked to read a set of unrelated sentences which were presented on a tablet computer screen. The reading passage was composed of 21 sentences with 12 target words: 6 words potentially containing /wɑ/ variation (variants: monophthong or diphthong), including *janggwan* 'minister', *gigwan* 'agency', *gyohwan* 'exchange', *sagwa* 'apple', *gyeolgwa* 'result', and *jeonhwa* 'phone call' and 6 words potentially exhibiting tone variation (variants: NKK tone patterns or Seoul prosody), including *norae* (HL) 'song', *meori* (HL) 'head', *gogi* (HL) 'meat', *namu* (LH) 'tree', *dari* (LH) 'bridge', and *maru* (LH) 'floor.'

The reading passage data were acoustically analyzed. For the 6 words containing /wɑ/, measurements of F1 and F2 were taken at two time points during the /wɑ/ syllable: at the vowel midpoint to capture the central tendency of the vowel /ɑ/, and at the onset of the /wɑ/ syllable to determine whether a glide is present (see Figure 3).

The glide [w] in Korean is characterized by a low F1 and low F2; the low central vowel [ɑ] has a higher F1 and F2. Therefore, if the glide is realized before the vowel /ɑ/, both F1 and F2 values at syllable onset will be lower than those at vowel midpoint. Meanwhile, if there is full monophthongization, then there will be little to no difference between the onset and midpoint measures.

Thus, to get a measure of diphthongization along each dimension, each onset formant measure was subtracted from each midpoint measure for each token, with higher resulting numbers indicating more diphthongized vowels. For convenience, the value calculated from each instance of subtraction will be called DIPHTHONGIZATION; the difference between F1 at midpoint and F1 at syllable onset will be called F1 DIPHTHONGIZATION (i.e., F1 value at the midpoint—F1 value at onset), and the difference between F2 at midpoint and F2 at syllable onset will be called F2 DIPHTHONGIZATION (i.e., F2 value at the midpoint—F2 value at onset).

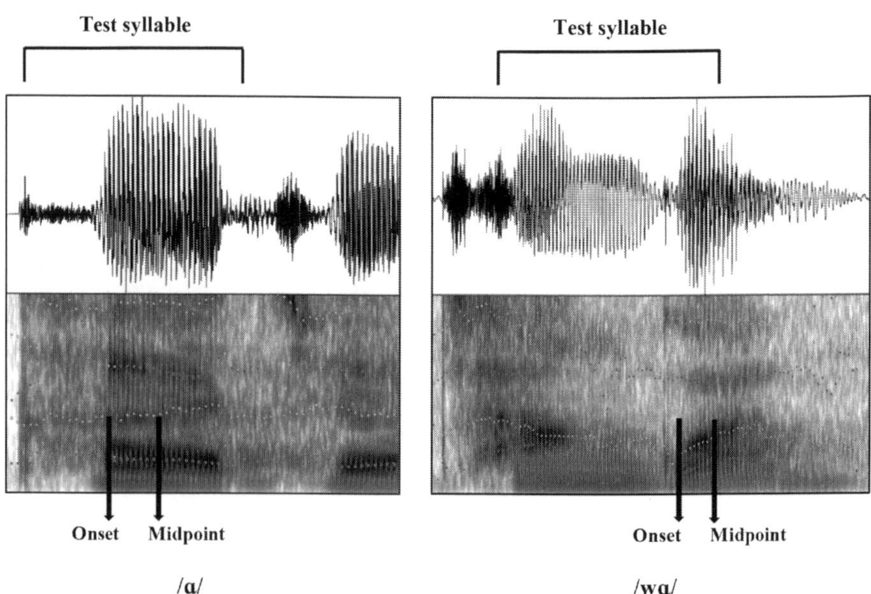

Figure 6.3. Examples of /ɑ/ and /wɑ/ produced by a female SK speaker with two measurement points (i.e., syllable onset and vowel midpoint)

For the 6 words potentially exhibiting tone contrasts, I followed the tone-assignment method for Korean suggested by Lee, Jongman, and Zhang (2016). First, each target word was segmented into syllables, including a vowel only. Next, the mean F0 values (Hz) for the vocalic component of each of the two syllables were measured. The syllable with the higher mean F0 value was selected, and an H was assigned to that syllable. Finally, to assign a tone for the other syllable, a percentage criterion was used: if the mean F0 for the other syllable differed by less than 5% from the highest pitch, it was also considered to be an H syllable and assigned an H. Any syllable with more than a 5% F0 difference from the syllable with the highest mean F0 was assigned an L.

Awareness and Salience Tasks

After completing the reading passage task, I explained to participants how the use of tones and production of /wa/ differ across the SK and NKK. I also described two other features that differ across the varieties, NKK-like word-initial tensification (e.g., [k*upta ~ kupta] 'to bake', [t*aruun ~ taruun] 'different') and NKK-like merger of /ɯ/ and /ʌ/, to assess how salient /wa/ variation and use of tones are among different features of NKK and SK. (These other two features will not be further discussed here.) The participants were asked to identify any features that they had known about as differences between SK and NKK prior to participating in the study (Awareness Task). If the participants identified some of these features, I asked them to rank those features in order of which most typifies the D2 (Salience Task). The aim of these activities was to assess whether participants had a conscious awareness of the two features of interest in this study and to elicit stereotypes directly by having the participants rank and comment on the variables examined in this study. All tasks were conducted in Korean.

Attitude Questionnaire

Finally, the participants were asked to complete a questionnaire to examine the effect of attitudes towards the D1 and D2 on the acquisition of D2 features (table 6.1); the questionnaire was presented and completed in Korean. The questionnaire consisted of a subset of statements drawn from Vousten's (1995) instrument, which itself adapted Gardner's (1985) Attitude and Motivation Test Battery (AMTB) for use in studies of D2 acquisition. Twelve statements were selected to represent three categories from the Vousten's list: *integrative orientation, instrumental orientation,* and *subjective perception of motivational support by the dialect speaking peer group.* The *integrative orientation* category assesses the degree to which participants seek to learn the D2 to fit in with the D2 community. The *instrumental orientation* category assesses the extent to which participants want to learn the D2 for pragmatic reasons. *Subjective perception of motivational support by the dialect speaking peer group* assesses the extent to which participants believe local dialect speakers would support them in using the D2. Besides those three categories, the *fear of speaking the dialect* category was selected and divided into two sub-categories: *fear of speaking the D1,* assessing the degree to which participants are afraid of using their D1 in the D2 region, and *fear of speaking the D2,* assessing the extent to which participants feel fear

Table 6.1. Language attitude and motivation questionnaire results

		Kyungsang-in-Seoul speakers	Seoul-in-Kyungsang speakers
		Mean (SD)	
Integrative orientation	I think it is important to be able to speak the new dialect because it makes it easier for me to make friends.	2.5 (1.0)	2.9 (1.1)
	I think it is important to be able to speak the new dialect because then I feel more comfortable with people who speak the new dialect.	3.8 (1.4)	2.7 (1.3)
	I think it is important to be able to speak the new dialect because then I will be part of the group.	3.1 (1.4)	3.0 (1.3)
Overall mean		**3.1**	**2.9**
Instrumental orientation	I think it is important to be able to speak a new dialect because the people who speak the dialect can understand me better.	4.4 (1.2)	2.6 (1.1)
	I think it is important to be able to speak a new dialect to adjust to living in a new region.	4.2 (1.2)	2.9 (1.3)
Overall mean		**4.3**	**2.8**
Fear of speaking the D1	I'm afraid people will laugh at me when I speak my first dialect.	3.8 (1.2)	2.1 (1.3)
	I feel insecure when I speak my first dialect.	3.6 (1.3)	1.9 (1.3)
Overall mean		**3.7**	**2.0**
Fear of speaking the D2	I'm afraid people will laugh at me when I speak the new dialect.	2.6 (1.2)	3.9 (1.1)
	I don't like to speak the new dialect because I'm afraid it sounds weird.	2.5 (1.3)	3.5 (1.3)
	I feel insecure when I speak the new dialect.	2.1 (1.3)	4.1 (1.0)
Overall mean		**2.4**	**3.9**

		Kyungsang-in-Seoul speakers	Seoul-in-Kyungsang speakers
		Mean (SD)	
Subjective perception of motivational support by the dialect speaking peer group	I think people would like me to speak their dialect.	2.1 (0.9)	2.3 (1.0)
	I think people would like to help me learn their dialect.	3.6 (0.9)	3.7 (1.0)
Overall mean		2.9	3.0

using the D2 in the D2 region. Each statement was assessed by participants using a 5-point Likert scale (1 = strongly disagree, 2 = disagree, 3 = neither disagree nor agree, 4 = agree, 5 = strongly agree). Most of the statements in table 6.1 reflect a positive attitude toward the D2 and motivation to acquire it. In terms of calculating the scores for the questionnaire, when the participants evaluated these statements with 5, five points were given, four points for 4, three points for 3, two points for 2, and one point for 1. The three statements representing "fear of speaking the D2," however, reflect a negative attitude toward the D2 and reluctance to acquire it; for these statements, the point allocation was accordingly reversed, with one point given for 5, two points for 4, and so on. Thus, the maximum score for the questionnaire is 60, and the minimum score is 12.

Results and Discussion

In the discussion that follows, I categorize each speaker in a binary way, as having acquired or not acquired each D2 feature. This categorization is done in reference to the two lifelong control groups. For the /wɑ/ words, the Kyungsang controls mean F1 DIPHTHONGIZATION value in the reading passage task is 27 Hz, and their mean F2 DIPHTHONGIZATION value is–75 Hz. The Seoul controls mean F1 DIPHTHONGIZATION value is 195 Hz in the same context, and their mean F2 DIPHTHONGIZATION value is 368. This indicates that the Seoul control group produced diphthongized vowels of [wɑ] in the reading passage task but the Kyungsang control group showed relative monophthongization of /wɑ/ to [ɑ] in the same context.

A dividing line for each DIPHTHONGIZATION measure was set at the midpoint of the range exhibited by the two control groups and used to categorize the mobile speakers from each sample. So, any mobile speaker with a mean F1 DIPHTHONGIZATION value of below 111 Hz (halfway between the value of 27 for the NKK controls and 195 for the SK controls) was assigned "monophthongization," and

Table 6.2. Distribution of the Kyungsang-in-Seoul speakers (left) and the Seoul-in-Kyungsang speakers (right) in terms of their behavior for the two variables

	D1 [ɑ]	D2 [wɑ]		D1 [wɑ]	D2 [ɑ]
D1 tone	0	0	D1 no tone	17	13
D2 no	9	23		(12W, 5M)	(3W, 10M)
tone	(4W, 5M)	(16W, 17M)	D2 tone	0	0

speakers with a mean F1 DIPHTHONGIZATION value of over 111 Hz were assigned "diphthongization." Similarly, any speaker with a mean F2 DIPHTHONGIZATION value of below 146 Hz was assigned "monophthongization," and speakers with a mean F2 DIPHTHONGIZATION value of over 146 Hz were assigned "diphthongization." Then, speakers who were assigned "diphthongization" for either (or both) F1 DIPHTHONGIZATION and F2 DIPHTHONGIZATION values were finally coded as "SK-leaning," while speakers who were assigned "monophthongization" for both F1 DIPHTHONGIZATION and F2 DIPHTHONGIZATION values were finally coded as "NKK-leaning."

For the use of tones, the Kyungsang control speakers show an expected NKK tonal distinction in the six disyllabic test words in the reading passage context, while the Seoul control speakers exhibit a final-rising accent pattern in the same task. Mobile speakers were thus coded as "NKK-leaning" for this feature if the tone assignment method resulted in these words receiving the expected HL or LH assignment, and "SK-leaning" if not.

Table 6.2 shows a summary of the distribution of speakers using these criteria. Twenty-three of the 32 Kyungsang-in-Seoul speakers show use of both of the two D2 features, and 9 of them show evidence of having acquired one of the two D2 features. The Seoul-in-Kyungsang speakers show the opposite pattern: 17 of the 30 Seoul-in-Kyungsang speakers use neither of the two D2 features, and only 13 of them have acquired one of the two D2 features—specifically, /wɑ/.

All 32 Kyungsang-in-Seoul speakers show evidence of having lost the NKK tones, and 23 of them have acquired the SK-like /wɑ/ diphthongization. Unlike the Kyungsang-in-Seoul speakers, all of the Seoul-in-Kyungsang speakers show evidence of having maintained their D1 prosody, not acquiring the NKK tones. Only 13 of the 30 Seoul-in-Kyungsang speakers have acquired the NKK-like /wɑ/ monophthongization. These patterns are consistent with my prediction that Kyungsang-in-Seoul speakers will acquire the SK prosody and lose their distinct NKK tones, whereas Seoul-in-Kyungsang speakers will not acquire the NKK tones and maintain their D1 accent pattern because the NKK tones are a stereotype of NKK, and they are subject to conscious awareness. These findings are also consistent with how we would expect these speakers to pattern given the relative complexity of each change: the more complex lexical tone of NKK is not acquired, while the lack of tone is easily adopted.

However, with respect to the results for /wɑ/ variation, the results are not consistent with my expectation that the Seoul-in-Kyungsang speakers will acquire the

NKK-like /wɑ/ monophthongization because the /wɑ/ monophthongization may be a simple phonetic change, while the Kyungsang-in-Seoul speakers will not acquire the SK-like /wɑ/ diphthongization because acquiring diphthongization may be a more complex rule.

These results may partly be explained by the different salience of the two features, as revealed in the results of the salience task. In the salience task, both the Kyungsang-in-Seoul and Seoul-in-Kyungsang speakers say that the use of tones is the most typical feature of the D2, while the least typical feature of the D2 is /wɑ/ variation. None of the Kyungsang-in-Seoul and Seoul-in-Kyungsang speakers use the NKK tones in the reading passage task. Meanwhile, a relatively small number of the Kyungsang-in-Seoul speakers exhibit the SK-like /wɑ/ diphthongization, while about half of the Seoul-in-Kyungsang speakers show the NKK-like /wɑ/ monophthongization.

Trudgill (1986) suggests that features with high salience are more likely to be acquired. However, if features are too salient, they will not be accommodated. This apparently contradictory statement that a too-salient feature will inhibit the accommodation has been criticized as being ad hoc and circular (Auer, Barden and Grosskopf 1998; Hinskens 1996; Kerswill and Williams 2002).

For these results, I do not suggest that salience alone will encourage acquisition or loss of dialect features; rather, it is simply interesting to observe how the more salient features behave in these particular dialect contact situations. In these particular contexts where people relocate between two regions, one urban and characterized by a prestigious dialect, and one rural, whose dialect is stigmatized, all of the Kyungsang-in-Seoul speakers show evidence of having acquired the most salient D2 feature of the prestigious dialect. In contrast, none of the Seoul-in-Kyungsang speakers show evidence of having adopted the most salient D2 feature. These results suggest that accommodation is not automatic but agentive and socially mediated and that prestige, as well as salience, is implicated.

Another striking aspect of table 6.2 is that there is no Kyungsang-in-Seoul speaker who has maintained D1 forms for both features, and all of them have acquired at least one SK feature. In contrast, there is no Seoul-in-Kyungsang speaker who has acquired both NKK features, and all of them have maintained D1 forms for at least one feature.

This overall result—that the majority of Kyungsang-in-Seoul speakers have acquired the SK features but the majority of Seoul-in-Kyungsang speakers have not acquired the NKK features—cannot be explained simply by appealing to salience or the assumption that mobile speakers never acquire features of a less prestigious dialect. Even linguistic complexity (Chambers 1992) does not provide a full explanation.

In this study, the complexity of acquiring the other dialect's /wɑ/ system depends on the direction of mobility; for the Kyungsang-in-Seoul speakers who exhibit /wɑ/ monophthongization in their D1, acquiring the SK-like diphthongization of /wɑ/ would be complex because the Kyungsang-in-Seoul speakers have to learn which of their native /ɑ/ words should be diphthongized. In contrast, for the Seoul-in-Kyungsang speakers, whose D1 exhibits the /wɑ/ diphthongization, acquiring the NKK-like /wɑ/ monophthongization would be a simple phonetic change, substituting [wa] for their [ɑ] pronunciation of the monophthong.

With respect to the use of tone, for the Seoul-in-Kyungsang speakers who do not use tone differences for lexical distinctions in their D1, acquiring the NKK tones is complex because this feature is lexically conditioned, and thus they need to learn it word by word. In contrast, for the Kyungsang-in-Seoul speakers, losing the NKK tone patterns and acquiring the SK-like final rising accent pattern is relatively simple. One possibility to consider is that the Seoul-in-Kyungsang speakers cannot perceptually hear tone differences within words, especially considering that their D1 does not use tone differences for lexical distinctions. However, results of a pilot study suggest otherwise. In a pilot study, I tested whether non-mobile SK speakers had difficulties in perception of pitch accent contrasts. In this perception task, 30 words were played in a random order, and participants heard each word twice. The task was a two-alternative forced-choice; participants were asked to judge whether there was a tone difference between the first and the second syllable. The result shows that of the 15 SK speakers, 13 of them received a perfect score on the test, and two of them scored above 93% in total on the test. This result suggests that SK speakers in general have no major difficulties in perception of pitch accent contrasts.

The result that all of the Kyungsang-in-Seoul speakers have lost the NKK tones and acquired the SK-like prosody, while none of the Seoul-in-Kyungsang speakers have acquired the NKK tones, is consistent with Chambers's argument that simple rules are acquired faster and earlier than complex rules. However, the result that the majority of the Kyungsang-in-Seoul speakers show acquisition of even the complex feature that involves making a new lexically conditioned contrast between /wɑ/ and /ɑ/ is somewhat unexpected in terms of Chambers's argument. Hence, relative prestige of dialects and their features cannot be discounted in the process of D2 acquisition.

In addition to appealing to salience, prestige, and complexity, the Kyungsang-in-Seoul speakers' overall pattern of acquisition and the Seoul-in-Kyungsang speakers' lack of acquisition can be related to other extralinguistic reasons, as indicated by the results of the questionnaire (table 6.1). The Kyungsang-in-Seoul speakers have more instrumental motivation to learn SK for pragmatic reasons than the Seoul-in-Kyungsang speakers; the Kyungsang-in-Seoul speakers think it is important to be able to speak SK because the people who speak SK can understand them better. They also think it is important to be able to speak SK to adjust to living in Seoul. In contrast, the Seoul-in-Kyungsang speakers seem to have a low instrumental motivation to learn NKK. Moreover, the Kyungsang-in-Seoul speakers seem to be afraid of speaking their D1, while they have a relatively low fear of speaking the D2. The Kyungsang-in-Seoul speakers think people will laugh at them when they speak their D1, and they also feel insecure when they speak their D1. By contrast, the Seoul-in-Kyungsang speakers seem to be afraid of speaking the D2, while they do not have a fear of speaking their D1.

These results underscore the prestige associated with the Seoul dialect and the stigmatization of the Kyungsang variety and suggest that the Kyungsang-in-Seoul speakers show linguistic insecurity to some extent (Labov 1966). This linguistic insecurity comes from the belief that "the speech of a socially subordinate group will be interpreted as linguistically inadequate by comparison with that of the socially dominant group" (Wolfram and Schilling-Estes 2016, 7). Kyungsang Korean speakers' linguistic insecurity was also found in my previous perceptual dialectology and language attitude study (Kang and Kim 2015). In a large-scale study that examined 488 Kyungsang Korean speakers' perceptions about the Korean language spoken in Korea and their language attitude toward Kyungsang Korean and Seoul Korean, my coauthor and I found that the Kyungsang Korean speakers viewed their own dialect negatively but viewed Seoul Korean very positively. Moreover, one interesting result of the language attitude questionnaire and interviews was that the majority of Kyungsang Korean speakers perceived accent imitation by Seoul Korean speakers as insulting and believed Seoul Korean speakers imitate the Kyungsang accent to covertly index negative stereotypes of Kyungsang Korean speakers. This can also be seen as evidence of Kyungsang Korean speakers' linguistic insecurity; even though they do not know whether accent imitation by Seoul Korean speakers comes from malicious intentions or well-meaning efforts to accommodate to Kyungsang speakers, most of the Kyungsang Korean speakers strongly believed that Seoul Korean speakers imitate their accent with bad intent.

Thus, it might be possible that the Kyungsang-in-Seoul speakers have acquired the D2 more successfully than the Seoul-in-Kyungsang speakers partly because of their high instrumental motivation and their linguistic insecurity. At the same time, the Seoul-in-Kyungsang speakers' failure to acquire the D2 may be due not only to the higher social value of the Seoul dialect but also to avoid making NKK speakers feel like they are being imitated.

With respect to speakers' social factors, it is striking that among the 23 Kyungsang-in-Seoul speakers who have acquired both SK features, 16 of them are females (table 6.2). Among the 17 Seoul-in-Kyungsang speakers who have maintained both D1 features, 12 of them are females, while among the 13 Seoul-in-Kyungsang speakers who have acquired one of the two NKK features, 10 of them are males. These results are in line with those of previous sociolinguistic studies suggesting that women are more sensitive to what is considered standard and non-standard and often more oriented toward the standard, while men may be more oriented toward nonstandard forms (Labov 1966; Trudgill 1972).

In addition, the result that female Kyungsang-in-Seoul speakers have acquired the D2 features better and female Seoul-in-Kyungsang speakers have maintained the D1 features more might be related to their sense of identity as a Seoul Korean. A person's identity in relation to their birth origin and their current residence is not easily quantifiable and categorized. Moreover, while a person's identity and behaviors are deeply related, the effects of identity on production are more complex.

Despite these challenges, previous studies of SDA examined the effect of social identity on the acquisition of D2 features (Ivars 1994; Omdal 1994). To look at the role of identity on SDA in the current study, during the interview the mobile speakers were also asked, "Do you now consider yourself as a Seoul Korean or as a Kyungsang Korean?" The results are quite striking. Among the 32 Kyungsang-in-Seoul speakers who responded to the question regarding place identity, 20 reported seeing themselves as Seoul Koreans, while 12 considered themselves Kyungsang Koreans. Among the 27 Seoul-in-Kyungsang speakers who responded to the same question, 21 regarded themselves as having a Seoul identity, while 6 claimed a Kyungsang identity. Of the 16 female Kyungsang-in-Seoul speakers who have acquired both D2 features,

12 identified as being Seoul Korean. Of the 12 female Seoul-in-Kyungsang speakers who have maintained both D1 features, 11 of them identified as still being Seoul Korean. This self-assessment of identity, then, seems to have an effect on the degree of D2 attainment for these speakers.

Conclusion

This study examines the acquisition of D2 features by mobile speakers relocating between two regions, one urban and characterized by a prestigious dialect (Seoul), and one rural, whose dialect is stigmatized (North Kyungsang). The overall results show that most Kyungsang-in-Seoul speakers have acquired both SK features, while most Seoul-in-Kyungsang speakers have acquired neither of the NKK features.

With respect to the effect of salience, all of the Kyungsang-in-Seoul speakers show evidence of having lost the NKK tones, the most salient D1 feature of the stigmatized dialect, while none of the Seoul-in-Kyungsang speakers show evidence of having acquired the NKK tones. With respect to linguistic complexity, the Kyungsang-in-Seoul speakers show some acquisition of complex features, such as the SK-like /wa/ diphthongization, whereas none of the Seoul-in-Kyungsang speakers have acquired the complex feature of NKK tones. With respect to extralinguistic factors, the Kyungsang-in-Seoul speakers show high instrumental motivation to acquire SK and linguistic insecurity, while the Seoul-in-Kyungsang speakers have low instrumental motivation to learn NKK. In addition, a clear majority of the Kyungsang-in-Seoul speakers reported that they see themselves now as Seoul Korean, but only a small number of the Seoul-in-Kyungsang speakers claimed to have Kyungsang identity.

These findings suggest that linguistic complexity may or may not play a role, but the combination of linguistic complexity and stigmatization totally blocks the acquisition of a complex feature; that is, a complex but non-stigmatized feature allows for D2 acquisition, but a complex and stigmatized feature blocks it. Other factors that seem to come into play involve people's attitudes regarding the utility of acquiring and linguistic insecurity pertaining to speaking stigmatized varieties, whether their own native dialect or that of a region into which they have relocated.

Several questions remain unanswered at present. Future research should be undertaken to investigate the effect of age of arrival on SDA. Previous work has shown that age of arrival is an important factor in the degree of acquisition in SDA (Berthele 2002; Ivars 1994; Tagliamonte and Molfenter 2007). Since the speakers in this study moved to the D2 region after the age of 20, the effect of age of arrival was not examined. A further study with more focus on the effect of age of arrival is therefore suggested. Moreover, further investigations are needed to disentangle the factors of salience, prestige, complexity, attitude, and identity, given that these are often correlated with one another.

Note

*Some figures in this chapter are available on the publisher's website (press.georgetown.edu) to make it easier to view the data.

References

Ahn, Miae. 2010. *Daegu ji-yeog-eo-ui mo-eum-che-gye-e dae-han sa-hoe-eum-seong- hag-jeog yeon-gu*. [A sociophonetics study on the vowel system of Daegu dialect]. Unpublished PhD dissertation, Kyungpook National University, Daegu, South Korea.

Auer, Peter, Birgit Barden and Beate Grosskopf. 1998. Subjective and objective parameters determining "salience" in long-term dialect accommodation. *Journal of Sociolinguistics* 2: 163–87. doi: 10.1111/1467-9481.00039

Bayard, Donn. 1995. Peers versus parents: A longitudinal study of rhotic-non-rhotic accommodation in an NZE-speaking child. *New Zealand English Newsletter* 9: 15–22.

Berthele, Raphael. 2002. Learning a second dialect: A model of idiolectal dissonance. *Multilingua* 21: 327–44. doi: 10.1515/mult.2002.014

Chambers, Jack K. 1992. Dialect acquisition. *Language* 68: 673–705. doi: 10.2307/416850

Gardner, Robert C. 1985. *Social psychology and second language learning: The role of attitudes and motivation*. London: Edward Arnold.

Giles, Howard and Nikolas Coupland. 1991. *Language: Contexts and consequences*. Milton Keynes, UK: Open University Press.

Giles, Howard and Peter F. Powesland. 1975. *Speech style and social evaluation*. London: Academic Press.

Hinskens, Frans. 1996. *Dialect levelling in Limburg: Structural and sociolinguistic aspects*. Tübingen: Niemeyer.

Hong, Miju. 2011. *Daegu ji-yeog-eo-ui eum-un-byeon-i-e dae-han sa-hoe-eon-eo-hag- jeog yeon*-gu. [A sociolinguistic study on phonological variation of Daegu dialect]. Unpublished PhD dissertation, Kyungpook National University, Daegu, South Korea.

Ivars, Ann-Marie. 1994. Bidialectalism and identity. In Nordberg Bengt (ed.), *The Sociolinguistics of urbanization: The case of the Nordic countries*. Berlin: Walter de Gruyter, 203–22. doi: 10.1515/9783110852622.203

Jeon, Lisa. 2013. *Drawing boundaries and revealing language attitudes: Mapping perceptions of dialects in Korea*. Unpublished MA thesis, University of North Texas, Denton.

Jun, Sun-Ah. 1998. The accentual phrase in the Korean prosodic hierarchy. *Phonology* 15: 189–226. doi: 10.1017/S0952675798003571

Kang, Yoojin and Deok-Ho Kim. 2015. Perceptual dialectology and language attitudes: A view from Gyeongsang dialect speakers. *The Journal of Linguistic Science* 75: 1–22.

Kerswill, Paul. 1994. *Dialects converging: Rural speech in urban Norway*. Oxford: Clarendon Press.

Kerswill, Paul and Ann Williams. 2000. Creating a new town koine: Children and language change in Milton Keynes. *Language in Society* 29 (1): 65–115. doi: 10.1017/S0047404500001020

Korea. 2017. Korean Standard Language Act. 1.1. Ministry of Culture, Sports and Tourism.

Labov, William. 1966. *The social stratification of English in New York City*. Washington, DC: Center for Applied Linguistics.

Lee, Hyunjung Allard Jongman, and Jie Zhang. 2016. Variation and change in the nominal pitch-accent system of South Kyungsang Korean. *Phonology* 33: 325–51. https://www.jstor.org/stable/26337994

Lee, Munkyu. 2000. Seong-jo bang-eon-ui un-yul yu-hyeong. [The prosody of tone language]. *The Society of Korean Culture and Convergence* 22 (1): 43–68.

Long, Daniel and Young-Cheol Yim. 2002. Regional differences in the perception of Korean dialects. In Daniel Long and Dennis Preston (eds.), *Handbook of perceptual dialectology* (vol. I). Amsterdam: Benjamins, 199–226. https://doi.org/10.1075/z.hpd2.19lon

Nycz, Jennifer. 2013. Changing words or changing rules? Second dialect acquisition and phonological representation. *Journal of Pragmatics* 52: 49–62. https://doi.org/10.1016/j.pragma.2012.12.014

Omdal, Helge. 1994. From the valley to the city: Language modification and language attitudes. In Bengt Nordberg (ed.), *The Sociolinguistics of Urbanization: The case of the Nordic countries*. Berlin: De Gruyter, 11–48. doi: 10.1515/9783110852622.116

Payne, Arvilla C. 1980. Factors controlling the acquisition of the Philadelphia Dialect by out-of-state children. In William Labov (ed.), *Locating language in time and space*. New York: Academic Press, 143–78.

Pickering, Martin and Simon Garrod. 2004. Toward a mechanistic psychology of dialogue. *The Behavioral and Brain Sciences* 27: 169–90. doi: 10.1017/S0140525X04000056

Song, Jae Jung. 2012. South Korea: Language policy and planning in the making. *Current Issues in Language Planning* 13 (1): 1–68. doi: 10.1080/14664208.2012.650322

Starks, Donna and Donn Bayard. 2002. Individual variation in the acquisition of postvocalic /r/: Daycare and sibling order as potential variables. *American Speech* 77: 184–94. doi: 10.1215/00031283-77-2-184

Tagliamonte, Sali A. and Sonja Molfenter. 2007. How'd you get that accent?: Acquiring a second dialect of the same language. *Language in Society* 36 (5): 649–75. doi: 10.1017/S0047404507070911.

Trudgill, Peter. 1972. Sex, covert prestige and linguistic change in the urban British English of Norwich. *Language in Society* 1 (2): 179–95. doi: 10.1017/S0047404500000488

Trudgill, Peter. 1986. *Dialects in contact*. Oxford: Blackwell.

Trudgill, Peter. 2008. Colonial dialect contact in the history of European languages: On the irrelevance of identity in new-dialect formation. *Language in Society* 37: 241–80. https://www.jstor.org/stable/20108124

Vousten, Rob. 1995. *Dialect als tweede taal. Linguïstische en extra-linguïstische aspecten van de verwerving van een Noordlimburgs dialect door standaardtalige jongeren.* [Dialect as a Second Language: Linguistic and Extra-linguistic Aspects of the Acquisition of a North Limburg Dialect by Standard-speaking Youngsters] Unpublished PhD dissertation, University of Nijmegen, the Netherlands.

Wolfram, Walt and Natalie Schilling. 2016. *American English: Dialects and variation* (3rd ed.). Oxford: Blackwell.

Interaction, Confounding Effect, and Collinearity in the Analysis of Brazilian Internal Migrants' Speech

LIVIA OUSHIRO
Universidade Estadual de Campinas

Introduction

Variationist studies prize generalizability, the search for regular patterns of language variation and change embedded in linguistic and social structure (Weinreich, Labov and Herzog 1968).[1] The sociolinguistic enterprise has unveiled several recurrent patterns of the social stratification of different languages in various communities, formally summarized in "principles" (Labov 1994, 2001, 2010; Chambers 1992) which describe the regular effect of social predictors (speakers' gender, social class, ethnicity, age, etc.) and of internal predictors (phonological context, word class, word frequency, etc.) on variable phenomena and changes in progress in the speech community.

Studying the speech of mobile populations is, of course, no different. The same general tenets of the study of language variation and change, namely, *orderly heterogeneity* and *inherent variability*, are also empirically observed in migrants' speech. However, the great majority of the studies that have motivated the articulation of regular patterns and principles such as those found in Labov (2001) were primarily interested in community natives. There is not, as of yet, a well-developed theoretical sense of what to expect from the linguistic behavior of migrants. For instance, should mobile female speakers be expected to employ more standard variants of stable variables than mobile males in Western urban communities? Systematically analyzing the speech of different migrant groups—a significant portion of the population in most communities today—will certainly shed light on the extent to which previous generalizations will hold or need to be revised.

But analyzing migrants' linguistic patterns often involves a more complex scenario, in which there is a possibly larger set of variants to which speakers are exposed—those from speakers' place of origin, those from the host community and from any other social groups with which they have had contact—as well as a larger set of sociodemographic factors playing into the mechanisms of dialect contact and new dialect acquisition, for instance, age of arrival and length of residence at the new community, not analyzed in the speech of lifelong residents.

A question that arises is how to adequately model and interpret the effect of several predictors in migrants' speech. Labov's (1972) definition of the "speech community" takes into account both shared evaluations and shared norms among individual members. This implies that speakers who do not share the community's evaluations and patterns of usage, even if of a mutually intelligible dialect, are by definition not part of that speech community. Migrants then may not follow the same expected patterns, and individual mobile speakers may have variously either acquired, partially acquired, or not acquired them at all, leading to more dispersion within the migrant group.[2]

Further, cases of interdependence between predictor variables, reported in studies of natives to the community (e.g., Labov 1990; Sigley 2003; Tagliamonte and Baayen 2012), seem to be particularly frequent in migrants' speech. The interdependence is often found among sociodemographic factors and refers to statistical patterns reflecting complex social embedding, since the effect of a single predictor—say, speakers' gender—may not always be reliably accounted for in isolation from other social constraints.

This chapter discusses the effect of gender, level of education, age of arrival, and length of residence in a number of cases where the effect of a predictor variable is not independent from the effect of another: (1) cases of interaction between gender and level of education, (2) cases of a confounding effect of length of residence on the effect of age of arrival, and (3) cases of collinearity between length of residence and attitudes. Two samples of migrants' speech from Projeto Acomodação ("Accommodation Project"; Oushiro 2020b), both representing speakers from the Brazilian Northeastern states of Alagoas and Paraíba living in the Southeastern state of São Paulo, are used as the basis for this discussion: one is a sample of 32 speakers living in the city of São Paulo and balanced for gender, age, and level of education (henceforth "São Paulo Sample"; Oushiro 2020a); the other is a sample of 40 speakers living in the Campinas Metropolitan Region (about 100 km Northwest of the city of São Paulo), balanced for gender, age of arrival (before 18 y.o. [years old]; 19 + y.o.), and length of residence in the host community (9 or less years; 10+ years) (henceforth "Campinas Sample"; Oushiro 2020b). Analyses of these samples are discussed in light of the results found in other studies of lusophone migrants in Brazil, in an attempt to find adequate interpretations for these results.

The next section presents a general background of Brazilian dialectal variation and migration movements, in which regional and socioeconomic differences are closely intertwined. The following section discusses the effect of speakers' gender and its interaction with level of education. The section "Age of Arrival, Length of Residence, and Attitudes: Confounding Effect and Collinearity" turns to cases of confounding and collinear variables, for which the interpretation of the effect of length of residence may be clouded by the accidental or intrinsic interdependence between predictor variables. All of these cases put in check general expectations and generalizations for these predictors. Finally, the conclusion calls attention to the need for a detailed look at migrants' social experience to uncover these frequent cases of interdependence. The adequate statistical modeling and interpretation of patterns of language variation in migrants' speech need to be richly informed by the complex and intersecting context of the dialect contact situation.

Background

Works on dialect contact in Brazil have largely concentrated on contact between long-established focused varieties (i.e., regional dialects perceived as different; Bortoni-Ricardo 1991), especially between Brazilian Northeasterners and Southeasterners (Oushiro forthcoming). The dialectal differences between North and South have been considered the greatest dialectal division in Brazilian Portuguese since one of the earliest dialectological proposals of Brazilian isoglosses by Antenor Nascentes in the 1920s ([1922] 1953). In Nascentes's proposal, the Southern dialect is subdivided into *fluminense* (roughly around the state of Rio de Janeiro), *mineiro* (part of the state of Minas Gerais), and *sulista*—the latter encompassing the state of São Paulo—and the Northern dialect is subdivided into the *amazônico* (the Amazon region), the *baiano* (encompassing the North of the state of Minas Gerais and the state of Bahia), and the *nordestino*—including the other states in Northeast Brazil. A significant portion of a sparsely populated area in the Central-West region is named *território incaracterístico* (uncharacteristic territory).

The main basis for Nascentes's ([1922] 1953, 19–20) dialectological division is the realization of pretonic midvowels /e/ and /o/ (e.g., *relógio* 'watch', *romã* 'pomegranate') as mid-closed [e, o] in the South/Southeast and mid-open vowels [ɛ, ɔ] in the North/Northeast. Another dialectal difference, at least between part of the Southern and Northeastern dialects, is the realization of coda /r/ (e.g., *porta* 'door', *mulher* 'woman') as respectively more fronted [ɾ, ɹ] in the South or more backed [χ, h] in the North (Callou, Moraes and Leite 1996). Coda /r/ is probably the main shibboleth in Brazilian Portuguese and can be considered a highly salient feature. At the morphosyntactic level, Southern and Northern dialects employ structures of sentential negation (simple: *não vi*; double: *não vi não*; post-verbal: *vi não* 'I haven't seen') at different rates: double and post-verbal negation are relatively more frequent in the Northeast (Furtado da Cunha 2001; Schwenter 2005). North-South dialectological distinctions such as these are generally not proscribed in a normative sense; i.e., they are not considered "wrong" nor overtly commented upon as features to be corrected, but the phonetic features may be negatively evaluated outside their dialectal region, especially the São Paulo retroflex [ɹ] and the Northeastern mid-open pretonic vowels [ɛ, ɔ].

Additionally, most works on dialect contact in Brazil discuss the situation of migrants who have moved from economically less developed rural areas to metropolitan regions, such as the capital city Brasília, in the Center-West region (see, e.g., Adant 1989; Bortoni-Ricardo 1985); and the Southeastern cities of Rio de Janeiro (see, e.g., Marques 2006; Soares 2009), and São Paulo (see, e.g., Oushiro 2020a, 2020b; Santana 2021; Silveira 2022). These migrants have generally moved in search of better life conditions (Oushiro forthcoming). In Projeto Acomodação's samples, most speakers' motivation for moving from the Northeast to São Paulo is "to find a better job," followed by the motivation "to be close to the family," which is the case of many female speakers who moved after their husbands settled in São Paulo. Eight speakers in the São Paulo Sample, namely, those with higher levels of education, also expressed having sought "better university education" and "better quality of life." These motivations reflect the main migratory movements in Brazil throughout the twentieth century (Baeninger 2005).

Rural-urban distinctions in Brazilian Portuguese include the realization of /t, d/ before [i] (e.g., *tia* 'aunt', *dia* 'day') more frequently as affricates [t͡ʃ, d͡ʒ] in urban areas and predominantly as stops [t, d] in rural areas (see Corrêa 2019; Pozzani and Albano 2016); and variation between the standard and non-standard forms of nominal agreement (e.g., *as casas* vs. *as casa* 'the houses'), first-person plural verb agreement (e.g., *nós vamos* vs. *nós vai* 'we go'), and third-person plural verb agreement (e.g., *eles vão* vs. *eles vai* 'they go'). The agreement variables are also sharply stratified according to speakers' education and social class (Guy 1981; Mendes and Oushiro 2015; Scherre and Naro 2014). Because of their association with lower social strata, most rural features tend to be stigmatized and considered "bad Portuguese," especially the morphosyntactic non-standard forms.

These observations entail that, in most cases, contact involves not only *regional* differences between varieties but also *socioeconomic* differences and contact between *rural and urban* dialects. To illustrate this situation, consider the excerpt of an interview with a 44-year-old woman from Paraíba living in the city of Rio de Janeiro, where she is telling what it was like to commute to work on her first day as a housemaid in Copacabana:

> and my first job was in Copacabana and . . . I took the wrong bus many times because I didn't know anything yet let alone how to read . . . (interviewer: uhum) I knew nothing . . . nothing . . . (interviewer: wow) nothing I only knew . . . how to sign my name.[3] (Rosalinda M.)

Literacy is not just the ability to read and write but encompasses all aspects of a person's life. The excerpt shows that the implications of illiteracy go beyond the academic realm or the job market. For instance, because of Rosalinda's social class and the fact that she came from a rural area, she went to the movies for the first time in her life when she was 43 years old, just a year before this recording in 2015. This type of social and geographical mobility creates a situation of cultural contact that contrasts with much of the literature on dialect contact in Anglophone and other Global North communities, which has largely focused on middle-class speakers (see e.g., Bowie 2000; Chambers 1992; Nycz 2011; Tagliamonte and Molfenter 2007; Trudgill 1986). Thus, one of Chambers's (1992, 697) eight principles posited for dialect acquisition predicts that "orthographically distinct variants are acquired faster than orthographically obscure ones," based on the observation that "in dialect acquisition, unlike first-language acquisition and, typically, second-language acquisition, the acquirers are literate." One such hypothesis naturally needs to be taken under advisement in culturally distinct settings. Although Chambers (1992, 677) provided for this hypothesis when formulating the principles as "testable hypotheses," it further reinforces the need to broaden the scope of communities and speakers under investigation to characterize patterns of variation and change.

Dialect contact in developing countries such as Brazil will often depict speakers in a complex contact setting. For most migrants in Brazil, especially in the subset of works here reviewed, it is nearly impossible to isolate geographical mobility from socioeconomic mobility, and socioeconomic from rural-urban differences. This calls for a careful analysis of a possibly larger set of intersecting predictors.

Gender and Level of Education: A Case of Interaction

Gender is one of the most studied predictors in sociolinguistics with generally consistent patterns across communities. These findings were summarized in Labov's (2001, 293) "Gender Paradox": "Women conform more closely than men to sociolinguistic norms that are overtly prescribed, but conform less than men when they are not."

However, Bortoni-Ricardo (1985), in an early work on dialect contact in Brazil, consisting of her famous study of the speech of rural migrants from Minas Gerais living in Brazil's capital city (Brasília), found that these speakers did not follow the gender generalization for first- and third-person-plural subject-verb agreement, whose non-standard variants are overtly stigmatized in Brazilian Portuguese and, in her sample, favored by women. This result is also found for third-person verb agreement in the speech of rural migrants in São Paulo (Rodrigues 1987). The reverse pattern was explained as a consequence of the speakers' social networks: while men usually had greater chance to have contact with natives from the host community because they worked outside their neighborhood, women mostly worked within the household, as either housewives or maids, thus having only indirect contact with the urban dialect via their spouses and children. One could question whether these women truly did not conform to the Gender Paradox or rather simply did not have the same exposure to the overt prescribed variant (most of Bortoni-Ricardo's female speakers were in fact illiterate or had low levels of formal education).

But gender differentiation in migrant communities has shown quite mixed results. Subsequent studies have found women to be ahead of men in the acquisition of urban or host community's traits (e.g., Cardoso 2009; Possatti 2020; Silva 2016; Soares 2009, among others), and others still have found no significant differences between women and men (e.g., Corrêa 1998; Guedes 2019; Oliveira 2020; Santana 2021, among others). For instance, within the same sample of speakers, Bortoni-Ricardo (1985) also describes women's preference for the standard variant of post-tonic diphthongs, as in *armár*[iw] 'cabinet', in relation to its non-standard monophthongized form *armár*[u], and no significant gender difference in the case of /ʎ/ vocalization, as in *filho* (standard) vs. *fio* (non-standard) 'son'. The author suggests that these different results are due to differences in the variables' salience and speakers' awareness (which hints at an interaction between gender and style), arguing that while monophthongization is below the level of consciousness for these speakers, the verb agreement variables are not. But this explanation still leaves unanswered the lack of correlation for /ʎ/ vocalization and whether the degree of awareness is different between males and females. Overall, studies do not reveal a clear motivation for the gender effect in

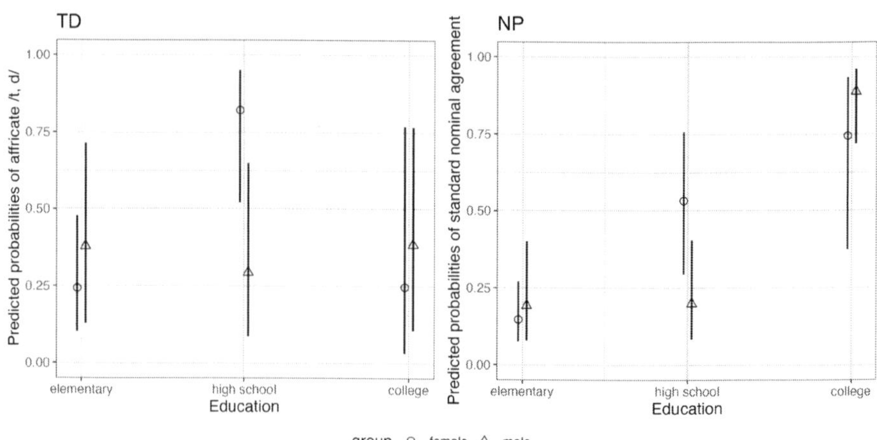

Figure 7.1. Interactions between gender and level of education for variable /t, d/ before [i] (left) and variable NP agreement (right) in the speech of 32 Northeastern migrants living in São Paulo, in mixed-effects models performed on the São Paulo Sample of Projeto Acomodação (Source: Adapted from Oushiro 2020a, 59–60)*

different communities and even in the same migrant community regarding different linguistic features.

On the technical side, interactions are observed when "the effect of one explanatory variable on the outcome depends on the value of another variable. The effect can be reinforced, weakened, or even reversed" (Levshina 2015, 162). A well-known case of interaction in variationist studies is the one between gender and social class (Labov 1990), as differences between female and male speakers are not held constant through the course of language change, in cases of stable variation, nor in different socioeconomic groups.

A systematic interaction between gender and level of education was described by Oushiro (2020a) in an analysis of six variables in the São Paulo Sample: pretonic mid-vowel height /e/ and /o/, coda /r/, /t, d/ affrication, sentential negation, and nominal agreement (see the "Background" section). From this set, /t, d/ indexes rural-urban distinctions, nominal agreement indexes rural-urban and level of education differences, and the other variables index Northern-Southern dialects. There were significant interactions between gender and education in mixed-effects models only for /t, d/ affrication and nominal agreement (figure 7.1); for all other variables, no significant effect of gender was found (figure 7.1 and subsequent figures are available in a larger size at the publisher's website).

In figure 7.1, the left panel shows the results for the predicted probabilities of /t, d/ affrication, and the right panel shows the probabilities of usage of standard nominal agreement (the preferred host community variants), all with their respective error bars. Each panel shows the females on the left (lines with circle) and the males on the right (lines with triangle), and both groups are subdivided into speakers' level of education: elementary, high school, and college. The different patterns for females and males indicate the interactions: for both affricate /t, d/ and standard nominal agreement, women with a high school level of education favor the host community variants in relation to men of similar education, compared to speakers with an elementary or a university degree.[4]

The inverted "U-shaped" curve for /t, d/ affrication in women's speech is worthy of attention: women with a high school level lead in the acquisition of the host community variant. The same pattern is not observed for males, nor for nominal agreement in general. Nominal agreement, instead, follows a more consistent pattern of greater usage of the urban form according to higher level of education, though the difference between males with elementary or high school level is not significant.

In the Campinas Sample, containing no speakers with a university degree (most had an incomplete high school level of education), women were found to favor affricate /t, d/ (F: 45.6% vs. M: 29.5%) and standard nominal agreement (F: 48.3% vs. M: 29.7%). There was no significant gender difference for coda /r/ and sentential negation (Oushiro 2020b, 83).

These results were interpreted in terms of the variables' social meanings: /t, d/ stopping and non-standard nominal agreement are associated with *rural* speakers (as they are also present in the São Paulo countryside), while aspirate /r/ and double/post-verbal negation are associated with *Northeasterners*. Thus, it is apparent that women are moving away from the rural variants but not the Northeastern ones. The difference in the overall curve for /t, d/ and nominal agreement may also be accounted for by their indexicalities: while women with college education do tend to employ the overtly prescribed standard nominal agreement, they do not necessarily reject /t, d/ stopping, which may also index regional variation. This rejection of /t, d/ stopping, however, takes place among women with high school education, perhaps a symptom of greater linguistic insecurity and a more fragile socioeconomic status than for college educated women. Hence speakers' social position and variables' social meanings (in addition to their salience and degree of awareness; Bortoni-Ricardo 1985), ought to be considered in explaining differences in dialect accommodation.

On the other hand, Oushiro's (2020a) interpretation of gender differences does not account for Bortoni-Ricardo's (1985) and Rodrigues's (1987) previous results, where non-standard rural variants of verb agreement were *favored* by women, not disfavored. One possibility for understanding these discrepancies is the difference in statistical methods applied in these studies, as mixed-effects models are a relatively new implementation in linguistic studies and were not applied by Bortoni-Ricardo in the 1980s.

Oushiro's (2020a) systematic comparison of fixed- and mixed-effects models may shed light onto these conflicting results. In fixed-effects models, gender showed a significant main effect on pretonic midvowel /o/, sentential negation, and nominal agreement—all pointing to men's lead in the accommodation to the host community's variant. These effects for gender, however, are only apparent, as they disappear when speaker is included in the models as a random effect. Regarding the interaction with level of education, results also change when not including speaker (figure 7.2).

Figure 7.2 shows much narrower error bars in contrast with figure 7.1, which is indicative of the crucial role of individuals for explaining much of the observed

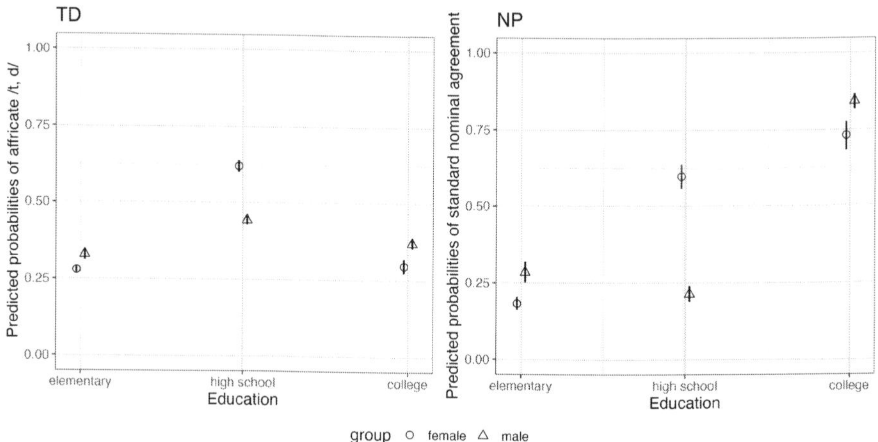

Figure 7.2. Interactions between gender and level of education for variable /t, d/ before [i] (left) and variable NP agreement (right) in the speech of 32 Northeastern migrants living in São Paulo, in fixed-effects models performed on the São Paulo Sample of Projeto Acomodação (Source: Adapted from Oushiro 2020a, 59–60)*

dispersion in the data. Although the overall shapes of the curves are roughly the same as in the mixed-effects models, in figure 7.2 gender differences arise not only for speakers with high school education but also for more and less educated speakers. Bortoni-Ricardo's (1985) participants were mostly illiterate or had very low levels of education, while most speakers in the São Paulo Sample have at least completed elementary school. In figure 7.2, if considering only the less-educated speakers, the comparison between males and females in the fixed-effects models could indeed lead to the conclusion that men are ahead of women in the accommodation to affricate /t, d/ and standard nominal agreement, which is the same result that Bortoni-Ricardo (1985) found for rural speakers. Thus the difference in the observed behavior for women and men in Bortoni-Ricardo's (1985) and Oushiro's (2020a) studies may be accounted for by both the differences in statistical models and the general educational level of their participants.

Most important, though, this systematic comparison of studies and models shows that (1) there is great dispersion among individuals, which may be particularly enhanced in dialect contact situations (see Silveira 2022), and hence it is imperative to analyze migrants' speech in mixed-effect models to adequately infer the role of fixed-effects; (2) migrants do not behave homogeneously in relation to different variables, and various patterns of correlation with gender (either men or women in the lead, or yet no correlation) may be observed, especially considering variables' social salience, indexicalities ("Northeastern," "rural," "stigmatized," etc.), and speakers' awareness; and (3) gender patterns are closely related to gender roles variously defined in different communities, and it is likely that migrants' gender interacts with other external predictors, such as speakers' education, social class, and style.[5]

Age of Arrival, Length of Residence, and Attitudes: Confounding Effect and Collinearity

The social predictor that has been most analyzed in Brazilian dialect contact studies is length of residence. Significant correlations have been found between this variable and migrants' speech, all on phonetic variables (e.g., pretonic midvowels in Marques 2006; coda /s/ in Lima and Lucena 2013; coda /r/ in Leite 2004 and Bieler da Silva 2015; /t, d/ before [i] in Pozzani and Albano 2016, among others). Marques (2006) compared patterns of accommodation in the speech of Northeasterners from Paraíba living in Rio de Janeiro and Brazilians living in Portugal, and found that a 10-year period is sufficient to perceive accommodation for the internal migrants but not across the national varieties, signaling that length of residence is not independent from other external factors.

Most of these studies, however, did not control for speakers' age of arrival. Since it is often the case that the ones who have lived the longest in the new community are also the ones who arrived earlier, it is important to control both of these variables in a sample (Oushiro forthcoming). Age of arrival is regarded in second language and second dialect acquisition as the single-most-important predictor for attainment of host community's patterns (Bortoni-Ricardo 1991; Siegel 2010), especially in the case of complex phonetic variation, such as vowel backing in Southern England English (Chambers 1992).

The Campinas Sample of Projeto Acomodação was built especially to disentangle the effect of age of arrival and length of residence. The effect of these social predictors was systematically compared in the analyses of four of the six sociolinguistic variables analyzed for the São Paulo Sample (see the section "Gender and Level of Education: A Case of Interaction"): coda /r/, /t, d/ before [i], sentential negation, and nominal agreement. These results are shown in figure 7.3 (from Oushiro 2020b).

Figure 7.3 shows regression lines relating speakers' rates of usage of the host community's typical variants (tap or retroflex /r/, affricate /t, d/, simple negation, and standard nominal agreement) and their age of arrival (left) and length of residence (right). The probabilities in log odds were estimated in mixed-effects logistic regression models, including speakers' gender, age of arrival, and length of residence as fixed effects, and speaker as a random effect. Coda /r/ significantly correlates with both variables: speakers tend to employ the local /r/ the younger they were when arriving at the new community and the longer they have been in Campinas, as shown by the descending and ascending slopes, and negative and positive estimates. In comparison, /t, d/ affrication only correlates with age of arrival, also in the expected direction: smaller rates of [t͡ʃ, d͡ʒ] as age of migration increases. Finally, sentential negation and nominal agreement, the two morphosyntactic variables, correlate with none of these social predictors (Oushiro 2020b).

Silveira (2022), analyzing accommodation to 17 prosodic parameters in the subset of Alagoans of the same sample, similarly did not find correlations with length of residence but found a significant interaction between age of arrival and gender: males were closer to the local Campinas patterns for six of the nine intonational variables (standard deviation of f0, f0 peaks, mean positive f0 change rate, mean negative

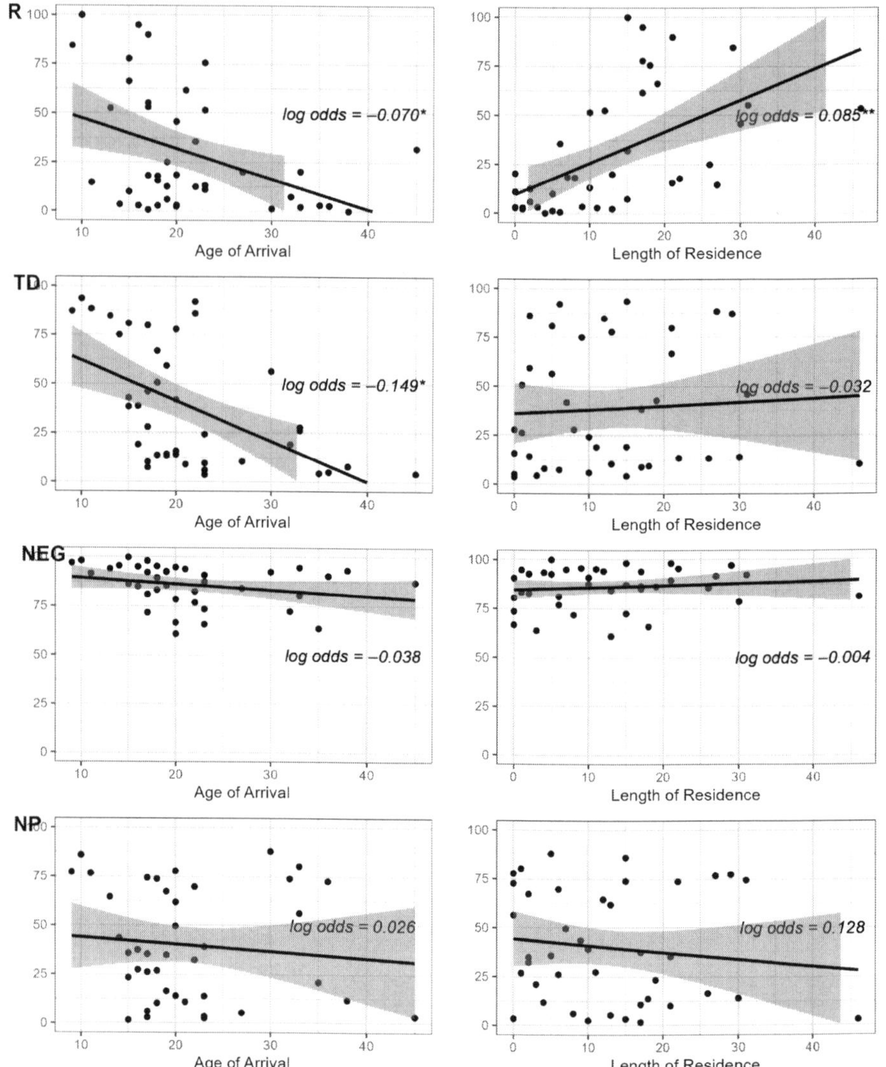

Figure 7.3. Regression lines between speakers' rate of usage of São Paulo's typical variants and age of arrival (left) and length of residence (right) for coda /r/, /t, d/ before [i], sentential negation, and nominal agreement in the Campinas Sample. Log odds are from mixed-effects logistic regression models, with speakers' gender, age of arrival, and length of residence as fixed effects and speaker as a random effect (Source: Adapted from Oushiro 2020b, 83)*

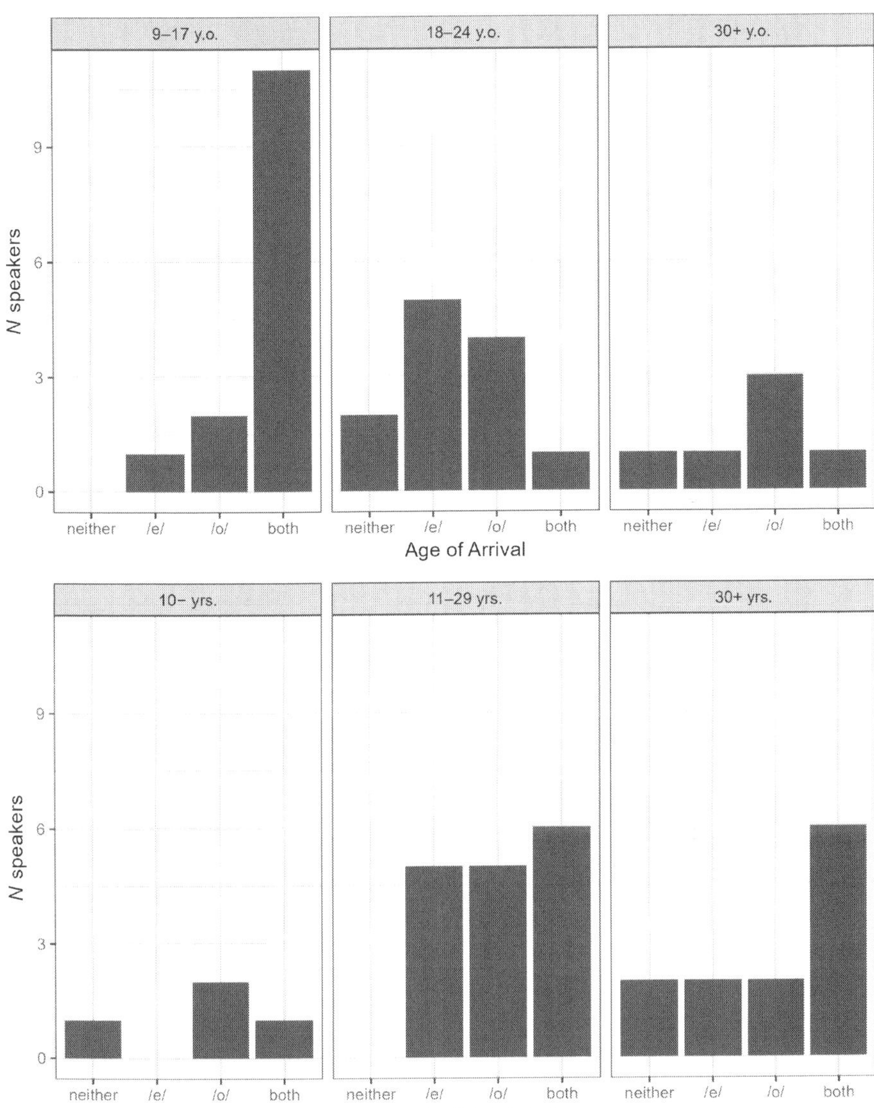

Figure 7.4. Number of speakers in the São Paulo Sample accommodating to Paulistas' pretonic midvowels /e/ and /o/ according to migrants' age of arrival (top) and length of residence (bottom) (Source: Adapted from Oushiro 2019, 688)*

f0 change rate, standard deviation of positive f0 change rate, and standard deviation of negative f0 change rate) the younger they were when they moved to the new community, but women did not exhibit the same pattern.

Figure 7.4 (adapted from Oushiro 2019) shows the results for pretonic midvowels in the São Paulo Sample. Recall that this group of migrants is stratified according to their gender, age, and level of education, so speakers' age of arrival and length of residence are not balanced and were thus analyzed separately. The ad hoc categories for age of arrival (9–17 y.o.; 18–24 y.o.; 30+ y.o.) were partially determined by life phase (roughly teenage years; young adults; adults) and partially by number of speakers, so that each level would have approximately the same number. The second criterion was also applied to length of residence (less than 10 years, 11–29 years, 30+ years). Figure 7.4 compares the number of speakers in each category who have accommodated to the Paulista pretonic /e/, pretonic /o/, to neither or to both vowels.

Accommodation was measured by comparing the migrants' speech with a control-sample of seven native Paulistas. Speaker was analyzed as a fixed-factor, and a migrant individual was considered to have accommodated to the host community's pattern when there was no significant difference of this speaker's vowel height compared to the average F1 for /e/ and /o/ of the seven native speakers. While there is no difference in accommodation according to length of residence (bottom), the panel at the top shows that more speakers who migrated at an earlier age accommodated to both vowels.

Taking multiple variables into account, the generalization is that age of arrival is more important than length of residence in the case of phonetic and prosodic variables—the only exception being coda /r/, correlated with both social predictors. Morphosyntactic variables, at least for the ones analyzed so far, are not affected by these predictors.

The consistent correlations found in previous studies between phonetic variables and length of residence may well have been cases of a confounding effect: when controlling for the simultaneous effect of age of arrival, the effect of length of residence disappears for most of them. A confounding effect is a variable that influences both the response and another predictor variable, and as such may mask the actual effect being detected (Gries 2021). In this example, length of residence is a confounding effect of age of arrival in studies that did not control for both predictors. It is one of the motivations for the statistics mantra "correlation does not imply causation." The main takeaway is a corollary of this statement: results cannot be interpreted as prima facie motivation.

Length of residence is usually taken as a proxy for the amount of linguistic input a speaker has had from the host community. A different interpretation has also been presented for the observed correlations with length of residence, questioning its motivating role but also arguing that underlying this effect are speakers' *attitudes* toward the varieties in contact. In fact, a number of works in Brazilian contact studies have argued that this is the key factor driving dialect accommodation in mobile speakers.

In reviewing three works that found length of residence to be a significant predictor of dialect accommodation, Lucena (2017) argues that length of residence is a confounding effect of the migrants' *attitudes* toward the host community. In other words, length of residence would not be the true motivation for the observed correlation. For instance, in Silva and Lucena's (2015; *apud* Lucena 2017) study on the vocalization of the post-vocalic lateral /l/ (*a*[ɫ]*ma* vs. *a*[w]*ma* 'soul') among seven lusophone Africans in João Pessoa, the authors found rates of accommodation as low as 4.2% and as high as 89%. Although finding a significant correlation with length of residence, Lucena (2017) relates the speaker who mostly accommodated to the Brazilian vocalized /l/ (89%) to their positive attitudes toward the country and the one who least accommodated (4.2%) to their evaluation of Brazilian Portuguese as less prestigious than European Portuguese. The latter speaker also expressed their intention to go back to Guinea-Bissau and get involved in Guinean politics. When asked where he plans to live, he says: "Preferably in my own country. I wanna live in my country, work in my country [. . .] my dream, as I always joke . . . is . . . to become the president of the republic in twenty years' time" (Lucena 2017, 70–71).[6]

This interpretation, though plausible, may conceal yet a deeper relation between length of residence and attitudes: that they are simply not independent predictors, and both have a joint effect on one another. The longer a person stays in a community, the more likely they will develop positive attitudes toward it; and the more positive the attitude toward the community, the more likely it is they will stay. Ascertaining the effect of each of these predictors or yet their interdependence is an empirical question for dialect contact studies, and not without its difficulties. While speakers' age of arrival and length of residence may be objectively determined, assessing speakers' attitudes is not. Qualitative analyses of speakers' attitudes may end up being partial and biased, at least to some extent, since these are not static traits. In most cultures, denying one's roots is socially frowned upon, so migrants are likely to express high identification with their place of origin, even when they have high rates of dialect accommodation. The following excerpt from an interview with a married couple from Paraíba living in São Paulo exemplifies this point:

JOSANE V: Sometimes I complain to him. I say, "you've been here in São Paulo for so many years and you still don't know how to speak you can't learn it?"

HENRIQUE A: It's not that I can't learn . . . [. . .] my roots . . . I will never leave them. . . . [M]y accent I will never leave it.[7]

Attitudes such as those expressed by Josane V and Henrique A can be analyzed qualitatively, but quantifying them is somewhat harder. An attempt at capturing them more systematically was done in data collection of the Campinas Sample. In this sample of 40 Alagoans and Paraibans, participants were asked at the end of the interview to self-attribute a grade from 0 to 10 to their degree of identification with their home state and São Paulo. The distributions of these answers are shown in figure 7.5.

Unsurprisingly, 39 out of 40 speakers self-attributed high grades (7–10) to how Alagoan and Paraiban they considered themselves. This means that handpicking statements of how proud a migrant is of their place of origin to explain a lower rate of accommodation is not enough: it is likely that nearly all migrants, given a specific context, will report a positive attitude toward their home region. Interestingly, though, their answer to the question of how Paulista they considered themselves (figure 7.5, bottom) is more evenly distributed from 0 to 10, indicating that their attitudes toward the host community may be more important than those toward the community of origin as a predictor of their linguistic behavior.

These scales are surely not intended to represent speakers' identities, a complex and dynamic construct that goes beyond a number on a scale. These questions were

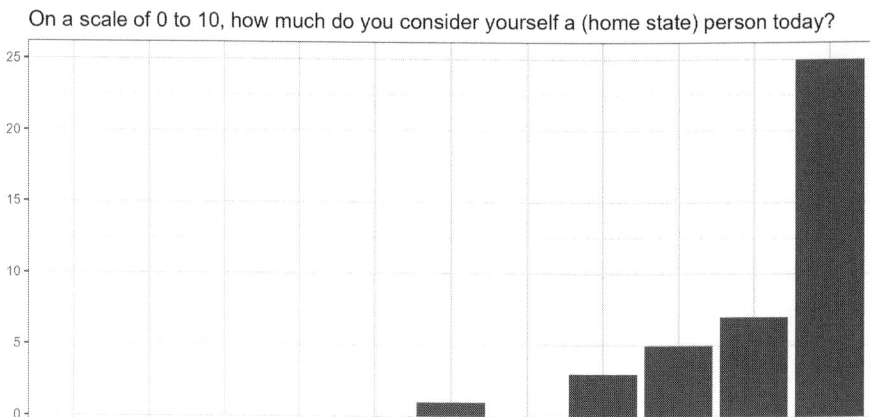

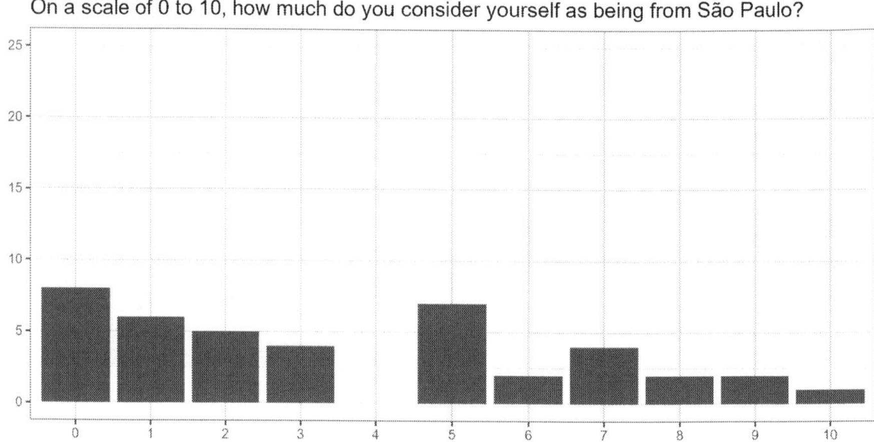

Figure 7.5. Participants' self-attributed degree of identification with home state (top) and host community (bottom) (Source: Adapted from Oushiro 2020b, 85.)*

simply aimed at probing speakers' attitudes toward the different regions in the highly localized instance of the sociolinguistic interview. In fact, one of the speakers in the sample—who was recorded in two different occasions in 2016 and 2018, with slightly different interview schedules—self-attributed grade 5 in 2016 and grade 3 in 2018 to how Paulista they considered themself, clearly showing that this is only an indirect measure of their attitudes at a specific conversation, with a specific interlocutor, at a specific place and time.

More noteworthy is a correlation found between the Paulista scale and length of residence (Pearson's $r = 0.35$, $p = 0.02$); i.e., the greater the length of residence in São Paulo (in years), the greater the tendency to self-attribute a higher grade in the Paulista scale. Although not that strong a correlation, this signals that length of residence and attitudes toward the host community are not independent from one another—so this is yet *another* case of lack of independence between predictors.

This is a case of collinearity, which Levshina (2015, 159) defines as "a phenomenon that can be observed when some variables relate to the same underlying causal effect." It occurs when a predictor variable in a regression model can be linearly predicted from another predictor variable, configuring their lack of independence. Unlike the case of confounding effect reported earlier, in which a carefully designed sample made it possible to disentangle the effects of age of arrival and length of residence, it is often the case that collinear variables will remain so no matter the degree of control imposed on the data. Hence it does not seem to be the case to determine whether it is length of residence or attitudes that motivate dialect accommodation in certain sociolinguistic variables, but to recognize their interdependence and mutual effect on one another and on the response variable.[8]

Conclusion

Studies on dialect contact require the careful examination of a possibly larger set of predictor variables, which are frequently non-orthogonal with one another. Internal migration in the Global South often entails not only regional dialectal variation but also rural-urban and socioeconomic differences in mobile speakers' rich linguistic repertoire. This sets up a complex contact situation at its outset, even if pertaining to contact between mutually intelligible dialects.

This chapter presented examples of an interaction, of a confounding variable, and of collinearity—between gender and level of education, age of arrival and length of residence, and length of residence and attitudes—in dialect contact studies of Brazilian Portuguese. The observation of lack of independence among predictor variables is quite common in dialect contact and points to the need for careful interpretation of the observed patterns.

In certain cases, a sample of speakers who have been reasonably balanced for specific predictors may allow for an examination of their individual, interactive, or apparent effect on a response variable; in others, it may be simply the case that their effect cannot be disentangled, as they are part of a larger intertwined whole—and one needs to recognize its complexity.

Identifying these sets of interdependent predictors is not just a matter of statistically exploring the data but rather knowing the speakers and their communities. For instance, why did males in Bortoni-Ricardo's (1985) study favor the overtly prestigious variants? Why is it that women with lower and higher levels of education behave similarly in relation to /t, d/ affrication, and women with intermediary schooling stand out in the usage of the urban variant? Why is coda /r/ differently attained in dialect contact, correlating both with age of arrival and length of residence, unlike other phonetic variables?

Further ethnographic studies will shed light on individual speakers' roles, stances, and multiple identities, in specific conversational interactions and as part of a larger pattern of linguistic variation. The examples of statistical interaction, confounding effect, and collinearity among social predictors also call for an examination of several dimensions of the migrant's social and political identities simultaneously. Adequately modeling and interpreting mobile speakers' patterns cannot be separated from their overlapping social identities and complex social experience.

Notes

*Some figures in this chapter are available on the publisher's website (press.georgetown.edu) to make it easier to view the data.

1. This research was funded by Fundação de Amparo à Pesquisa do Estado de São Paulo (FAPESP 2016/04960-7). I am thankful for the many generous comments and suggestions by the audience at Georgetown University Round Table 2022 and by the anonymous reviewers to the manuscript.

2. Payne's (1976) study of the acquisition of phonetic and phonological features by children who moved to King of Prussia, Pennsylvania shows that some phonological features, such as the distribution of tense /æ/, may not be fully acquired even if migration took place at a very early age.

3. Original excerpt: "e o meu primeiro emprego foi lá em Copacabana e . . . peguei ônibus errado muitas vezes porque não sabia nada ainda e muito menos ler . . . (uhum) não sabia nada . . . nada . . . nada só . . . assinar o meu nome."

4. Although the error bars for females and males with a high school education overlap, the logistic regression models detected a significant interaction, as patterns are different for each educational level.

5. For other cases of interaction with gender in Brazilian Portuguese, see Silveira (2022), who reports an interaction between speakers' gender and age of arrival in analyses of 17 prosodic variables; and Oushiro (2021), who reports interactions between gender and style for coda /r/ and coda /s/.

6. Original excerpt: "De preferência no meu país. Eu quero morar no meu país. Trabalhar no meu país. [. . .] é o meu sonho, que eu sempre falo na brincadeira . . . é . . . daqui a vinte anos: presidente da república."

7. Original excerpt: "JosaneV: às vezes eu reclamo pra ele (eu digo) tantos anos que tu tá aqui em São Paulo tu não sabe falar tu não aprende isso?" HenriqueA: "não é que não aprende . . . [. . .] a minha raiz . . . eu não vou deixar nunca. . . . [O] meu sotaque eu não vou deixar nunca."

8. For cases of multicollinearity among different variables, a merged predictor from a Principal Component Analysis could also be set up.

References

Adant, Josepha. 1989. Difusão dialetal: O caso dos alagoanos em Brasília. In F. Tarallo (ed.), *Fotografias sociolinguísticas*. Campinas, Brazil: Editora da Unicamp, 181–97.

Baeninger, Rosana. 2005. São Paulo e suas migrações no final do século XX. *São Paulo em Perspectiva* 19 (3): 84–96. doi: 10.1590/S0102-88392005000300008

Bieler da Silva, Mariane Esteves. 2015. *Entre duas metrópoles: (-r) em Itanhandu*. Unpublished MA thesis, University of São Paulo.

Bortoni-Ricardo, Stella Maris. 1985. *The urbanization of rural dialect speakers*. Cambridge: Cambridge University Press.

Bortoni-Ricardo, Stella Maris. 1991. Dialect contact in Brasília. *International Journal of Sociolinguistics* 89: 47–59.

Bowie, David. 2000. *The effect of geographic mobility on the retention of a local dialect*. Unpublished PhD dissertation, University of Pennsylvania, Philadelphia.

Callou, Dinah, João Moraes and Yonne Leite. 1996. Variação e diferenciação dialetal: A pronúncia do /r/ no português do Brasil. In Ingedore Koch (ed.), *Gramática do português falado* (vol. VI). Campinas, Brazil: Editora da Unicamp, 463–489.

Cardoso, Daisy Barbara Borges. 2009. *Variação e mudança do imperativo no português brasileiro: gênero e identidade*. Unpublished PhD dissertation, Universidade de Brasília.

Chambers, Jack K. 1992. Dialect acquisition. *Language* 68 (4): 673–705. doi: 10.2307/416850.

Corrêa, Cíntia da Costa. 1998. *Focalização dialetal em Brasília: Um estudo das vogais pretônicas e do /s/ pós-vocálico*. Unpublished MA thesis, Universidade de Brasília.

Corrêa, Thaís Regina de Andrade. 2019. *A variação na realização de /t/ e /d/ na comunidade de práticas da UFS: mobilidade e integração*. Unpublished MA thesis, Universidade Federal de Sergipe.

Furtado da Cunha, M. A. 2001. O modelo das motivações competidoras no domínio funcional da negação. *D.E.L.T.A.* 17. doi: 10.1590/S0102-44502001000100001

Gries, Stefan Th. 2021. *Statistics for linguistics with R: A practical introduction* (3rd ed.). Berlin / New York: Mouton De Gruyter. doi: 10.1515/9783110718256

Guedes, Shirley. 2019. Emprego do artigo definido em situação de contato dialetal: Um estudo da fala de migrantes paraibanos em São Paulo. *Domínios da Linguagem* 13 (4): 1401–32. doi: 10.14393/DL40-v13n4a2019-4

Guy, Gregory R. 1981. *Linguistic variation in Brazilian Portuguese: Aspects of the phonology, syntax, and language history*. Unpublished PhD dissertation, University of Pennsylvania, Philadelphia.

Labov, William. 1972. *Sociolinguistic patterns*. Philadelphia: University of Pennsylvania Press.

Labov, William. 1990. The intersection of sex and social class in the course of linguistic change. *Language Variation and Change* 2 (2): 205–54. doi: 10.1017/S0954394500000338

Labov, William. 1994. *Principles of linguistic change: Internal factors*. Oxford and Cambridge: Blackwell.

Labov, William. 2001. *Principles of linguistic change: Social factors*. Oxford and Cambridge: Blackwell.

Labov, William. 2010. *Principles of linguistic change: Cognitive and cultural factors*. Malden, MA: Wiley-Blackwell. doi: 10.1002/9781444327496

Leite, Cândida M. Britto. 2004. *Atitudes linguísticas: A variante retroflexa em foco*. Unpublished MA thesis, University of Campinas, Brazil.

Levshina, Natalia. 2015. *How to do linguistics with R: Data exploration and statistical analysis*. Amsterdam/Philadelphia: John Benjamins. doi: 10.1075/z.195.website

Lima, Izete de Souza and Rubens Marques de Lucena. 2013. Influência de variáveis não linguísticas no processo de acomodação dialetal do /s/ em coda silábica por paraibanos em Recife. *Letrônica* 6 (1): 161–78.

Lucena, Rubens Marques de. 2017. Um olhar quali-quantitativo sobre o efeito da variável tempo de exposição em fenômenos de acomodação dialetal. *Gragoatá* 22 (42): 62–84. doi: 10.22409/gragoata.2017n42a33463

Marques, Sandra Maria Oliveira. 2006. *As vogais médias pretônicas em situação de contato dialetal*. Unpublished PhD dissertation, Universidade Federal do Rio de Janeiro.

Mendes, Ronald Beline and Livia Oushiro. 2015. Variable number agreement in Brazilian Portuguese: An overview. *Language and Linguistics Compass* 9 (9): 358–68. doi: doi.org/10.1111/lnc3.12156

Nascentes, Antenor. (1922) 1953. *O linguajar carioca*. Rio de Janeiro: Organização Simões.

Nycz, Jennifer. 2011. *Second dialect acquisition: Implications for theories of phonological representation*. Unpublished PhD dissertation, New York University.

Oliveira, Marcelo Augusto Junqueira de. 2020. *Dialetos em contato: Acomodação dialetal por migrantes baianos habitantes da cidade de Bauru, São Paulo*. Unpublished MA thesis, Universidade Estadual Paulista, São Paulo.

Oushiro, Livia. 2019. Linguistic uniformity in the speech of Brazilian internal migrants in a dialect contact situation. In Sasha Calhoun, Paola Escudero, Marija Tabain and Paul Warren (eds.), *Proceedings of the 19th International Congress of Phonetic Sciences*. 686–690. doi: 10.5281/zenodo.3510276

Oushiro, Livia. 2020a. As variáveis sexo/gênero e indivíduo em situação de contato dialetal. In Danniel Carvalho and Dorothy Brito (eds.), *Gênero e língua(gem). Formas e usos*. Salvador: EDUFBA, 43–65.

Oushiro, Livia. 2020b. Contrasting age of arrival and length of residence in dialect contact. *University of Pennsylvania Working Papers in Linguistics* 25 (2): 79–88.

Oushiro, Livia. 2021. Converging to local and supralocal norms: stylistic variation in migrants' speech. Paper presented at New Ways of Analyzing Variation 49. Austin, Texas, October.

Oushiro, Livia. Forthcoming. Dialect contact in lusophone communities. In Ana Maria Carvalho and Livia Oushiro (eds.), *The Oxford handbook of the Portuguese language*. Oxford: Oxford University Press.

Payne, Arvilla Chapin. 1976. *The acquisition of the phonological system of a second dialect*. PhD dissertation, University of Pennsylvania, Philadelphia.

Possatti, Lucas. 2020. *Acomodação dialetal de cariocas residentes em João Pessoa: Uma análise sociolinguística*. Unpublished MA thesis, Universidade Federal da Paraíba.

Pozzani, Denise and Eleonora C. Albano. 2016. Gradientes alofônicos de oclusivas alveolares do português brasileiro em uma situação de contato dialetal. *Veredas* 2: 62–79.

Rodrigues, Angela C. S. 1987. *A concordância verbal no português popular em São Paulo*. Unpublished PhD dissertation, Universidade de São Paulo.

Santana, Amanda de Lima. 2021. A pronúncia variável de /t, d/ diante de [i] na fala de migrantes sergipanos em São Paulo. *Estudos Linguísticos* 50 (3): 1283–1304. doi: 10.21165/el.v50i3.2969

Scherre, Maria Marta Pereira and Anthony Julius Naro. 2014. Sociolinguistic correlates of negative evaluation: Variable concord in Rio de Janeiro. *Language Variation and Change* 26: 331–357. doi: 10.1017/S0954394514000143

Schwenter, Scott. 2005. The pragmatics of negation in Brazilian Portuguese. *Lingua* 115: 1427–56. doi: 10.1016/j.lingua.2004.06.006

Siegel, Jeff. 2010. *Second dialect acquisition*. Cambridge: Cambridge University Press. doi: 10.1017/CBO9780511777820

Sigley, Robert. 2003. The importance of interaction effects. *Language Variation and Change* 15: 227–253. doi: 10.1017/S0954394503152040

Silva, Mikaylson Rocha da. 2016. *Contato dialetal: Atitudes do falar paraibano em São Paulo*. Unpublished MA thesis, Universidade Federal da Paraíba.

Silveira, Gustavo de Campos Pinheiro. 2022. *The prosody of speech in a dialect contact situation: A sociophonetic study of the speech of Alagoan migrants in São Paulo*. Unpublished MA thesis, University of Campinas, Brazil.

Soares, Viviane dos Ramos. 2009. *A negação no contato entre dialetos*. Unpublished MA thesis, Universidade Federal do Rio de Janeiro.

Tagliamonte, Sali and R. Harald Baayen. 2012. Models, forests, and trees of York English: *Was/were* variation as a case study for statistical practice. *Language Variation and Change* 24: 135–178. doi: 10.1017/S0954394512000129

Tagliamonte, Sali and Sonja Molfenter. 2007. How'd you get that accent? Acquiring a second dialect of the same language. *Language in Society* 36 (5): 649–675. doi: 10.1017/S0047404507070911

Trudgill, Peter. 1986. *Dialects in contact*. Oxford: Basil Blackwell. doi: 10.1017/S0047404507070911

Weinreich, Uriel, William Labov and Marvin I. Herzog. 1968. Empirical foundations for a theory of language change. In W. P. Lehmann and Y. Malkiel (eds.), *Directions for historical linguistics*. Austin: University of Texas Press, 95–195.

Chapter 8

On the (Non-)Uniformity of Contact Outcomes:
A Comparison of Spanish in New York City and Boston

DANIEL ERKER
Boston University

THIS STUDY EXAMINES THE linguistic outcomes of dialectal and language contact among Spanish speakers in two settings, New York City (NYC), New York, and Boston, Massachusetts. The feature used to assess contact outcomes is the variable presence vs. absence of subject personal pronouns—e.g., *(yo) canto,* both 'I sing'—which constitutes a site of crosslinguistic (Spanish vs. English) as well as dialectal difference (i.e., pronoun use varies geographically within the Hispanophone world). Multivariate variationist sociolinguistic analysis of subject pronoun use with 88,512 finite verbs collected from 220 speakers (140 New Yorkers and 80 Bostonians) reveals both similarities and differences between the two settings. The prevailing trend in both locales is intergenerational structural continuity. In both cities, Spanish speakers with differing contact experiences—recent arrivals, well-established immigrants, and US-born individuals— demonstrate remarkably similar sensitivity to the same set of linguistic conditioning factors. Alongside evidence of stability are also indications of linguistic innovation, in the form of contact-induced structural convergence with English as well as dialectal leveling. Evidence of change is clearer and stronger in the New York data, where increased contact experience is associated with both higher rates of pronoun use as well as the erosion, among established immigrants and US-born speakers, of a regional contrast (Mainland Latin America vs. the Caribbean) that is present in the speech of recent arrivals. In the Boston data, evidence of structural convergence with English pronominal norms is restricted to speakers of Caribbean origin. Additionally, in the Boston data there is no evidence of dialectal leveling between speakers of Caribbean and Mainland origins. The regional contrast that seems to fade away among New Yorkers is intergenerationally maintained among Bostonians. The study's results underscore the complexity of linguistic contact and the difficulty of generalizing across contact settings, even when they are highly similar. In addition, results serve to caution against the casual association of linguistic contact with linguistic change. Contact may promote change but does not guarantee it.

Introduction

Imagine children at play, painting with watercolors and marveling at the new hues they can create by mixing their materials. If they combine yellow and red, they get orange. By mixing blue and yellow, they can make green, and when they add black to white, they get make gray. Over time, children will learn to expect the outcomes of particular color combinations, because they are deterministic in nature. This predictability in the outcomes of combining paints—where mixing color X with color Y reliably produces color Z—contrasts sharply with the topic of the present study, which is about the mixing of people with different ways of speaking, or *linguistic contact.*[1] Indeed, the outcomes of this phenomenon have proven difficult to predict, such that scholars have struggled to answer some of the central questions in the field of contact linguistics. These include *What happens when speakers of Language X mix with speakers of language Y?*, and *What happens when speakers of different varieties of language Z interact?*

A common answer to these questions is, *Change of some kind.* That is, linguistic contact is often viewed as a catalyst of linguistic innovation. This is for good reason, as it would be impossible to account for a host of linguistic phenomena—from the origins of the English lexicon to the very existence of languages like Papiamentu or Palenquero—without considering historical contact between groups with different linguistic traditions. Indeed, that contact *can* trigger language change is unquestionable. However, it remains unclear whether contact *must* do so. To quote Poplack and Levey (2010, 412; original italics): "Contact-induced change is *not* an inevitable, nor possibly even a common, outcome of language contact." Furthermore, even if language change has occurred in some setting, and even if it has been triggered by contact, there is no guarantee[2] that the innovation would happen again under similar circumstances in another setting. To quote Thomason (2020, 33): "The combinations of social and linguistic factors that favor the success of one innovation and the failure of another are so complex that we can never (in my opinion) hope to achieve deterministic predictions in this area. Tendencies, yes; probabilities, yes; but we still won't know why an innovation that becomes part of one language fails to establish itself in another language (or dialect) under apparently parallel circumstances."

This view—that the outcomes of linguistic contact are difficult to predict, heterogeneous, and possibly even unlikely to include change—motivates the present chapter. Here, this perspective is brought to bear on one of the larger linguistic contact events unfolding in the world today, namely, contact in the United States (US) between speakers of Spanish and English, on the one hand, and between Spanish speakers of varying regional backgrounds, on the other. Studies that have examined these contact phenomena—which represent a simultaneous case of *language contact* and *dialectal contact*, respectively—have indeed produced mixed results. To illustrate, consider previous US-based studies of two well-known variable phenomena in Spanish: (1) the weakening of syllable-final /s/ and (2) the variable use of subject personal pronouns. These variables represent sites of cross-linguistic difference, distinguishing the grammatical norms of Spanish and English. They also constitute sites of dialectal variation in the Hispanophone world, which for present purposes will be restricted to a broad division between Caribbean/coastal and Mainland Latin American locales.

The first phenomenon, /s/ weakening, refers to the pronunciation of words like *más* 'more', *mismo* 'same', and *hablas* 'you speak', in which /s/ is realized across a spectro-temporal continuum, ranging from robust frication to complete deletion. English speakers tend not to systematically weaken syllable-final /s/. Within the Hispanophone world, rates of /s/ weakening are higher among speakers with origins in the Caribbean and coastal Latin America than among speakers with origins in the Latin American mainland (Lipski 1994, *passim*). The second variable, subject pronominal variation, refers to the presence vs. absence of subject pronouns with finite verbs; for example, *yo canto* and *canto* both mean 'I sing.' English speakers tend to use subject pronouns with finite verbs at very high rates—on the order of 90 percent of the time (Shin and Montes-Alcalá 2014). Rates of subject pronoun use among Spanish speakers are much lower, typically ranging from 20 to 40 percent, with higher rates observed in Caribbean compared to Mainland communities (Carvalho, Orozco, and Shin 2015, *i.a*).

Several studies of /s/ among Spanish speakers in the US have reported evidence of contact-induced change, primarily in the form of dialectal leveling whereby speakers with origins in communities known for relatively higher rates of /s/ weakening shift toward the norms of speakers who weaken /s/ infrequently. These include studies carried out in Los Angeles (Parodi 2003; Villarreal 2014), Houston (Aaron and Hernández 2007; Hernández and Maldonado 2012), Miami (Lynch 2009), and New York City (Erker 2012). However, several other studies of /s/ observe the intergenerational maintenance of dialectal differences, including among Spanish-speaking residents of Chicago (Potowski and Torres 2022), Boston (Erker and Reffel 2021), New York (Lamboy 2004), and rural Ohio (Ramos Pellicia 2012).

A similarly non-uniform picture emerges with respect to subject pronoun use among Spanish speakers in the US, with several studies reporting evidence of change (Orozco 2018; Otheguy and Zentella 2012; Otheguy, Zentella and Livert 2007) and others emphasizing stability (Bayley and Pease-Alvarez 1997; Flores-Ferrán 2004; Torres-Cacoullos and Travis 2018). Let us consider two of these studies of pronominal variation in detail, as they shape the research questions pursued here. In their 2018 study, Torres Cacoullos and Travis examined subject pronoun use among Spanish speakers in New Mexico, a site of centuries-old and ongoing language contact. Using two speech samples—one drawn from interviews with present-day New Mexicans and another from speakers born between 1897 and 1918—Torres Cacoullos and Travis modeled the underlying structure of variant choice in Spanish subject pronoun use by assessing the effect of several linguistic conditioning factors. Their comparative analysis revealed striking similarity between the two groups of speakers. Remarking on their findings, Torres Cacoullos and Travis write that "the alignment in direction of effects refutes a scenario of linguistic change. Such perfect alignment is rather testament to grammatical continuity" (147). They conclude both that "the hypothesis of convergence [between Spanish and English pronominal norms] is firmly rejected" (203) and that "grammatical change through contact is far from a foregone conclusion in bilingual communities, where speakers are adept at keeping their languages together, yet separate" (1).

These conclusions contrast with those of Otheguy, Zentella, and Livert, who, on the basis of their 2007 study of Spanish-speaking New Yorkers, write: "A variationist approach to rates of overt pronouns and variable and constraint hierarchies, comparing speakers from different dialect regions (Caribbeans vs. Mainlanders) and different generations (those recently arrived vs. those born and/or raised in New York), reveals the influence of English on speakers from both regions. In addition, generational changes in constraint hierarchies demonstrate that Caribbeans and Mainlanders are accommodating to one another. Both dialect and language contact are shaping Spanish in New York City" (770). It should be noted that Otheguy and Zentella, in their 2012 book-length treatment of pronoun use among a larger sample of New Yorkers, go to great lengths to emphasize that their evidence for change emerges within a larger context of intergenerational continuity. That is, they make it clear that Spanish-speaking New Yorkers with differing contact experiences are much more alike than they are different in terms of pronoun use overall. Nonetheless, the evidence of contact-induced change in their data remains robust, making for a sharp contrast between the results of studies in New Mexico and New York.

What accounts for this kind of variability in contact outcomes? Why, for instance, do some studies of /s/ show patterns of dialectal leveling while others do not? And why do some investigations of subject pronoun use reveal evidence of contact-induced change while others do not? One possibility is that the lack of uniformity in these and other contact outcomes arise from the relative scarcity of replication studies in linguistic research in general and in contact linguistics in particular. That is, while different linguists are often interested in answering similar (or even identical) questions, the details of how they pursue these questions vary. Torres Cacoullos and Travis (2018, 9), for their part, lament that "discord in contact linguistics has been exacerbated by the problems of meager data and disparate standards of proof." It is possible, perhaps likely, that even small differences in how language phenomena are defined and how data are collected and analyzed could be a factor contributing to variation in observed outcomes. Another potential source of non-uniformity in contact outcomes is the fact that "languages do not interact in a single way, but rather in many different ways, depending on the social setting of the contact . . . and speakers are influenced by different constraints on language behavior, given the different circumstances in which they find themselves and the languages involved" (Muysken 2013, 710). This observation—that every contact setting is characterized by a unique set of sociolinguistic factors—highlights the inherent difficulty of cross-community comparison, even of the same phenomena in the same languages. Indeed, it is not hard to imagine, for example, that the very different social and linguistic dynamics of urban vs. rural settings (such as those of NYC and New Mexico) are an important piece to the puzzle of non-uniformity in contact outcomes observed among Spanish speakers in the United States.

These issues give shape to the present study, which constitutes a *conceptual* replication of Otheguy and Zentella's analysis of pronominal variation among Spanish-speaking New Yorkers. The current project, a comparative variationist analysis of subject pronoun use among Spanish-speaking Bostonians, is a replication of Otheguy and Zentella's in that it carefully adopts their methodology for pronominal data collection, coding, and analysis, which is extensively documented in a coding manual appendix to their 2012 book. Additionally, the present study also employs the same questionnaire that Otheguy and Zentella used to gather sociodemographic, language usage, and attitudinal information from study participants.

Along with adopting the methodology of Otheguy and Zentella's study, the present analysis of subject pronoun use also focuses on a contact setting that, in contrast to the one examined by Torres Cacoullos and Travis in New Mexico, has much in common with the one in NYC. While New Yorkers and Bostonians might bristle at the thought, the two cities are very similar as sites of language and dialectal contact as far as Spanish is concerned. Both cities are large, international, densely populated, and located on the Northeastern seaboard of the United States. They are both popular destinations for Spanish-speaking immigrants as well as home to substantial intergenerational communities whose members are of Caribbean and Mainland Latin American origins. Furthermore, in both cities, the historical settlement of Caribbeans largely pre-dates that of Mainlanders by roughly a generation. In addition, in both cities a substantial fraction of residents makes daily use of extensive mass-transit systems, which, combined with high-density housing, promotes regular contact between a wide array of citizens. Finally, while Spanish speakers live and work throughout both Boston and NYC, each city is home to a number of neighborhoods that are strongly linked with Latin American cultural heritage and are home to high concentrations of Spanish speakers, who regularly use the language in daily public life, for example, Loisaida, Spanish Harlem, Washington Heights, and Sunset Park in NYC, and East Boston and Chelsea in Boston.

Despite these similarities, the present investigation remains a *conceptual* replication. While the studies share a methodology and the aim to understand contact dynamics in settings that are similar in important ways, this is not a controlled experiment. The data come from spontaneous speech collected in the context of interviews. Additionally, the individuals in the two studies are not the same people. And for all of the similarities between NYC and Boston listed above, there are many potentially meaningful differences, not least of which is the difference in the absolute size of the Spanish-speaking population in the two cities: Spanish-speaking New Yorkers in the five boroughs alone number close to 3 million individuals, a figure that rivals the entire population of the Metro-Boston area. All of this being said, the present project manages to go a good way toward minimizing the two potential sources of non-uniformity in contact outcomes that were highlighted above, namely, (1) methodological variation across studies and (2) significant differences in the sociolinguistic factors that shape contact settings. Therefore, when it comes to the question of to what extent patterns of subject pronoun use among Spanish-speaking New Yorkers and Bostonians are comparable with respect to contact outcomes, the goal here is to test what may be called a *Strong-Uniformity Hypothesis*, articulated as follows: variation in subject pronoun use among Spanish-speaking Bostonians should reveal comparable patterns of continuity and change, aligning Boston with NYC. Specifically, the expectation is for structural convergence via language contact at the level of overall rates—that is, an increase in pronoun use alongside increased contact experience—and regional leveling via dialectal contact to be found in the details of the underlying structure of variant choice. The next section presents the study's methodology for testing this hypothesis. This is followed by a presentation and discussion of the study's results, including some conclusions and directions for future research.

Methods

To test the hypothesis of Strong-Uniformity outlined above, the study examines subject pronoun use in a dataset consisting of 88,512 finite verbs collected from 220 Spanish-speaking adults in the context of sociolinguistic interviews. A total of 63,457 verbs were collected from 140 New Yorkers by a research team led by Ricardo Otheguy and Ana Celia Zentella between 2001 and 2005. A total of 25,055 verbs were collected from 80 Bostonians by a team led by the author of the present study, between 2014 and 2018, in accordance with Otheguy and Zentella (2012, 221–73). Each verb included in the data either occurred or could have[3] occurred with a subject pronoun, e.g., *tú hablas* or *hablas*, both 'you speak', *nosotros somos* or *somos*, both 'we are', etc. Verbs that occurred with a pronoun were coded as *pronoun present*. Those that did not but could have occurred with a pronoun were coded as *pronoun absent*. *Pronoun presence vs. absence* thus represents the dependent variable in the study. The study's independent variables are of two types: linguistic and social.

Linguistic Factors

Each verb was coded for the following linguistic factors, which have been shown elsewhere to shape variation in pronoun use (Bayley and Pease-Alvarez 1997; Carvalho, Orozco, and Shin 2015; Erker and Guy 2012; Orozco 2018; Otheguy and Zentella 2012; Otheguy, Zentella, and Livert 2007, *i.a.*).

- *Person and Number*—a categorical linguistic factor describing the person and number of verb tokens—with these values:
    - First-person singular, *canto*
    - First-person plural, *cantamos*
    - Second-person singular, *cantas*
    - Second-person plural, *cantaís*
    - Third-person singular, *canta*
    - Third-person plural, *cantan*
- *TMA*—a factor describing the tense, mood, and aspect of verb tokens—with these values:
    - Present indicative, *canto*
    - Preterit indicative, *canté*
    - Imperfect indicative, *cantaba, estaba cantando*

- ○ Periphrastic future, *voy a cantar*
- ○ Future indicative, *cantaré*
- ○ Conditional, *cantaría*
- ○ Present subjunctive, *cante*
- ○ Past subjunctive, *cantara*
- ○ Imperative, *canta, cante*
- ○ Perfective, *he cantado, había cantado*
- *Reflexivity*—a factor distinguishing reflexive and non-reflexive verbs—with these values:
  - ○ Reflexive, *me llamo* 'I call myself'
  - ○ Non-reflexive, *llamo* 'I call'
- *Switch Reference*—a factor describing whether a verb token represents a switch in subject referent from the immediately preceding finite verb—with these values:
  - ○ Same—the verb's subject does not constitute a switch in referent, e.g., (1) *soy Mexicano*, (2) *nací en Chiapas* 'I am Mexican, I was born in Chiapas'; the referent of (2) is the same as the referent of (1)
  - ○ Different—the verb's subject represents a switch in referent, (1) *soy Mexicano*, (2) *nació en Chiapas* 'I am Mexican, (s)he was born in Chiapas'; the referent of (2) is different than that of (1)
- *Priming*—a factor describing whether the immediately preceding site of pronominal variation occurred or did not occur with a subject pronoun—with these values:
  - ○ Preceding site pronoun present, e.g., (1) *Yo soy Mexicano*, (2) *nací en Chiapas*; the site of pronominal variation preceding (2) has a pronoun present
  - ○ Preceding site pronoun absent: (1) *Soy Mexicano*, (2) *nací en Chiapas*; the site of pronominal variation preceding (2) has a pronoun absent

This last variable, Priming, is one not studied by Otheguy and Zentella, but it was added to the coding schema for the Boston data on account of its clear influence on pronoun use in the work of Torres-Cacoullos and Travis. Two other variables that were included in Otheguy and Zentella's analysis—verbal lexical content and type of clause in which a verb occurred—were not coded for in the Boston data, on account of the weakness of their effects in NYC. These details will be revisited later.

Social Factors

The study's social[4] factors are based on information collected via the questionnaire mentioned above:

- *Regional Origin*—A factor with the values *Caribbean* and *Mainland*. Individuals were considered Caribbean if they had origins or ancestry in Cuba, the Dominican Republic, Puerto Rico, coastal Colombia, or coastal Venezuela. Participants categorized as Mainland were those with origins or ancestry in Ecuador, El Salvador, Guatemala, Honduras, Nicaragua, Mexico, Peru, Paraguay, or non-coastal Colombia.

- *Percent of Life Lived in the United States (PLUS)*—A variable calculated by dividing the number of years a participant had lived in the US by their age; e.g., a 20-year-old who arrived in the US at age 10 has a PLUS value of 50%. Note that for participants of Puerto Rican origin, this variable was calculated on the basis of years spent living in the continental US.
- *Apparent-time Generation*—A factor with the values *Newcomer, Established Immigrant*, and *US Born*. Newcomers arrived in the US after their 16th birthday and had spent less than six years there at the time of their interview. Established Immigrants arrived in the US after their 16th birthday and had spent more than 6 years there at the time of their interview. Participants were considered US Born if they arrived in the US prior to their 3rd birthday. The different generational groups are viewed as representing different degrees of contact experience: Newcomers with the least and US Born with the most. This variable is tightly linked to PLUS, such that participants with the lowest PLUS values are, by and large (though not exclusively), Newcomers, and those with the highest PLUS values are the US Born. In the analysis presented in the next section, these two variables are used side by side, offering complementary yet distinct ways of characterizing differences in contact experience.
- *Percent Spanish-only interlocutors*—A variable calculated on the basis of participants' answers to the following question:*¿Cuál(es) idioma(s) habla [o hablaba] con su(s): papá, mamá, hermanos, hijos menores, hijos mayores, amigos, jefe, compañeros de trabajo, compañeros de escuela, esposa/o o novia/o?* 'Which language(s) do [or did] you speak with your: father, mother, siblings, younger children, older children, friends, boss, coworkers, classmates, spouse or boy/girlfriend?' Participants were asked to answer *español* 'Spanish', *inglés* 'English', or *ambos* 'both' to this question. The total number of *español* answers was divided by the total number of interlocutors for whom a participant provided a response, e.g., an individual who answered *español* for five of ten interlocutors received a score of 50% Spanish-only interlocutors.

Results

Results are presented in two main parts. First is an analysis of variation in pronoun use at the level of overall rates, in which speakers are grouped by city as well as according to the study's social factors. The second part of this section reports the results of multivariate analysis of the linguistic conditioning factors outlined above.

Analysis of Rates

The overall rate of pronoun use in the NYC data is 33.6 percent, with a standard deviation of 11.5 and a median of 34.1. The lowest observed Pronoun Rate is 8.7 percent and the highest is 60 percent. In the Boston data, the overall Pronoun Rate is 27 percent, with a standard deviation of 12.3 and a median of 26. The minimum rate is 6 percent, and the maximum is 63.5 percent. Figure 8.1 contains a pair of histograms that show the distribution of overall Pronoun Rate for each city's data (this and subsequent figures are available in a larger size at the publisher's website).

We will now consider a series of additional figures, each accompanied by statistical tests that assess the significance of the patterns that they demonstrate. Figure 8.2 presents a pair of scatterplots, one each for the NYC and Boston data. On the x-axis of each plot is the variable PLUS. The variable Pronoun Rate is plotted on the y-axis. Each speaker is represented by a point, and their location in the figure is determined by the intersection of their PLUS value and their overall rate of pronoun use, as observed in their sociolinguistic interview. A line has been fit to each city's data using the *ggplot2* package in R (Wickham 2016). Correlation tests—one for each city—returned significant results. In both datasets we observe weak-to-modest, statistically

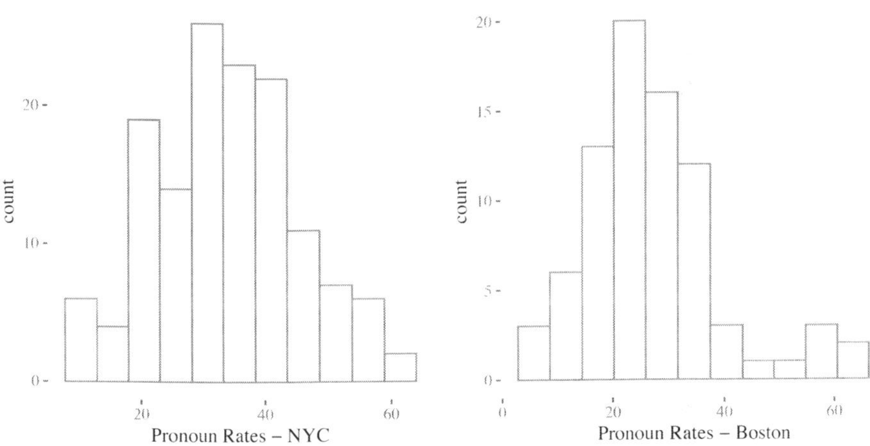

Figure 8.1. Pronoun Rate for each city*

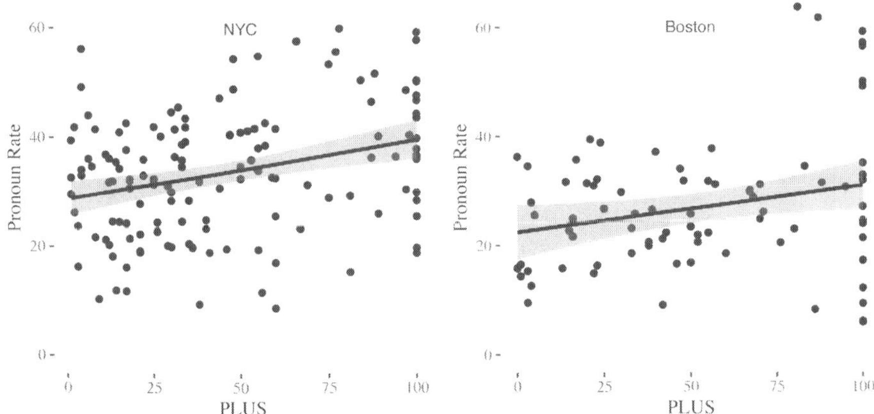

Figure 8.2. Pronoun Rate by PLUS for each city*

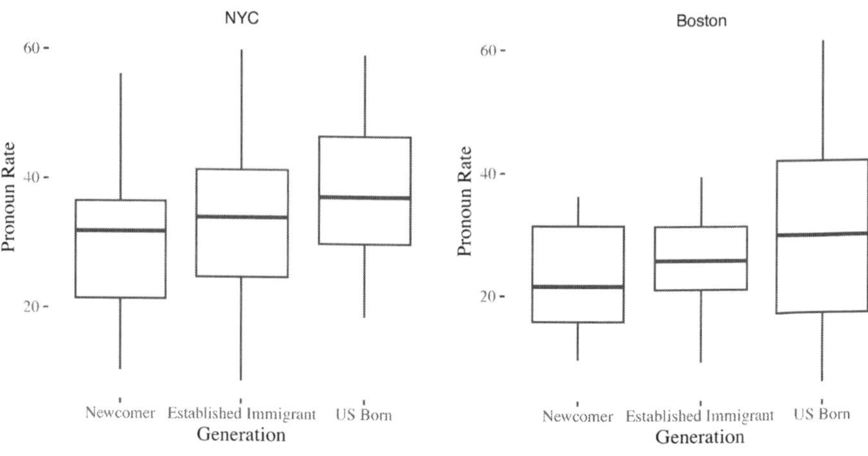

Figure 8.3. Pronoun Rate by Generation for each city*

significant positive correlations: for the NYC data, r(138) = .30, p < .001, and for the Boston data r(78) = .24, p < .03. Figure 8.2 and its associated quantitative analysis indicate that greater US life experience, as measured by the variable PLUS, is associated with higher rates of pronoun use.

The categorical variable Generation, plotted in a pair of box plots in figure 8.3, provides a complementary view. In each city Newcomers have lower pronoun rates on average than Established Immigrants, who in turn have lower rates than the US Born. For the NYC data, the mean Pronoun Rate of the three groups is 30, 34, and 38 percent, respectively. An ANOVA comparing the means of the three groups returns significant results, $F(2,137) = 4.45$, p < .01. Bonferroni post-hoc tests indicate that the only significant pairwise contrast in the NYC data is between Newcomers and the US Born, p < .01. In the Boston data, the Pronoun Rate of Newcomers, Established Immigrants, and US Born, respectively, is 23, 27, and 30—the same pattern of intergenerational increase observed for NYC speakers. However, in contrast to the NYC data, an ANOVA run on the Boston data did not return significant results for this variable, $F(2,77) = 1.96$, p < .14.

Now let us consider the relationship between pronoun rates and the regional origins of study participants. The reader may recall that the research literature generally reports higher rates of pronoun use among Spanish speakers with origins in Caribbean and coastal locales than among those who hail from the interior of Mainland Latin America. Both the NYC and Boston data are consistent with this pattern, as can be seen in figure 8.4. A pair of Welch Two Sample t-tests comparing the mean Pronoun Rate of the two regional groups returns significant results for each city's data: For NYC, the mean Pronoun Rate for Caribbeans and Mainlanders is 39 and 27.5, respectively, $t(138) = 7.03$, p < .001, 95% CI (confidence interval) = [15, 8.5]. For Boston, the mean Pronoun Rate is 35 for Caribbeans and 23 for Mainlanders, $t(78) = 3.5$, p < .001, 95% CI = [18, 4.8].

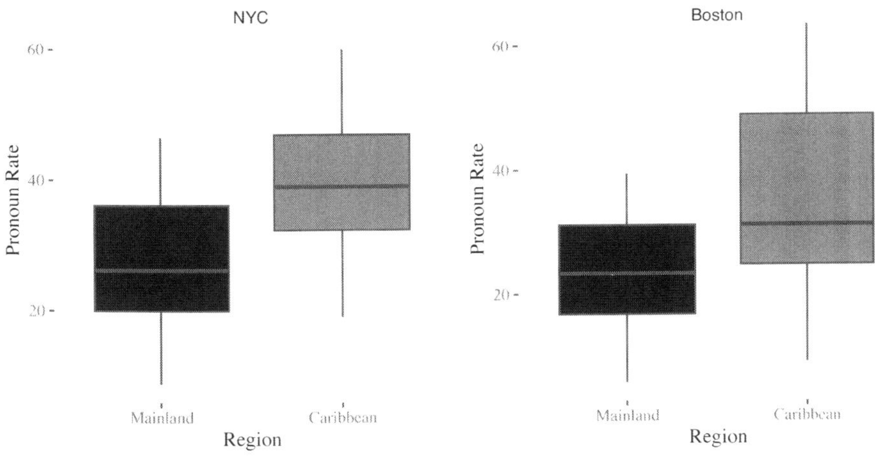

Figure 8.4. Pronoun Rate by participant regional origin for each city*

How does the regional difference between Caribbeans and Mainlanders relate to the trend observed above, whereby increased US life experience was associated with higher rates of pronoun use? To answer this question, we can replicate figures 8.2 and 8.3 while grouping speakers by regional origin. This has been done in figures 8.5 and 8.6. In the NYC data, each regional group recapitulates the patterns found in the overall NYC dataset. Among Caribbeans (in gray) as well as Mainlanders (in black), greater US life experience, as measured by the variables PLUS and Generation, is associated with higher Pronoun Rate. The correlation between PLUS and Pronoun Rate among NYC Caribbeans is $r(70) = .38$, $p < .001$. For NYC Mainlanders it is $r(66) = .25$, $p < .03$. The mean Pronoun Rate among NYC Caribbeans, for Newcomers, Established Immigrants, and the US Born is 36, 39, and 44 percent, respectively. For NYC Mainlanders among the same generational groups, the means are 24, 28, and 33. These trends are consistent with an interpretation of structural convergence via language contact for both regional groups in the NYC data. To quote Otheguy, Zentella and Livert's (2007) interpretation of these results: "We attribute the increase in pronoun rates to the widespread bilingualism of the [US born] (795) . . . contact with English is causing an increase in the use of overt pronouns in Spanish" (783). With respect to dialect contact, there appears not to be any evidence of regional leveling in the NYC data at the level of rates. While the rates of both Caribbeans and Mainlanders increase with PLUS and Generation, they remain separate from each other. That is, the gap between the two regional groups does not close across apparent-time generation, even as rates increase overall.

When we shift our attention to the Boston data, we observe a striking distinction between the two cities. In the NYC data, rates of pronoun use increased with US life experience for both regional groups. In the Boston data, this pattern is restricted to Caribbeans: while there is a significant positive correlation between PLUS and Pronoun Rate among Bostonian Caribbeans [$r(23) = .69$, $p < .001$], a comparable

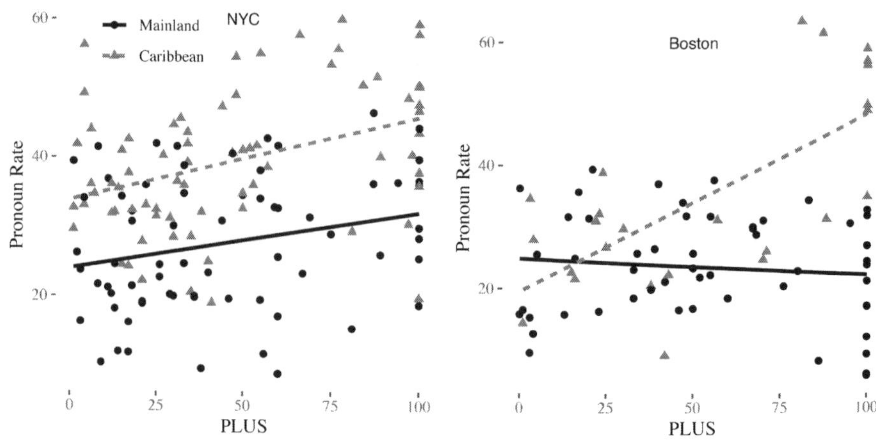

Figure 8.5. Pronoun Rate by PLUS by participant-regional origin for each city*

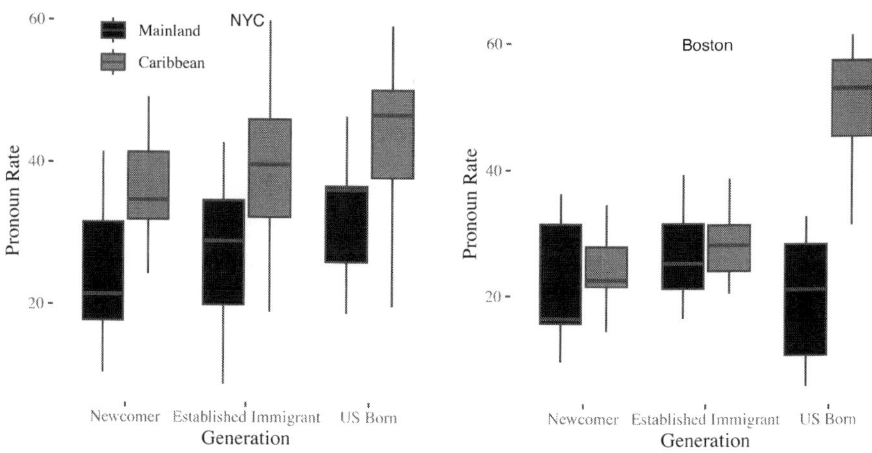

Figure 8.6. Pronoun Rate by Generation by participant regional origin for each city*

pattern fails to emerge for Boston Mainlanders [r(51) = −.1, p = .46]. The variable Generation provides a parallel, if perhaps more revealing, perspective, suggesting that the seeming exceptionalism of Mainland Bostonians is largely due to the behavior of the US Born. Indeed, median pronoun rates in the Boston data actually increase from Newcomers to Established Immigrants in both regional groups, as they do in the NYC data. While this pattern continues (and intensifies) from Established Immigrants to US Born among Caribbean Bostonians, it appears to reverse among Mainland Bostonians. Mean rates across the generational groups are, for Bostonians Caribbeans, 24, 30, and 49, for participants who are Newcomers,

Established Immigrants, and US Born, respectively. Among Mainland Bostonians, the corresponding means are 21, 26, and 20. The regional bifurcation among the Bostonian US Born contrasts with the gradual and regionally uniform intergenerational increase in rates in the NYC data.

To summarize the preceding analysis of rates, we may state the following:

- In both cities, individuals with more contact experience, as measured by PLUS and Generation, have higher pronoun rates on average, a pattern consistent with an interpretation of structural convergence via language contact.
- However, while evidence in line with an interpretation of contact-induced structural convergence is apparent among both regional groups in NYC, it is restricted to Bostonians of Caribbean Origin. That being said, it is worth underscoring that the only clear exception to the trend of increased rates with increased contact experience are the US-Born Bostonian Mainlanders.
- In neither city is there evidence of regional leveling via dialectal contact.

The Strong-Uniformity Hypothesis proposed above fares moderately well at the level of rates. The prediction that the Boston data would mirror the NYC data in terms of dialectal contact (i.e., no clear evidence at this level of analysis) is borne out. The prediction that the Boston data would mirror the New York data in terms of language contact—that is, patterns of pronoun use suggestive of contact-induced structural convergence with the grammatical norms of English—is partially borne out, in that evidence of convergence is apparent but is restricted to Bostonian Caribbeans. Let us now shift to an analysis of the effects of the study's linguistic factors.

Analysis of Constraints

Analysis of the effects of the study's linguistic factors, or constraints, is guided by the view that they reveal the underlying structure of variant choice, in this case the use or non-use of a subject pronoun. More precisely, multivariate quantitative modeling of sets of conditioning factors offers a window into probabilistic linguistic competence, which guides language users in the selection of variants (Weinreich, Labov and Herzog 1968; Poplack and Levey 2010). What unifies or differentiates groups or communities of speakers is the extent to which they share sensitivity to conditioning factors, both in terms of the relative importance of a given factor and the nature of its effects. Guided by this perspective we will first examine constraint rankings and then examine the details of the strongest conditioning factor in the data, namely, verbal Person and Number. Results show that while the various regional and generational groups have a great deal in common, they differ enough to permit a serious test of the hypothesis of Strong-Uniformity in contact outcomes.

New York City Constraints

In order to assess the statistical effects of the study's linguistic factors—which included verbal Person and Number, TMA, Reflexivity, Switch Reference, Clause Type, Lexical Content, and Priming—multivariate logistic regression models were fit to generational and regional subsets of the data (recall that the NYC data were not coded for Priming and that the Boston data were not coded for Clause Type or verbal Lexical Content). We focus here on the two ends of the contact spectrum, that is, on Newcomers and the US Born. First, let us consider regression results for NYC Newcomers, asking how the models for Caribbeans and Mainlanders compare in terms of constraint significance and strength (i.e., ranking). A third dimension, constraint directionality—that is, how the levels of the various constraints either favor or disfavor pronoun use—will be addressed separately. To assess the first two properties, the significance and strength of constraints, we can use a test statistic that quantifies the relative contribution of each constraint to its respective model. The larger the test statistic value is for a given constraint, the more robust its contribution to patterns of pronoun use for the group in question. Otheguy and Zentella (2012) relied on Wald statistics to carry out their analysis, and we will recapitulate their approach here.

Consider the left panel of figure 8.7, which plots the Wald statistics associated with the models for Newcomer New Yorkers; once again Caribbeans are represented by gray and Mainlanders by black. The *y*-axis plots Wald values, and the *x*-axis lists the linguistic factors included in the regression model. For each regional group, the largest Wald statistic was observed for the variable Person and Number. This was followed, in order of decreasing constraint strength, by Switch Reference, TMA, Clause Type, Lexical Content of the target verb form, and verbal Reflexivity. Each of the six constraints significantly contributed to its respective model. The rankings, or *variable hierarchies*, of the two groups are identically structured. These results show that among Newcomers there is little to no dialectal variation in terms of the relative importance of these linguistic factors. Now consider the right panel of figure 8.7, which presents the regression results for US-Born New Yorkers. Their variable hierarchies are identical in rank to each other as well as to those of their Newcomer counterparts with one exception: Reflexivity and Lexical content of the verb—the two weakest predictors—have switched rankings among the US Born. Remarking on these results, Otheguy and Zentella (2012, 182) write that "the patterns are the same

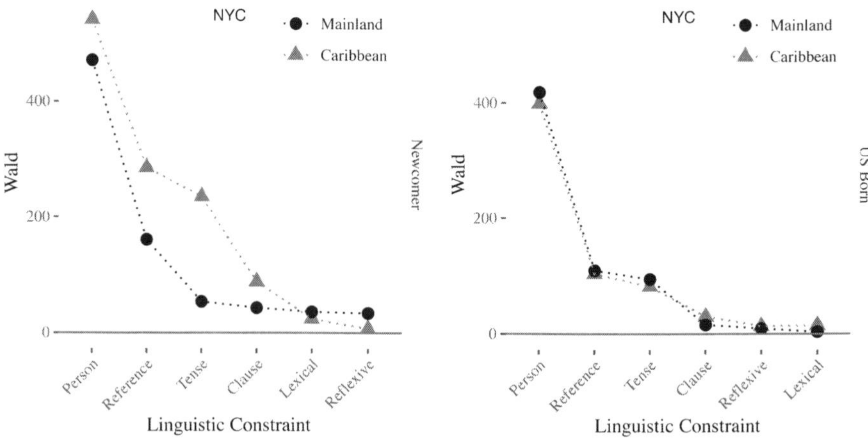

Figure 8.7. NYC variable hierarchies*

in both regions in both generations." It is on the basis of this fact that they emphasize intergenerational continuity in pronoun use that appears alongside the changes in rates presented above.

Boston Constraints

Now consider analogous variable hierarchies among Bostonians. Here, instead of Wald values, the variable hierarchies for Bostonians are based on Akaike Information Criteria (AIC) values. The larger the AIC value for a given variable, the stronger the variable is in reducing error in its model. Two additional methodological differences between the NYC and Boston hierarchies are that the latter exclude the variables Lexical Content and Clause Type and include the variable Priming. The same qualitative pattern for variable hierarchies observed in the NYC data—that is, intergenerational continuity and the absence of dialectal differences—emerges in the Boston data (see figure 8.8). All four Boston groups share rankings, the order of which, from strongest to weakest constraint is Person and Number, Switch Reference, Priming, TMA, and Reflexivity. In terms, then, of the results of variable hierarchy comparisons, the prevailing trend in the data is one of intergenerational continuity in each city. While contact with English may be driving significant increases in overall rates of pronoun use among New Yorkers and Caribbean Bostonians, this change appears not to have resulted in generational reconfiguration of variable hierarchies in either city. At this level of analysis, thus, there is strong evidence of uniformity across the two locales.

Person and Number

We have now examined rates and variable hierarchies across the two datasets. As a third and final exercise in comparison, let us now turn our attention to the question

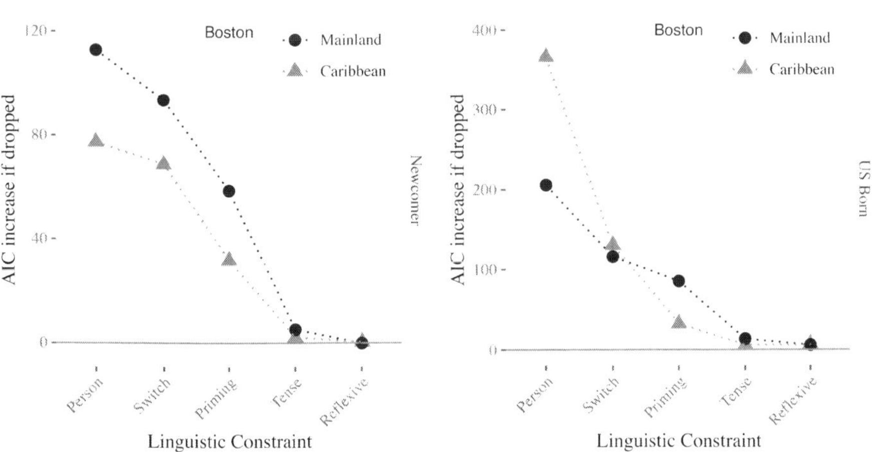

Figure 8.8. Boston variable hierarchies*

of the nature of constraint effects, focusing specifically on the constraint that emerged as the strongest predictor in each of the eight regression models just discussed, Person and Number. It is with respect to this variable that Otheguy and Zentella uncovered some of their strongest evidence for intergenerational dialectal leveling. To understand how it is possible to employ constraint effects as a means for diagnosing contact-induced change, consider the following from Lim and Guy:

> The linguistic unity of speech communities lies in shared linguistic practices and evaluations. Where variable processes are concerned, this linguistic unity extends to shared constraint effects . . . Philadelphians show a common effect of the following pause constraint on /t,d/ deletion, treating it as a conservative environment which disfavors deletion. On the other hand, New Yorkers exhibit an opposite effect of the same constraint, such that it favors deletion. Since the effects are distinct in the two communities, they cannot be attributed to universal factors. But since they are consistent within each community, they reflect shared linguistic practices, which can be characterized as shared grammars. Hence variable constraint effects can be treated as a feature of the grammar. (2005, 1)

The variable Person and Number represents a site of regional contrast in subject pronouns that is analogous to the difference that Lim and Guy observe for English speakers in Philadelphia and New York. That is, while both Caribbeans and Mainlanders are highly sensitive to verbal Person and Number when making decisions about pronoun use—it is uniformly the strongest predictor variable—they *exhibit an opposite effect of the same constraint*, specifically in second-person singular verbs like *hablas* 'you speak' and *cantas* 'you sing.' Consider figure 8.9, which plots on the *x*-axis the parameter estimates (i.e., the beta-values or log odds) associated with the level *second-person singular* for the variable Person and Number in the regression models discussed above. The location of the points along the *x*-axis indicates whether second-person singular forms favor or disfavor pronoun use for the respective groups. Points that are located to the right of the dotted line at zero indicate that second-person singular forms favor pronoun use for that group, while points to the left of the horizontal line mean that the second-person singular forms disfavor pronoun use. The stars next to the points represent the *p*-value associated with the estimate, i.e., $p < .001$ is represented by '***.'

Starting with the top-left panel of figure 8.9, we see that second-person singular forms significantly disfavor pronoun use among NYC Newcomer Mainlanders while they significantly favor pronoun use among NYC Newcomer Caribbeans. Shifting down to the lower-left panel, we see that second-person singular forms no longer significantly condition pronoun use among the US-Born Caribbean New Yorkers. Otheguy and Zentella interpret these results as evidence of the intergenerational erosion of a dialectal difference via contact. In the Boston data, represented in the top- and bottom-right panels, there is no evidence of a comparable pattern. The dialectal difference in speakers' treatment of second-person singular forms—in which Bostonian Caribbeans favor while Bostonian Mainlanders disfavor pronoun use—persists intergenerationally. This represents a significant contrast in contact

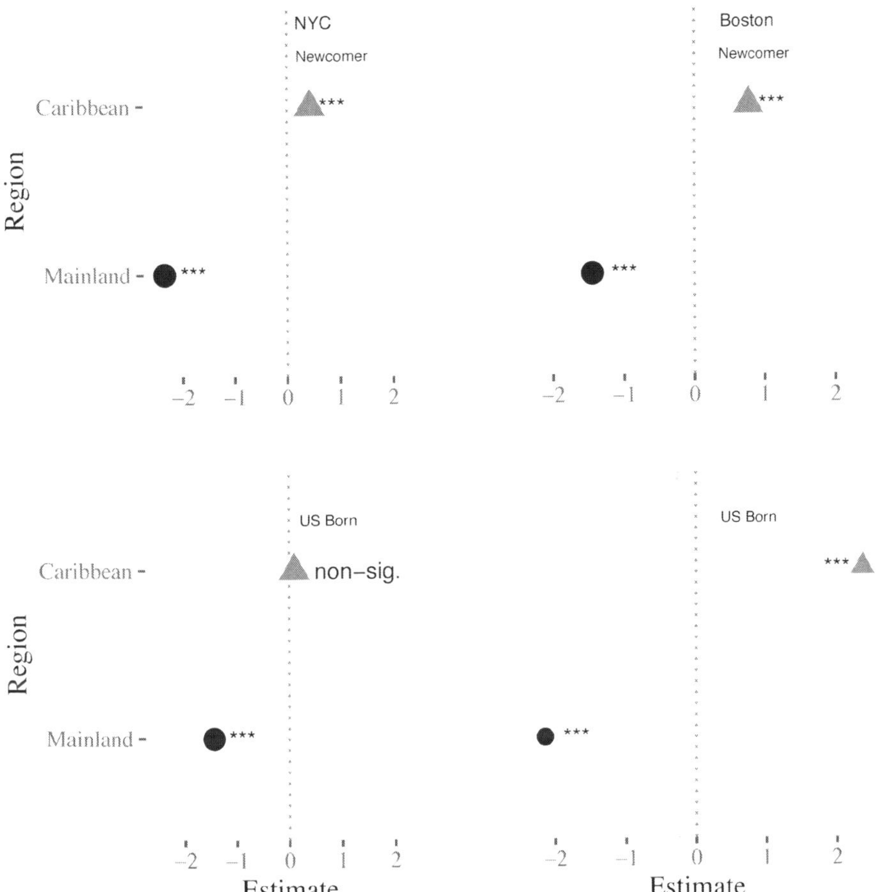

Figure 8.9. Second-person singular parameter estimates by city and region*

outcomes in the NYC and Boston data, and it is a challenge to the Strong-Uniformity Hypothesis.

Discussion

Let us summarize the main results reported above and take stock of how the Strong-Uniformity Hypothesis fares in light of them.

- At the level of rates, there is evidence of contact-induced structural convergence in both cities; i.e., increased contact experience is associated with higher pronoun rates. But this pattern is clearer and stronger in the NYC data. Results at this level of analysis amount to what may be called *moderately uniform outcomes* in the two contact settings.

- At the level of variable hierarchies, there is strong evidence of structural continuity. There is zero indication of intergenerational reconfiguration of variable hierarchies in either dataset. These results amount to *strongly uniform outcomes*.
- At the level of constraint effects, and in particular the environment *second-person singular* for the variable Person and Number, there is evidence in the NYC data of change in the form of dialectal leveling, with Caribbeans shifting toward Mainland norms across generations. No such pattern arose in the Boston data. These amount to *strongly non-uniform* outcomes in the two settings.

The predictions of strong uniformity that framed the study are thus borne out to some extent overall. Spanish speakers in Boston and New York are, with respect to variation in subject pronoun use, similar in that in both locales, linguistic innovation occurs alongside structural stability. Greater contact experience appears to drive an increase in pronoun rates among New Yorkers and also some Bostonians. Yet, this change in rates leaves unperturbed the overall structure of variable hierarchies that reflect speaker norms for variant selection. It is not obvious how to understand these trends. Indeed, the relationship between rates and variable hierarchies is complex and disputed. Some scholars are dubious of the utility of rates as measures of contact-induced change: "The outcome of contact-induced change is ambiguous as concerns overall rates" (Torres-Cacoullos and Travis 2018, 8). While this is certainly a reasonable (if conservative) position, the sheer empirical heft of the evidence here makes it difficult to entirely dismiss rates as a signal of linguistic innovation. Further discussion of this topic must be reserved for future research.

Two other topics that merit additional attention relate to the non-uniform outcomes that were observed, that is, the exceptionalism of US-Born Bostonian Mainlanders at the level of rates and the absence of dialectal leveling for the environment second-person singular in the Boston data. One way to probe these issues further is to examine potential differences in habitual language use. Perhaps the Bostonian US-Born Mainlanders use English less frequently in their daily lives, comparatively minimizing the influence of English pronominal norms on their use of pronouns in Spanish. And perhaps in Boston, Mainlanders and Caribbeans interact less with each other than in NYC. While a full investigation of these questions is beyond the scope of the present analysis, the possible exceptionalism of US-Born Bostonian Mainlanders may be briefly pursued here.

Spanish-Only with Interlocutors

Recall that the study included a variable Percent Spanish-Only Interlocutors that quantified patterns of participants' language choices across interlocutors. Values for this variable are, unsurprisingly, strongly negatively correlated with the variable PLUS for both regional groups in both cities, as shown in figure 8.10. For all four groups—that is, NYC Caribbeans, NYC Mainlanders, Boston Caribbeans, and Boston Mainlanders—the overall fraction of interlocutors with whom participants speak only Spanish decreases as PLUS increases: For NYC Caribbeans, $r(68) = -.58$,

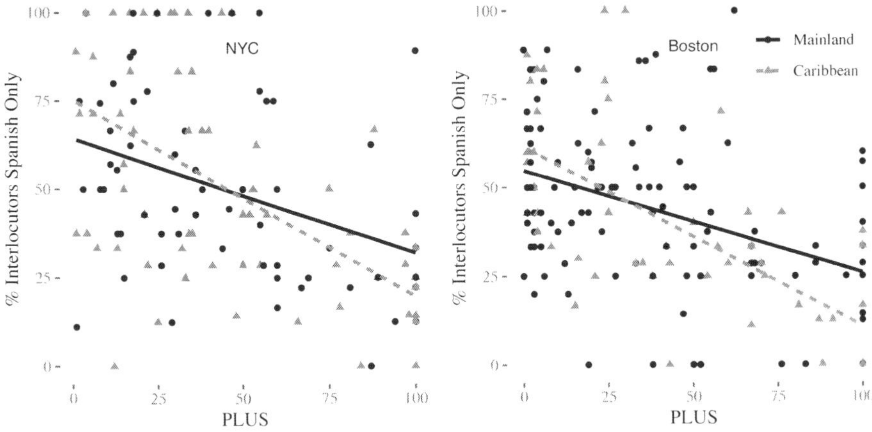

Figure 8.10. Percent Spanish-Only Interlocutors*

$p < .001$, and for NYC Mainlanders $r(62) = -.37$, $p < .002$. For Boston Caribbeans $r(54) = -.67$, $p < 001$., and for Boston Mainlanders $r(112) = -.42$, $p < .001$. While the correlation coefficients are stronger for Caribbeans in both cities, the Bostonian Mainlanders show a stronger correlation coefficient than the NYC Mainlanders. In other words, there is strong uniformity across the two locales such that increased US life experience is associated with a shift away from exclusive Spanish interaction with interlocutors. The hypothesis that Bostonian Mainlanders are less exposed to the grammatical norms of English does not hold up well in light of these results.

Filled Pauses

Yet another scenario to consider is that for some reason that is beyond the reach of the study's variables, Boston Mainlanders are simply less susceptible to the innovation-promoting forces of linguistic contact. Consideration of a different variable phenomenon strongly suggests otherwise. A related research initiative of the present project is a study of variation in vowel quality in filled pauses among Spanish-speaking Bostonians (see Erker and Bruso 2017 for detailed analysis). Variants include [e] as well as two central variants, [a] and [schwa]. The [e] variant is favored among individuals with less life experience in Boston and among those with a larger fraction of Spanish-only interlocutors. In contrast, the centralized variants, [a] and [ə], are preferred among those with greater US life experience and fewer Spanish-only interlocutors. These preferences in vowel quality, which indicate that the pause-filling norms of Spanish speakers have been reconfigured under contact, are observed among both regional groups.

Figure 8.11 contains two scatterplots, each of which has on its *y*-axis Rate of Centralized Filled Pauses. This refers to the percentage of a speaker's filled pauses that were produced with either [a] or [ə], rather than [e]. For example, if a participant produced 100 filled pauses during their interview (the same ones that were used to

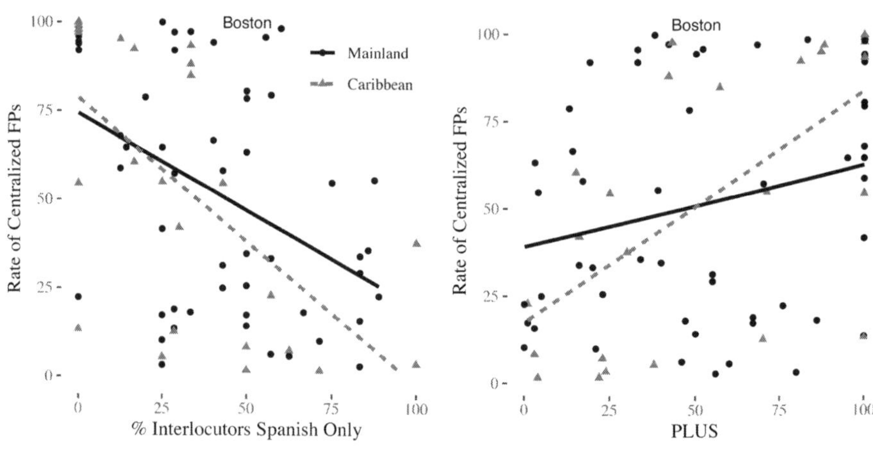

Figure 8.11. Rates of Centralized Filled Pauses by Spanish-Only Interlocutors and PLUS*

collect subject pronominal data) and 70 of them were *eh* while 20 were *ah* and 10 were *uh/um*, the rate of centralized filled pauses for that participant would be 30 percent. On the *x*-axes of the two scatterplots in figure 8.11 are the now familiar contact measures Percent Spanish-Only Interlocutors and PLUS, in the left and right panels respectively. Correlation tests support what the figure suggests: There is a significant negative correlation between rates of Centralized Filled Pauses and Percent Spanish-Only Interlocutors for both Bostonian Caribbeans [r(23)=−.62, $p < .001$] and Bostonian Mainlanders [r(50)=−.43, $p < .002$]. There is a significant positive correlation between rates of Centralized Filled Pauses and PLUS for Caribbeans [r(23)=.62, $p < .001$] and a near-significant correlation for Mainlanders r(50)=.24, $p < .08$. These results—whereby increased US life experience and decreased use of Spanish are associated with greater use of centralized vowels—strongly support the conclusion that a process of structural convergence with the pause-filling norms of English, in which central vowels are favored in filled pauses, is underway among both Bostonian regional groups. This contrasts with the trends illustrated in figures 8.5 and 8.6, which indicate contact-induced convergence in subject pronoun rates for Bostonian Caribbeans but not for Mainlanders. These are challenging results, and there is no obvious way to reconcile them. They suggest the tantalizing possibility that even among the same individuals, contact-induced change may unfold in different ways in different components of linguistic systems.

Conclusion

This study examined the linguistic outcomes of dialectal and language contact among Spanish speakers in two settings, NYC and Boston. The linguistic feature used to assess contact outcomes was the variable presence vs. absence of subject personal pronouns, a site of cross-linguistic as well as dialectal differences. Multivariate variationist sociolinguistic analysis revealed both similarities and differences between the two settings. A uniform trend in both locales is that of intergenerational structural continuity in variable hierarchies. In both cities, Spanish speakers with differing contact experiences—recent arrivals, well-established immigrants, and US-born individuals—demonstrate remarkably similar sensitivity to the same set of linguistic conditioning factors. Alongside evidence of stability were also shared indications of linguistic innovation, in the form of contact-induced structural convergence with English. Evidence of change is clearer and stronger in the NYC data, where increased contact experience is associated with both higher rates of pronoun use as well as the erosion, among established immigrants and US-born speakers, of a regional contrast (Mainland Latin America vs. the Caribbean) that is present in the speech of recent arrivals. In the Boston data, evidence of structural convergence with English pronominal norms is largely restricted to speakers of Caribbean origin (though change is underway for both regional groups in other grammatical domains, i.e., filled pauses). Additionally, in the Boston data there is no evidence of dialectal leveling between speakers of Caribbean and Mainland origins. The study's results underscore the complexity of linguistic contact and the difficulty of generalizing across two (or more) contact settings, even when they are highly similar. But they also affirm the value of conceptual replication and the comparison of comparable settings and groups. Finally, the study's results serve as a reminder that the association of linguistic contact with linguistic change cannot be casually asserted. Rather, it must be demonstrated empirically, because contact may promote change, but it does not guarantee it.

Notes

*Some figures in this chapter are available on the publisher's website (press.georgetown.edu) to make it easier to view the data.

1. This term is meant to include what scholars have called *language contact* (Weinreich 1953, *i.a.*) as well as *dialect contact* (Trudgill 1986, *i.a.*).

2. Though see Trudgill et al. (2000) for an argument in favor of predictability in the case of dialectal mixture.

3. For full details regarding the envelope of variation, including exclusion criteria, see the appendix section of Otheguy and Zentella (2012, 221–73).

4. Spanish subject pronoun use has not been shown to reliably correlate with speakers' social class, sex, or age (Orozco and Hurtado 2021; Otheguy and Zentella 2012). The primary language-external correlates of the variable are speakers' geographic origins and factors relating to language and/or dialectal contact, thus the emphasis on these factors here.

References

Aaron, Jessi Elana and José Esteban Hernández. 2007. Quantitative evidence for contact-induced Accommodation. In Kim Potowski and Richard Cameron (eds.), *Spanish in Contact: Policy, Social and Linguistic Inquiries*. Amsterdam: Johns Benjamin Publishing Company, 327–41. doi: 10.1075/impact.22.23aar

Bayley, Robert and Lucinda Pease-Alvarez. 1997. Null pronoun variation in Mexican-descent children's narrative discourse. *Language Variation and Change* 9 (3): 349–71. doi: 10.1017/S0954394500001964

Carvalho, Ana M, Rafael Orozco and Naomi Lapidus Shin. 2015. *Subject pronoun expression in Spanish: A cross-dialectal perspective.* Washington, DC: Georgetown University Press. https://www.jstor.org /stable/j.ctt1657v9g

Erker, Daniel. 2012. *An acoustically based sociolinguistic analysis of variable coda/s/production in the Spanish of New York City.* Unpublished PhD dissertation, New York University.

Erker, Daniel and Joanna Bruso. 2017. Uh, bueno, em: Filled pauses as a site of contact-induced change in Boston Spanish. *Language Variation and Change* 29 (2): 205–44. doi: 10.1017/S0954394517000102

Erker, Daniel and Gregory R. Guy. 2012. The role of lexical frequency in syntactic variability: Variable subject personal pronoun expression in Spanish. *Language* 88 (3): 526–57. doi: 10.1353/lan.2012.0050

Erker, Daniel and Madeline Reffel. 2021. Describing and analyzing variability in Spanish/s: A case study of Caribbeans in Boston and New York City. In Eva Núñez-Méndez (ed.), *Sociolinguistic approaches to sibilant variation in Spanish.* London: Routledge, 131–63.

Flores-Ferrán, Nydia. 2004. Spanish subject personal Pronoun use in New York City Puerto Ricans: Can we rest the case of English contact? *Language Variation and Change* 16 (1): 49–73. doi: 10.1017/ S0954394504161048

Hernández, José Esteban and Rubén Armando Maldonado. 2012. Reducción de/s/final de sílaba entre transmigrantes salvadoreños en el sur de Texas. *Lengua y Migración / Language and Migration* 4 (2): 43–67.

Lamboy, Edwin M. 2004. *Caribbean Spanish in the metropolis: Spanish language among Cubans, Dominicans, and Puerto Ricans in the New York City area.* Oxford: Routledge.

Lim, Laureen T, and Gregory R Guy. 2005. The limits of linguistic community: Speech styles and variable constraint effects. *University of Pennsylvania Working Papers in Linguistics* 10 (2): 13. https:// repository.upenn.edu/pwpl/vol10/iss2/13

Lipski, John M. 1994. *Latin American Spanish.* New York: Addison-Wesley.

Lynch, Andrew. 2009. A Sociolinguistic analysis of final/s/in Miami Cuban Spanish. *Language Sciences* 31 (6): 766–90. doi: 10.1016/j.langsci.2008.08.002

Muysken, Pieter. 2013. Language contact outcomes as the result of bilingual optimization strategies. *Bilingualism: Language and Cognition* 16 (4): 709–30. doi: 10.1017/S1366728912000727

Orozco, Rafael. 2018. El castellano colombiano en la ciudad de Nueva York: Uso variable de sujetos pronominales. *Studies in Lusophone and Hispanic Linguistics* 11 (1): 89–129. doi: 10.1515/shll-2018-0004

Orozco, Rafael and Luz Marcela Hurtado. 2021. A variationist study of subject pronoun expression in Medellín, Colombia. *Languages* 6 (1): 5. https://doi.org/10.3390/languages6010005

Otheguy, Ricardo and Ana Celia Zentella. 2012. *Spanish in New York: Language contact, dialectal leveling, and structural continuity* (vol. 203). New York: Oxford University Press. doi: 10.1093/acprof: oso/9780199737406.001.0001

Otheguy, Ricardo, Ana Celia Zentella and David Livert. 2007. Language and dialect contact in Spanish in New York: Toward the formation of a speech community. *Language* 83 (4): 770–802. doi: 10.1353/ lan.2008.0019

Parodi, Claudia. 2003. Contacto de dialectos del Español en Los Ángeles. In G. Perissinotto (ed.), *Ensayos de lengua y pedagogía.* Santa Barbara: University of California Linguistic Minority Research Institute, 23–38.

Poplack, Shana and Stephen Levey. 2010. Contact-induced grammatical change: A cautionary tale. In Peter Auer and Jurgen Erich Schmidt (eds.), *Language and space: An international handbook of linguistic variation* (vol. I). Berlin / New York: Walter de Gruyter. doi: 10.1515/9783110220278.391

Potowski, Kimberly and Lourdes Torres. 2022. *Spanish in Chicago.* Oxford: Oxford University Press.

Ramos Pellicia, Michelle F. 2012. Retention and deletion of /s/ in final position: The disappearance of /s/ in the Puerto Rican Spanish spoken in one community in the U.S. Midwest. *International Journal of the Linguistic Association of the Southwest* 31 (1): 161–75.

Shin, Naomi Lapidus and Cecilia Montes-Alcalá. 2014. El uso contextual del pronombre sujeto como factor predictivo de la influencia del inglés en el Español de Nueva York [English influence on Spanish in New York: Evidence from subject pronouns in context]. *Sociolinguistic Studies* 8 (1): 85. doi: 10.1558/sols.v8i1.85

Thomason, Sarah. 2020. Contact explanations in linguistics. In Raymond Hickey (ed.), *The handbook of language contact*, 31–49. Hoboken, NJ: Wiley. doi: 10.1002/9781444318159.ch1

Torres-Cacoullos, Rena and Catherine E. Travis. 2018. *Bilingualism in the community: Code-switching and grammars in contact*. Cambridge: Cambridge University Press.

Trudgill, Peter. 1986. *Dialects in contact*. Oxford: Blackwell.

Trudgill, Peter, Elizabeth Gordon, Gillian Lewis and Margaret Maclagan. 2000. Determinism in new-dialect formation and the genesis of New Zealand English. *Journal of Linguistics* 36 (2): 299–318. doi: 10.1017/S0022226700008161

Villarreal, Belen MacGregor. 2014. Dialect contact among Spanish-speaking children in Los Angeles. Unpublished PhD dissertation, University of California, Los Angeles.

Weinreich, Uriel. 1953. *Languages in contact*. The Hague / New York: Mouton. doi: 10.1075/z.166

Weinreich, Uriel, William Labov and Marvin Herzog. 1968. Empirical foundations for a theory of language change. In W. P. Lehmann and Y. Malkiel (eds.), *Directions for Historical Linguistics*. Austin: University of Texas Press, 97–195.

Wickham, Hadley. 2016. *Ggplot2: Elegant graphics for data analysis*. New York: Springer-Verlag. https://ggplot2.tidyverse.org.

Chapter 9

T-Flapping in Singapore English: Americanization, Innovation, or Both?

WESLEY MARK LINCOLN
University of Pennsylvania

REBECCA LURIE STARR
National University of Singapore

Introduction

Recent phonological developments in Singapore English (SgE) have been described as the result of "Americanization" (Y. Tan 2016). For example, Standard Singapore English (SSE) is traditionally non-rhotic, but rising post-vocalic rhoticity has been observed in this variety and readily attributed to American English (AmE) influence, particularly through media exposure (Tan and Gupta 1992). On the other hand, Starr (2019, 2021a) argues that not all shifts represent American influence and may instead be independent innovations. Furthermore, AmE-linked features like the BATH-TRAP merger and T-flapping have not been shown to have taken hold in SgE (Starr 2019; Y. Tan 2016), undercutting any image of sweeping Americanization.

These debates around the trajectory of SgE phonology underscore the rich sociolinguistic context of Singapore, which is undergoing endonormative stabilization (Schneider 2003) while SgE speakers are inundated with exposure to AmE, a prestigious "Inner Circle" variety (Kachru 1985), via the media and interpersonal contact. This situation undoubtedly makes it tempting to assume that AmE features might diffuse into SgE. In order to interrogate this assumption, this study examines the use of T-flapping in SgE and SgE speakers' explicit, self-reported awareness of T-flapping in AmE, while also considering how these outcome variables may be shaped by interpersonal contact and media consumption. In doing so, the study also touches upon a perennial debate regarding the possible role of media exposure in the spread of language features in dialect-contact situations by spreading knowledge and/or triggering adoption of these features.

English in Singapore

English, once spoken only by a small elite in Singapore, is now the dominant language of school and the workplace and has become the country's most commonly spoken home language (Singapore Department of Statistics 2021). Owing to Singapore's history as a British colony, SgE has traditionally oriented toward British English (BrE) exonormative standards, with some phonological features reminiscent of Standard Southern British English (SSBE) such as non-rhoticity (Deterding 2007) and a conservative BATH-TRAP vowel distinction (Low 2020, 310; Wee 2004, 1024). SgE differs considerably from SSBE, however, in its overall phonological system, which is characterized by a merger of tense and lax vowels and BAT and BET vowels, among other features (Deterding 2007). SgE also features a range of distinctive morphosyntactic features, vocabulary, and discourse particles (Leimgruber 2011) and has been described by some scholars as a creoloid rather than a dialect of English (Platt 1975).

Linguistic descriptions of SgE have been shaped by a traditional distinction made in some prior literature between SSE and Colloquial Singapore English (CSE) (Gupta 1989; Platt 1977), known colloquially as "Singlish." However, this approach has long been viewed as problematic for phonology, where the split between colloquial and standard forms is argued to be less clear cut (Lim 2004, 54). Starr (2021a) and Leimgruber (2012) go further, arguing that variation in SgE has become too multifaceted to justify models that uphold an SSE vs. CSE dichotomy. Instead, they propose the adoption of a variationist framework that focuses on the range of social meanings that may be indexed by particular variants. Research on variation in SgE between features consistent with BrE versus AmE, such as studies of the BATH and TRAP vowels (Starr 2019), have highlighted the shortcomings of approaches that account only for distinctions between standard and colloquial norms.

In line with Schneider's (2003) placement of Singapore in the "Endonormative Stabilization" phase of his dynamic model of post-colonial Englishes, there is evidence of stabilization and growing acceptance of local norms in SgE. For example, in terms of phonology, Starr (2021a, 2021b) finds that local features like the COT-CAUGHT-COURT merger are increasingly used even in careful speech and rated as sounding equally as professional as BrE and AmE variants in formal contexts. Endonormativity manifests in not only the acceptance of local norms for SgE but also the increasing embrace and prominence of CSE features as markers of Singaporean identity across social classes (Alsagoff 2010; Cavallaro, Ng and Seilhamer 2014).

Against this backdrop of rising endonormativity—that is, as Singaporeans develop a sense of ownership over English and become less tethered to conservative BrE norms—SgE is also coming into increasing contact with AmE. Interpersonal exposure occurs both within Singapore, where over 30,000 people from the United States (US) live and work (US Department of State 2021), and in the US, a popular travel destination for Singaporeans, seeing 414,000 Singaporean visitors in 2018 (Singapore Department of Statistics 2019). Media exposure to AmE, via both mass media and social media, is also extensive (Starr 2019). This situation raises the question of whether, beyond the acceptance of local norms, certain aspects of SgE use may shift toward AmE norms, as is claimed to be occurring in World Englishes more generally (e.g., Gonçalves et al. 2018; Hänsel and Deuber 2013), especially given the continued ideological positioning of "Inner Circle" varieties like AmE as legitimate targets for speakers of "Outer Circle" varieties like SgE (Park and Wee 2009). Indeed, some linguists have interpreted certain phonological shifts in SgE, such as the rise in post-vocalic rhoticity, as "Americanization" of SgE (e.g., Tan 2016) and have attributed this phenomenon to media exposure (Tan and Gupta 1992).

Media and Interpersonal Interaction in Dialect Contact

Claims of media-driven shifts in phonology in SgE run counter to a core tenet of sociolinguistics that face-to-face interaction is key to the spread of language features and thus language change. According to this view, interpersonal interaction encourages accommodation in dialect-contact situations: speakers who use more traditional linguistic forms may accommodate those who use innovative forms by adopting the new features and/or abandoning the traditional ones. Speakers may begin using the innovative feature even in the absence of an addressee who uses it (long-term accommodation), and language change may occur if the feature then spreads into the community (Auer and Hinskens 2009; Niedzielski and Giles 1996; Trudgill 1986).

Given the assumed centrality of accommodation in the process of language change, early work on dialect contact doubted the relevance of media influence, primarily arguing that television viewers and radio listeners do not interact with media figures in a way that encourages accommodation (Trudgill 1986, 2014). An alternative view that has gained ground in more recent work, however, is that high levels of media engagement may facilitate consumer convergence and accommodation with language encountered via media exposure (Nycz 2019; Stuart-Smith 2012). Nycz (2019) points out that this factor is especially relevant with new media services such as YouTube, which allow consumers to contribute their own comments and content, thus rendering the distinction between content producer and consumer less rigid. Further nuance in this debate comes from the distinction between features such as lexical items that are readily taken "off the shelf"—and thus deemed to be easier to acquire through media influence—in contrast to more complex grammatical features that are posited to require prolonged social exposure for acquisition (Eckert 2003; Milroy 2007; Sayers 2014; Trudgill 2014). Regarding phonological features, while Milroy (2007) considers TH-fronting to be an "off-the-shelf" feature, T-flapping exhibits complex conditioning (see the following section, "Variable of Interest"), which could mean that its acquisition requires more extensive input and exposure via social networks. Beyond actual adoption of specific features, scholars have suggested other, indirect ways in which the media might shape sociolinguistic change: for example, by improving attitudes toward new language varieties and features (Trudgill 1986) or by raising cross-dialectal awareness of linguistic features (Milroy and Milroy 1985). Empirical work, however, casts doubt on the importance of the media in influencing either attitudes (Stuart-Smith and Timmins 2014; Stuart-Smith 2006) or awareness (Starr 2019; Stuart-Smith et al. 2011). Stuart-Smith and Timmins (2014) further propose that television input could speed up the adoption of features that have already spread into a language community through face-to-face contact. This possibility is relevant for SgE given the coupling of interpersonal and mediated exposure to AmE.

The study of phonological changes in SgE therefore links to various larger debates in sociolinguistics concerning language ideology in the Outer Circle as well as the role of the media in language change. Given the sociolinguistic context of Singapore and its high volume of US media consumption, it is tempting to treat recent phonological trends in SgE as Americanizations, as has been said of rising post-vocalic rhoticity (Y. Tan 2012, 2016; Tan and Gupta 1992). A causal account in which AmE exposure has triggered these changes, however, ought to be supported by evidence that the specific patterns being acquired are consistent with AmE and that there is a positive correlation between individuals' consumption of US media and/or interpersonal interaction with AmE speakers and adoption of these innovative features.

Variable of Interest

The feature investigated in the present study has been thought to saliently distinguish AmE from SSBE and SgE: T-flapping—a lenition process in AmE (and some other varieties) in which an underlying voiceless alveolar plosive /t/ is realized as a voiced alveolar tap or flap [ɾ] in certain intervocalic positions. Most prior descriptions of SgE phonology do not include T-flapping as a feature of this variety; what these works do highlight is that, due to phonological transfer from substrate languages, /t/ in SgE is typically unaspirated in syllable-initial position, while syllable-final /t/ tends to be unreleased, glottalized, or deleted (Deterding 2007, 19; Wee 2004, 1028). Y. Tan's (2016) study appears to be the only prior quantitative study of T-flapping in SgE. While she found negligible use of this feature, our own informal observations suggested that T-flapping does occur relatively consistently in SgE in certain lexical items not elicited by her reading tasks: specifically, decade numbers such as *thirty*, *forty*, and *eighty*. We had also observed that SgE T-flapping becomes more frequent in rapid and casual speech, and commonly occurs in informal lexical items like *whatever* and *shut up*. It is these informal impressions, on top of the dearth of prior study of SgE T-flapping, that motivated the investigation of this feature.

T-flapping is observed not only in AmE but also in some Northern British English varieties, Australian English, and New Zealand English; Alderton (2021) also finds a limited degree of T-flapping in "elite" Southern BrE varieties. Crucially, it is not immediately clear that T-flapping is an American import in all these cases. In fact, Meyerhoff and Niedzielski (2003) specifically argue that T-flapping in New Zealand English is a case of drift, in which T-flapping, already within the range of vernacular variation in New Zealand English, diffused to become a standard feature. This case study underscores that not all phonological shifts toward AmE-like features are necessarily the outcome of Americanization. Starr (2021a) similarly encourages sociolinguists not to make this assumption prematurely. In her study, she problematizes the account that SgE speakers are attempting to model AmE in their use of post-vocalic rhoticity and argues that this may be an independent innovation resulting from orthographic cues.

In the case of T-flapping, it is particularly important to consider the possibility of independent innovations since, cross-linguistically, intervocalic voiceless stops show a tendency to undergo lenition (Honeybone 2012; Ladefoged 1997), as also illustrated by T-glottalization in certain BrE varieties. This tendency may be due to universal articulatory factors. Specifically, vowel–voiceless stop–vowel sequences involve extreme transitions in both oral closure (i.e., shifting from no closure in vowels to complete closure in the voiceless stop) and in laryngeal configuration (i.e., from closed glottis in vowels to open glottis in the voiceless stop), making these sequences effortful. Intervocalic voiceless stops like /t/, then, are universally susceptible to lenition to reduce the effort associated with such sequences. Voicing of these stops is "as likely to represent separate development as it is geographical diffusion" (Trudgill 2014, 217). Thus, the occurrence of flapped /t/, although superficially an AmE-like form, requires more scrutiny before being classed as an Americanization since this may in fact be a case of convergent development.

This study quantifies SgE speakers' awareness and use of T-flapping as part of the broader inquiry into the supposed Americanization of this variety. By comparing what speakers believe about AmE T-flapping to their reported use of T-flapping, it will be possible to obtain clues as to whether Singaporeans are explicitly imitating AmE or whether SgE T-flapping could be an independent innovation. Any such comparison, however, would first require us to establish the constraints on AmE T-flapping, to which we now proceed.

T-Flapping in American English

T-flapping in AmE is a rather complex feature, subject to several constraints. It is generally described as the process by which an underlying voiceless alveolar plosive /t/ is realized as a voiced alveolar tap or flap [ɾ] in intervocalic positions. As is evident from Haugen's early (1938) analysis, however, the above description glosses over some further intricacies: "[Flapping] cannot occur unless it is *preceded* by a vowel or a sonorant (n, l, r), and is *followed* by an unstressed syllable-forming element (vowel, l, r, but not the homorganic n)" (Haugen 1938, 631; emphasis in original).

Most subsequent analyses of flapping seem to broadly agree with the constraint proposed by Haugen (see Vaux 2000 for a review of over 20 analyses of T-flapping), which proposes that flapped /t/ must precede an unstressed syllable, a condition that can be further divided into three other environments: post-primary stress (V́_V), post-secondary stress (V̀_V), and between unstressed syllables (V_V). Vaux (2000) and Turk (1992) posit that flapping is mandatory for V́_V and V̀_V environments, and optional in V_V, as supported by qualitative studies by Eddington and Elzinga (2008) and Zue and Laferriere (1979). Thus, as shown below, T-flapping is obligatory for words like *butter* and *innovative* in (1a–b) but optional for a word like *imaginative* in (1c). We refer to the stress-related constraints as "STR."

(1) a. *butter*   /ˈbʌtɚ/   →   [ˈbʌɾɚ]
     b. *innovative*   /ˈɪnəˌveɪtɪv/   →   [ˈɪnəˌveɪɾɪv]
     c. *imaginative* /ɪˈmæd͡ʒɪnətɪv/ →   [ɪˈmæd͡ʒɪnətɪv ~ ɪˈmæd͡ʒɪnəɾɪv]

Given the role of stress in T-flapping, it is not surprising that vowel quality has also been proposed to condition this phenomenon. Unstressed vowels are often reduced (e.g., [ə], [ɪ]), binding up following-vowel quality with flapping. In experimental work, Eddington and Elzinga (2008) examine the role of following-vowel quality using data from the Texas Instruments / Massachusetts Institute of Technology (TIMIT) corpus and native-speaker judgments of nonce word pronunciation. Among V́_V contexts, [ɾ] was more likely before [ə, ɚ, ɪ, i, l̩] and [tʰ] before [ɛ, ej, aj, ɑj, æ]. Morpheme-internally, flapping requires not just a pre-stress environment but also a reduced vowel if the following syllable nucleus is a vowel (de Jong 1998; Wells 2011). Thus, within a morpheme like *latex* in (2a), although the stress requirements for flapping are met, flapping is blocked due to the strong vowel [ɛ] following /t/. This is in contrast with *atom* (2b), where the following [ə] is a weak vowel, allowing flapping. To refer to the vowel-quality constraint on T-flapping, we use the abbreviation "VOW."

(2) a. *latex*   /ˈleɪtɛks/ → [ˈleɪtɛks]
   b. *atom*   /ˈætəm/ → [ˈæɾəm]

Haugen (1938) also states that only sonorant consonants /n, l, ɹ/ can precede flapped /t/; the exclusion of /m/ and /ŋ/ correctly predicts that flapping is blocked in place-names like *Sumter* and *Washington* (Vaux 2000). Vaux also calls flapping after /l/ "highly ungrammatical in Standard American English" (2000, 3). Quantitative work shows that post-lateral flapping is indeed very infrequent, with low rates of 9.3% in Hannisdal (2020) and less than 5% in Zue and Laferriere (1979). We use the abbreviation "SON" to refer to the restrictions on sonorant consonants that can precede flapped /t/.

Of these sonorant consonants, /n/ is of interest because words with /nt/ clusters in flapping environments fall into two categories with different realizations. The vast majority of such words have a nasalized flap [ɾ̃], such as *twenty* in (3a) below. We term this main category "NTa" words. On the other hand, the "NTb" category refers to a small, lexically arbitrary group consisting of *seventy*, *ninety*, and *carpenter*, which instead have an alveolar nasal and an alveolar flap [nɾ] (Hannisdal 2020; Vaux 2000), as illustrated by (3b).

(3) a. *twenty*   /ˈtwɛnti/   →   [ˈtwɛɾ̃i]
   b. *seventy*   /ˈsɛv.ən.ti/   →   [ˈsɛvənɾi]

The STR, VOW, SON, NTa, and NTb constraints and categories constitute the main factors that condition T-flapping in AmE. Since AmE is not monolithic, but instead exhibits wide-ranging regional and social variation (Kretzschmar 2004), AmE varieties may differ slightly in their flapping contexts. This analysis, however, is a necessary abstraction to predict which realizations of AmE /t/ are most likely in different phonological contexts, offering a benchmark to probe SgE speakers' beliefs about T-flapping in AmE and to compare AmE T-flapping to that of SgE.

Methodology

A wordlist, shown in table 9.1, was designed to represent different conditions in which the STR, VOW, and SON constraints would predict T-flapping to be obligatory, optional, or illicit in AmE. For example, under the STR constraint, the OBLIGATORY condition contains words with /t/ in V́_V contexts, where obligatory flapping is predicted. On the other hand, the ILLICIT words have /t/ in V_V́ contexts, which are predicted to block flapping.

To test the SON constraint, the list contains two words with the V́ɹ_V structure and two with Vɹ_V́. Although /ɹ/ is one of the sonorants that may precede flapped /t/, the STR constraint precludes flapping in Vɹ_V́; flapping is licit (OBLIGATORY) only in V́ɹ_V. On the other hand, the ILLICIT condition also contains words with /ŋ, m, l/ preceding /t/. Since there are no OBLIGATORY counterparts to these words, participants' intuitions can instead be compared to the V́ɹ_V words. If they accept flapping in V́ɹ_V but not V́ŋ _V, V́m _V, and V́l _V, then it can reasonably be inferred that they are aware which sonorant consonants may precede flapped /t/ in AmE.

To examine participants' intuitions about flapping of /nt/ clusters, a wordlist representing the NTa and NTb categories was created, shown in table 9.2. NTa words are predicted to be realized with [r̃], while NTb words are predicted to have [nɾ]. The choice of words in NTb was constrained by the very fact that it is a small, lexically arbitrary group with only three items reported in the literature. For all other categories, care was taken to choose words that SgE speakers would reasonably be familiar with. For instance, the non-standard form *eleventy*, which Vaux (2000) suggests would fall into NTb, was excluded because it is not used by SgE speakers and is rare even in AmE. Furthermore, words involved in initial-stress derivation were avoided. Examples include verbs that undergo nominalization or adjectivization by shifting

Table 9.1. Wordlist for the STR, VOW, and SON categories

Category	Licitness of flapping in AmE		
	OBLIGATORY	OPTIONAL	ILLICIT
STR	*atom, eighty, computer, sitter*	*imaginative, volatile, unity, punitive*	*potassium, attack, Italian, totality*
VOW	*ditto, buttocks, analytic, rattle, attic*		*detox, Botox, latex, retail, proton*
SON	*artist, forty*		/ɹ/: *particular, libertarian*
			/m/: *empty, symptom*
			/l/: *salty, filter*
			/ŋ/: *Washington, springtime*

Table 9.2. Wordlist for the NTa and NTb categories

Category	Items	Nasalized flap [r̃]	Nasal + flap [nɾ]	Nasal + stop [nt]
NTa	*winter, hunter, twenty, bounty*	licit	illicit	licit
NTb	*carpenter, ninety, seventy*	illicit	licit	licit

stress to the first syllable, giving pairs like *detáil*$_V$ ~ *détail*$_N$. Such words would affect the validity of the data since it would not be possible to infer whether each participant is reacting to pre-stress or post-stress /t/.

Online Survey Design

The study was carried out via an online survey hosted on the Qualtrics platform. The survey introduced participants to the variable of interest using the following preamble:

> It is often noted that when people from the United States (US) speak English, they pronounce the letter "T" in a way that sounds like "D." For example, the word *butter* sounds like *budder*, and the word *party* sounds like *pardy*.
>
> In this survey, you will be presented with some English words, plus a few possible ways to pronounce each word. In some of the pronunciations, "T" is pronounced like "D", but not others.

Following the lead of Starr (2019), participants were shown a list of single-word stimuli and asked for: (1) their intuitions about how AmE speakers pronounce the word, and (2) how they themselves pronounce the word. The AmE perception task was administered first, followed by the personal-use task on a separate page with the same list of words. Each target item was presented in block letters, followed by two or three informal transcriptions of possible pronunciations to be rated on a 4-point Likert scale with the options "Never," "Rarely," "Often," and "Always." The informal transcriptions were largely orthographic; ⟨T⟩ was capitalized for prominence, e.g., ⟨parTy⟩, and replaced with ⟨D⟩ in the flapped form, e.g., ⟨parDy⟩. There were three realizations for /nt/ clusters in words like *twenty*: nasal-flap sequence ⟨tweNDy⟩, unflapped ⟨tweNTy⟩, or nasalized flap ⟨tweNNy⟩. These representations exploit the popular perception that AmE speakers seemingly pronounce "T" like "D," as alluded to in the preamble. In strict terms, such representations are inaccurate, since ⟨D⟩ in English typically corresponds to the voiced alveolar plosive [d], distinct from the voiced alveolar flap [ɾ]. Nonetheless, this strategy circumvents the challenge of conveying flapping to non-linguist participants, who are unlikely to be familiar with the International Phonetic Alphabet (IPA) or to have formal knowledge of phonological processes.

Demographic Data

After the two survey tasks, participants were prompted to give basic demographic information—birthplace, gender, and ethnicity. They also provided information about their exposure to AmE: how often they consumed US media, how often they interacted with people from the US, and whether they had visited or lived in the US and, if so, for how long. As a portion of respondents were linguistics students, the survey also asked if participants had ever taken any university modules in linguistics, to subsequently check for any effect of linguistics experience on awareness of flapping.

Complete responses were received from 88 participants who were recruited from among the first author's personal contacts. Five participants were excluded from analysis because they were not born in Singapore and two others because they fell outside the target age range of 18 to 25. The final pool of subjects therefore consisted of 81 participants, of whom 78 provided demographic data, summarized in table 9.3.

Results: Awareness of AmE T-Flapping

Collectively, the 81 participants gave 6,877 ratings out of a possible total of 6,885, amounting to a response rate of 99.88%. For analysis, ratings were quantified by assigning each option a numerical score such that "Never" equates to 0 points, "Rarely" 1 point, "Often" 2 points, and "Always" 3 points. Ratings showed unimodal distributions within conditions, so the mean numerical rating was chosen as a summary statistic for comparing between conditions.

Figure 9.1 shows ratings as a ratio of the mean flapped rating to the mean unflapped rating per word, grouped according to the licitness of T-flapping in AmE. Points above the reference line, indicating a ratio of 1:1, indicate a belief that the flapped form is used in AmE, while points below this reference line indicate a belief that the unflapped form is used. All OBLIGATORY word ratings fall above the line, while the opposite is true for ILLICIT. This pattern immediately points to a general awareness among SgE speakers regarding which words may be flapped in AmE and which may not. Nonetheless, there is some variability between words, as demonstrated by the closeness in ratings for words like *Botox* (ILLICIT) and *analytic* (OBLIGATORY), pointing to less uniform intuitions about the AmE pronunciation of certain words.

Among OPTIONAL words, most ratings are as high as some OBLIGATORY words. This result means either that the participants thought these words are obligatorily flapped in AmE, or that they are aware that these words can optionally be flapped, but are biased to believe they are more likely to be flapped than not. The one exception in this condition is the word *volatile*, which is rated as low as the ILLICIT words. Here, participants were likely considering the SgE pronunciation /vɔ.lə.taɪl/, with an unreduced [aɪ] vowel in the third syllable that would block T-flapping according to VOW, rather than the AmE pronunciation /ˈvɑ.lə.tl̩/ which does allow T-flapping.

As for words with /nt/ clusters (figure 9.2), ratings show variability across both NTa and NTb categories, although one pattern that does emerge is the preference for [ɾ] to [nɾ]. Thus, participants are aware that most /nt/ words have [ɾ] and overextend

Table 9.3. Summary of participant demographics and AmE exposure ($N = 78$)[a]

Demographic categories	Number	Percentage (%)
Gender		
Male	29	37.2
Female	48	61.5
Non-binary	1	1.3
Age		
Mean	22.8	—
Range	19–25	—
Standard deviation	1.48	—
Race		
Chinese	58	74.4
Malay	9	11.5
Indian	7	9.0
Mixed	4	5.1
Education		
Post-secondary (non-tertiary)	0	0.0
Diploma	0	0.0
Undergraduate degree	73	93.6
Postgraduate degree	5	6.4
Media consumption level		
Never or almost never	3	3.8
Every few months	16	20.5
Every few days	33	42.3
Daily or almost daily	26	33.3
Frequency of personal interaction with AmE speakers		
Never or almost never	55	70.5
Every few months, every few days, or daily	23	29.5
Visited or lived in US		
No	45	57.7
Yes	33	42.3

[a]Three participants did not provide demographic data.

this generalization to NTb words. The exception here is *ninety*, for which participants are aware that the more likely AmE pronunciation is [nɾ]. It is perhaps unsurprising that participants would show less awareness of the lexically arbitrary group, especially in the case of *carpenter*, which is a low-frequency word, occurring only 3.54 times per million words (pmw) in the Corpus of Global Web-Based English (GloWbE, Davies 2013). The fact that the NTa realization [ɾ̃] is mistakenly applied to NTb words is evidence that SgE speakers have learned a rule about AmE pronunciation rather than developing word-by-word impressions.

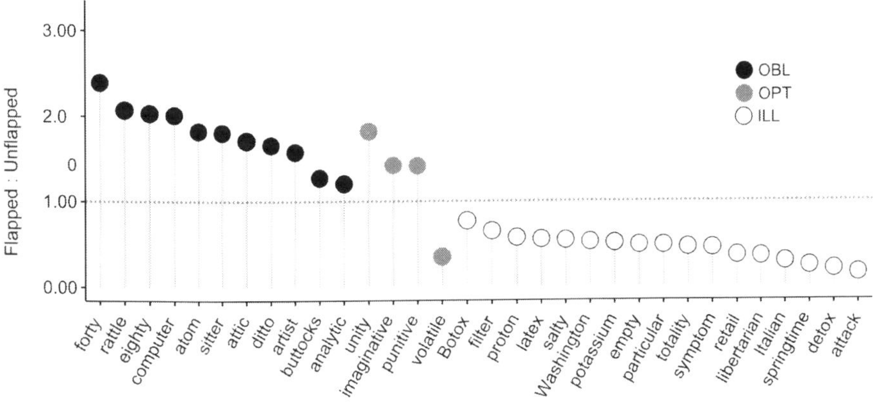

Figure 9.1. Participants' beliefs about T-flapping in AmE; for each word, the rating is given as the ratio of the mean flapped rating to the mean unflapped rating*

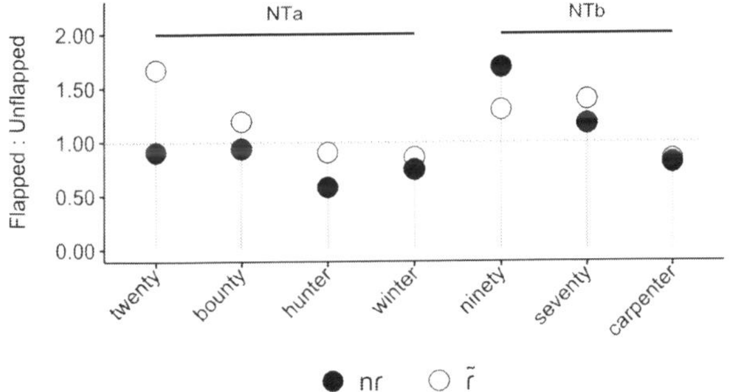

Figure 9.2. Participants' beliefs about flapping of /nt/ in AmE; for each word, the rating is given as the ratio of the mean flapped rating to the mean unflapped rating*

Awareness Metric

The data presented thus far reflect how SgE speakers as a group believe words are realized in AmE but may not be a clear indication of how accurate these perceptions are on an individual speaker level. To quantify the accuracy of individual participants' intuitions, each rating was scored based on whether it aligns with the AmE pronunciation predicted by the analysis that we adopt. In the OBLIGATORY condition, preference for the flapped pronunciation ("Always," "Often") is considered "correct" and receives 1 point, while dispreference ("Rarely," "Never") is scored 0 points. The reverse is true for the ILLICIT condition. If participants truly treat flapping as optional in the OPTIONAL condition, then intermediate responses ("Often," "Rarely") are expected for both pronunciations, so these options are both scored 1 point.

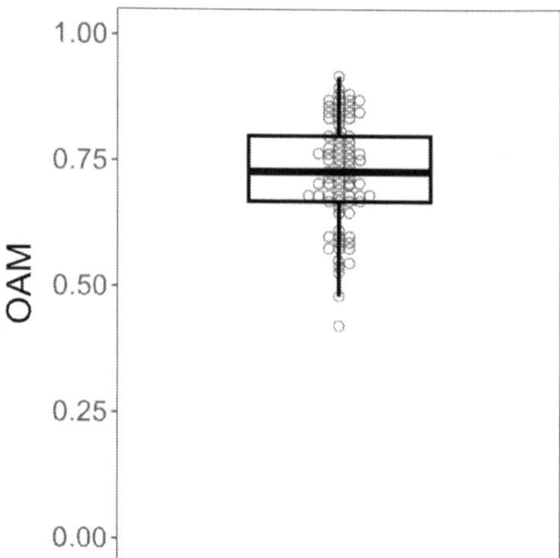

Figure 9.3. Boxplot showing the distribution of the Overall Awareness Metric

For NTa words, [ɾ̃] is considered grammatical and [nɾ] ungrammatical in AmE, so these pronunciations are scored 1 and 0 respectively. The reverse is true for NTb. For both NTa and NTb, the [nt] realization is possible in careful speech, so intermediate responses ("Rarely" and "Often") are scored 1 point each.

An Overall Awareness Metric (OAM) was computed for each participant by tallying the total number of points scored across all stimuli and dividing it by the total number of items. The distribution of OAM is shown in figure 9.3: this metric ranged from 0.424 to 0.918, with a mean of 0.727, meaning that participants have 72.7% accuracy on average—relatively high and yet imperfect awareness of T-flapping in AmE. The awareness data echoes Starr's (2019) study on Singaporeans' awareness of the BATH-TRAP merger. In that study, participants were asked to report whether /æ/ or /ɑ/ would be used in AmE for various BATH- and TRAP-class words. Despite general awareness of the merger, such that all words should rightfully have /æ/ in AmE, only 12.4% of participants showed complete accuracy; all others predicted a mix of /æ/ and /ɑ/. They did, however, report lower percentages of /æ/ for BATH-class words than TRAP-class words. Thus, participants had a general awareness of the vowel merger in AmE, but few were completely accurate in their predictions of AmE pronunciation. The OAM of the present study paints a similar picture: participants had considerable knowledge of AmE flapping, but none showed perfect knowledge, the highest OAM being 91.8%.

Predictors of Awareness

A linear regression model of OAM was constructed using the R package *stats* in RStudio (RStudio Team 2021). Age, sex, ethnicity, education, interpersonal interaction variables, and media consumption variables were included as fixed effects.

Table 9.4. Significant effects for the Overall Awareness Metric

Term	Mean	Estimate	SE	t-value	p-value
Intercept		0.723	0.074	9.773	7.73e^{-15}***
Dummy = 1 if education level is					
Undergraduate ($n = 73$)	0.718	−0.119	0.047	−2.553	0.013*
Dummy = 1 if US media consumption level is					
Every few months ($n = 16$)	0.724	0.120	0.063	1.910	0.060
Every few days ($n = 33$)	0.731	0.116	0.060	1.925	0.058
Daily or almost daily ($n = 26$)	0.736	0.131	0.061	2.149	0.035*

Note: ***$p < .001$; *$p < 0.05$.

Subject, when included as a random effect in a linear mixed-effects model, showed no significant effects and so was removed from the model. Table 9.4 shows the significant effects yielded by the model. Undergraduate students had significantly lower OAM scores than graduate students ($p = 0.013$); however, the pool of graduate students was minuscule ($n = 5$) compared to undergraduates ($n = 73$), potentially amplifying the differences due to sampling effects.

Notably, there was also a significant effect of daily or near-daily US media consumption ($\beta = 0.131$, $p = 0.035$): participants who reported this level of US media consumption scored on average 13.1 percentage points higher than counterparts who said that they never or almost never did so. For lower levels of media consumption, the effect size is comparable but only approaches significance (every few months: $\beta = 0.120$, $p = 0.060$; every few days: $\beta = 0.116$, $p = 0.058$). It cannot be disregarded, however, that for the group reporting the least amount of media consumption, the mean OAM already reaches an estimated 72.3% (intercept term). This figure suggests that even with little media consumption, SgE speakers have baseline knowledge about flapping. Indeed, learning the AmE flapping rule might be more intuitive a process given the naturalness of flapping in some environments due to articulatory factors (de Jong 2011). Greater consumption of US media, then, could have the effect of sharpening this baseline awareness.

Face-to-face interaction variables did not show any significant effects when included in the model (visited or lived in the US: $\beta = 0.009$, $p = 0.754$; higher interaction with people from the US: $\beta = 0.003$, $p = 0.922$). Thus, between US media consumption and personal interaction, it is only media that is associated with better awareness of the flapping feature. Such a result does not line up entirely with Starr's (2019) findings, which found time spent in the US and UK to be consistent predictors of Singaporeans' knowledge of BATH and TRAP use in those regions.

Results: Own Use of T-Flapping

Two participants skipped the survey section on their own use of T-flapping, but the remaining 79 participants had a 100% response rate, giving 6,715 ratings collectively. As with the AmE awareness data, qualitative ratings were quantified by assigning scores to each option. Mean personal-use ratings by word were computed to obtain a relative measure of the tendency to flap /t/ in each wordlist item, as shown in figure 9.4. In contrast with the awareness data shown in figure 9.1, all points fall below the reference line in this plot, indicating that the unflapped pronunciations are preferred across the board. This preference is expected since T-flapping is not traditionally used in SgE.

Nonetheless, there is some level of flapping reported in the OBLIGATORY and OPTIONAL categories. As with the AmE awareness data, *volatile* is an exception, with a relative rating lower than some of the ILLICIT words. Again, this result is likely a reflection of the SgE pronunciation /vɔ.lə.taɪl/. Flapped pronunciations for *eighty* and *forty* had the highest relative ratings, in line with the preliminary observation that decade numbers tend to be flapped in SgE. The high flapping rates of these items could arise from a frequency effect (*forty*: 28.2 tokens pmw, *eighty*: 58.3 tokens pmw in GloWbE), as could that of *computer* (115.03 tokens pmw). As for the low-frequency word *ditto* (2.45 tokens pmw), the high reported flapping may stem from a casualness effect. These results provide evidence that, while far from dominant, flapped /t/ is present in SgE. Its use also seems to be non-uniform across lexical items, partially corroborating Y. Tan's (2016) findings.

Data on SgE speakers' use of /nt/-flapping suggest a continuing preference for [nt] over both [ɾ̃] and [nɾ] as all relative ratings fall below the reference line in figure 9.5. In *twenty*, there is a clearer preference for [ɾ̃], while in *ninety*, [nɾ] was more likely. For all other words, relative ratings fall very close together, showing only a very

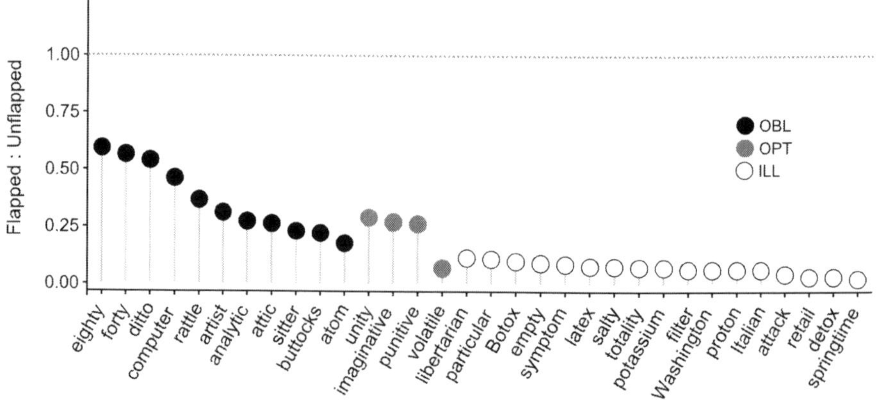

Figure 9.4. Participants' own use of T-flapping in SgE; for each word, the rating is given as the ratio of the mean flapped rating to the mean unflapped rating*

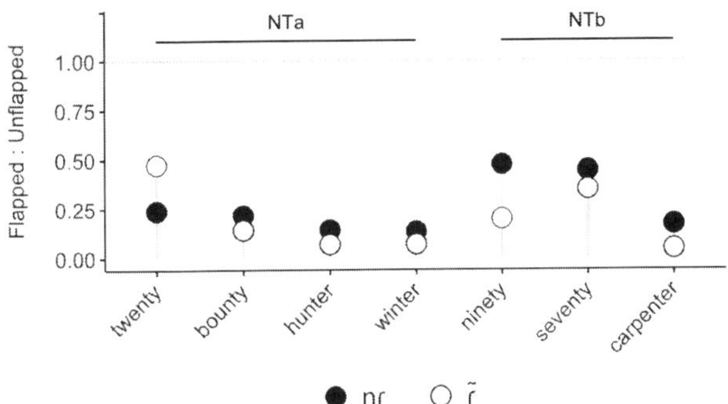

Figure 9.5. Participants' own use of flapping of /nt/ in SgE; for each word, the rating is given as the ratio of the mean flapped rating to the mean unflapped rating

weak preference for [ɾ̃]. It is unclear if this marginal preference is simply due to error in self-report. However, when juxtaposed against the AmE awareness data, these results show that while participants did think that [ɾ̃] was used in all AmE /nt/ words apart from *ninety*, they do not pronounce, or do not believe that they pronounce, most /nt/ words in the same way as AmE speakers.

Tendency Metrics

SgE speakers' relative tendency to use flapped forms was quantified by calculating the mean numerical rating for flapped pronunciations for words in the OBLIGATORY and OPTIONAL conditions. This statistic represents the use of flapping in the same environments as AmE and is thus termed Tendency$_{\text{AmE}}$. However, it would be premature to exclude the possibility of a unique "SgE style" of flapping distinct from that of AmE. Even in other Inner Circle varieties of English, flapping applies in environments where it would be illicit in AmE. In Australian English (Horvath 2004) and New Zealand English (Gordon and Maclagan 2004), "teen" numbers like *eighteen* and *thirteen* can be flapped, whereas the pre-stress position of /t/ would block flapping in AmE. To account for this possibility in SgE, a Tendency$_{\text{Inno}}$ statistic was also computed, equating to the mean numerical rating for flapped forms in the ILLICIT conditions.

The boxplot in figure 9.6 below summarizes the Tendency metrics. Tendency$_{\text{AmE}}$ had a mean of 0.716 ($SD = 0.533$) while Tendency$_{\text{Inno}}$ was lower, with a mean of 0.270 ($SD = 0.288$). These statistics reiterate that flapping is still a low-frequency feature in SgE while also suggesting that it is more likely to occur in the same environments where it is licit in AmE, which could reflect universal articulatory tendencies (de Jong 2011). Assuming that Tendency$_{\text{Inno}}$ reflects actual use of flapping in unique environments by Singaporeans, rather than being wholly due to inaccurate self-reporting, then the Tendency$_{\text{Inno}}$ data cast doubt on the hypothesis that flapping has simply been imported from AmE.

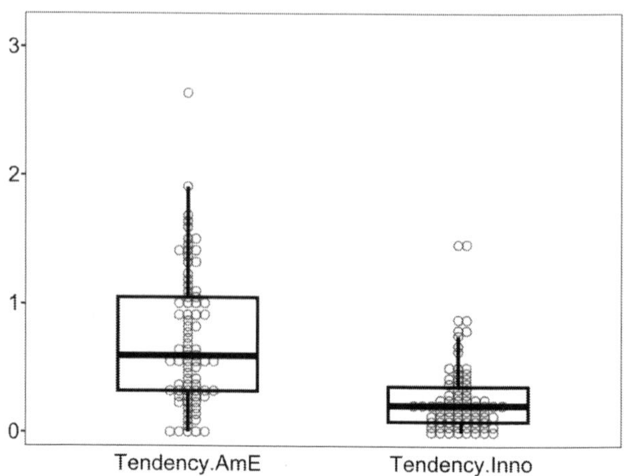

Figure 9.6. Boxplot showing the distribution of the tendency metrics

Predictors of Flapping Tendency

Linear regression models for the two Tendency statistics are summarized in tables 9.5 and 9.6. $\text{Tendency}_{\text{AmE}}$ was significantly predicted by personal interaction variables, i.e., greater interaction with people from the US ($\beta = 0.432$, $p = 0.001$) and having visited or lived in the US ($\beta = 0.316$, $p = 0.013$). When OAM (our metric for overall awareness of AmE flapping) was included in the model, it was found to have no significant effect on $\text{Tendency}_{\text{AmE}}$ ($p = 0.758$). The correlation between $\text{Tendency}_{\text{AmE}}$ and OAM was also very weak ($r = +0.177$); thus, respondents' degree of self-reported flapping was independent of their knowledge of AmE flapping.

As shown in table 9.6, $\text{Tendency}_{\text{Inno}}$ increased with $\text{Tendency}_{\text{AmE}}$ ($\beta = 0.396$, $p < 0.001$) but decreased with higher OAM ($\beta = -0.770$, $p = 0.001$) and greater interaction with people from the US ($\beta = -0.126$, $p = 0.024$). Thus, SgE speakers who flap in AmE flapping environments are more likely to also flap in non-AmE environments, but flapping in non-AmE environments decreases for people who have better awareness of AmE flapping and who interact more with people from the US.

When media consumption was included in the models, it did not provide a better fit for the data for $\text{Tendency}_{\text{AmE}}$ ($F = 2.597$, $p = 0.081$) or $\text{Tendency}_{\text{Inno}}$ ($F = 0.751$, $p = 0.476$). In other words, media consumption was not a significant predictor of personal use of flapping, even though, as discussed above, it did predict awareness of flapping. These results can be interpreted to mean that even if media sources may act as conduits through which sociolinguistic knowledge can flow, there is not necessarily a concomitant change in consumers' own language use. This result accords well with existing work on media and language change that admits the possible role of the media in promoting sociolinguistic awareness but not the adoption of specific features (e.g., Milroy and Milroy 1985; Stuart-Smith 2006, 2014).

One way in which this finding differs from those of Stuart-Smith (2006) and Stuart-Smith and Timmins (2014), however, is that in these prior studies, participants

Table 9.5. Significant effects for Tendency$_{AmE}$

Term	Mean	Estimate	SE	t-value	p-value
Intercept		0.503	0.071	7.089	6.33e^{-10}***
Visited or lived in US ($n = 21$)	0.970	0.316	0.124	2.540	0.013*
Interact with people from US ($n = 24$)	1.032	0.432	0.119	3.628	0.001***

Note: ***$p < .001$; *$p < 0.05$

Table 9.6. Significant effects for Tendency$_{Inno}$

Term	Mean	Estimate	SE	t-value	p-value
Intercept		0.576	0.160	3.595	0.001***
Tendency$_A$		0.396	0.048	8.273	3.95e^{-12}***
OAM		−0.770	0.222	−3.466	0.001***
Interact with people from US ($n = 23$)	0.295	−0.126	0.055	−2.298	0.024*

Note: ***$p < .001$; *$p < 0.05$

did not show clear awareness of specific segmental features and instead modified suprasegmental features when asked to mimic the accent of a TV character. The salience of T-flapping, a feature often discussed by laypersons, and the articulatory naturalness of its occurrence could together mean that knowledge of T-flapping is easier to pick up through media sources than other features. Alternatively, this discrepancy may simply be due to the fact that the present study explicitly highlighted a specific dialect feature, whereas Stuart-Smith's work focused on impressions of entire accents.

Americanization or Innovation?

Our survey found that SgE speakers have rather accurate, yet imperfect, awareness of T-flapping in AmE, correctly predicting T-flapping 72.7% of the time on average. US media consumption, but not face-to-face interaction with AmE speakers, correlated with higher awareness of the feature. On the other hand, participants reported limited use of T-flapping in their own SgE speech, which tended to occur in the same environments as AmE T-flapping. The source of AmE exposure that proved to be the strongest predictor of AmE-like flapping, as measured by Tendency$_{AmE}$, was interpersonal interaction, rather than media consumption.

While self-reported constraints on the use of T-flapping were largely consistent with AmE patterns, certain evidence in the data casts doubt on the account that T-flapping in SgE is adopted from AmE. First, Tendency$_{Inno}$ reflects divergences between flapping in SgE and in AmE, raising the possibility that T-flapping is an independent innovation in SgE that occurs in a wider, or at least different, set of environments. Face-to-face interaction with AmE speakers negatively predicted Tendency$_{Inno}$. This finding suggests that although T-flapping in SgE patterns differently from AmE, speakers who are more experienced with AmE align their use with AmE norms. Such a dynamic would be consistent with the high prestige accorded to AmE by Singaporeans, which encourages assimilation. The greater impact of interpersonal interaction over media consumption in the data also supports the view that interpersonal contact is the central driver of language change.

Participants' responses to words with /nt/ clusters also provide insights: even though participants are aware that [ɾ̃] is used in NTa words in AmE, they did not report such a preference in their own speech. In particular, participants mistakenly believed that the word *seventy* is pronounced like all other NTa words in AmE when, in fact, it belongs to NTb. They nonetheless preferred [nɾ] for their own pronunciation. While this response brings their self-report more in line with actual AmE pronunciation, their *belief* that they pronounce this word differently from AmE speakers suggests that they are not explicitly copying AmE speakers in every case.

These strands of evidence suggest contradictory aspects of language ideology and linguistic self-confidence among SgE speakers. Such complicated language ideological dynamics are expected in a context of endonormative stabilization, in which linguistic insecurity persists even as speakers develop linguistic self-confidence and a sense of ownership over English (Schneider 2003). Foo and Tan elaborate on the Singaporean context by positing that speakers feel a "new type of linguistic ownership in Singapore, one that does not invoke notions of authority or legitimacy" (2019, 606). Thus, while SgE speakers feel a strong enough sense of ownership over English to embrace local norms, including phonological innovations, SgE continues to be perceived as less legitimate relative to valorized and prestigious Inner Circle varieties such as AmE. Independent innovations, as we propose, may thus be shaped by norms emanating from the Inner Circle.

The self-report surveys used in this study provide information about participants' pronunciation and are useful in demonstrating that SgE speakers do not believe they are copying AmE speakers. Nonetheless, we acknowledge the potential for inaccurate self-reporting, either due to limitations in the intuitions that participants are able to probe and report, or due to a reluctance to report T-flapping despite its being associated with a valorized variety like AmE, since it would reduce spelling-pronunciation correspondence. This mismatch would run counter to SgE speakers' tendency to maximize the faithfulness to orthography as an index of correctness (Starr 2021a). To mitigate this potential drawback, we are building upon this work through the collection of production data to confirm the distribution and rate of T-flapping in SgE. The small sample size and demographic skew of the participants (e.g., the oversampling of participants with a high education level) also limit the generalizability of the data: a larger and more diverse participant pool will address this limitation while also revealing whether there is social variation in SgE T-flapping.

Beyond production studies, perception studies are also necessary to understand the social meanings of SgE T-flapping. In particular, they can reveal whether its use is perceived as markedly American or Singaporean. It is the first author's suspicion that T-flapping, especially in decade numbers and perhaps in phrases like *shut up* or *whatever*, may simply be evaluated as local variants; these pronunciations seem unremarkable to Singaporean speakers when asked informally. Just as Meyerhoff and Niedzielski (2003) observe for certain phonetic variables and lexical items in New Zealand English, it is possible that flapped /t/ in certain lexical items is simply part of the existing vernacular for SgE speakers and not a foreign import. Studies involving a wider age range of participants can also explore this possibility by determining whether T-flapping is used by older speakers as much as by younger ones.

Conclusion

SgE T-flapping invites further linguistic research; this study has provided evidence that this feature is indeed used in SgE, with lexical variation in its application. Our findings also suggest that while media exposure could improve cross-dialectal awareness of T-flapping, it does not correlate with actual use of the feature. The data also problematize claims of ongoing Americanization in SgE. First, T-flapping is not frequent in SgE, echoing previous findings that there is no wholesale move toward AmE phonological norms underway in Singapore (Starr 2019). Moreover, participants do not claim to use flapping in the exact same ways as AmE speakers, indicating that SgE speakers are not attempting to mimic this AmE feature. While SgE T-flapping tends to coincide with AmE T-flapping in its distribution, there are universal articulatory considerations that may account for this fact. It seems that, as in New Zealand English (Meyerhoff and Niedzielski 2003), T-flapping may have evolved independently in SgE; at the same time, given AmE's prestigious Inner Circle status, the patterning of AmE T-flapping may exert an influence on the use of this feature via interpersonal exposure. Overall, the findings suggest that Americanization of SgE phonology remains limited in scope and that the primary causes of the AmE-like phenomena observed in recent scholarship on SgE phonology are Singapore's status as a site of intense transnational mobility and the community's increasing shift in orientation away from BrE norms, rather than Singaporeans' high levels of US media consumption.

Note

*Some figures in this chapter are available on the publisher's website (press.georgetown.edu) to make it easier to view the data.

References

Alderton, Roy. 2021. T-tapping in Standard Southern British English: An "elite" sociolinguistic variant? *Journal of Sociolinguistics* 26 (2): 287–98. doi: 10.1111/josl.12541

Alsagoff, Lubna. 2010. English in Singapore: Culture, capital and identity in linguistic variation. *World Englishes* 29 (3): 336–48. doi: 10.1111/j.1467-971X.2010.01658.x

Auer, Peter, and Frans Hinskens. 2005. The role of interpersonal accommodation in a theory of language change. In Peter Auer, Frans Hinskens and Paul Kerswill (eds.), *Dialect change: Convergence and divergence in European languages*, eds., 335–57. Cambridge: Cambridge University Press. doi: 10.1017/CBO9780511486623.015

Cavallaro, Francesco, Bee Chin Ng and Mark F. Seilhamer. 2014. Singapore Colloquial English: Issues of prestige and identity. *World Englishes* 33 (3): 378–97. doi: 10.1111/weng.12096

Davies, Mark. 2013. Corpus of Global Web-Based English: 1.9 billion words from speakers in 20 countries (GloWbE). https://corpus.byu.edu/glowbe/.

de Jong, Kenneth J. 1998. Stress-related variation in the articulation of coda alveolar stops: Flapping revisited. *Journal of Phonetics* 26: 283–310. doi: 10.1006/jpho.1998.0077

de Jong, Kenneth J. 2011. Flapping in American English. In Marc van Oostendorp, Colin J. Ewen, Elizabeth Hume and Keren Rice (eds.), *The Blackwell companion to phonology*. Hoboken, NJ: Wiley & Sons, 1–19. doi: 10.1002/9781444335262.wbctp0113

Deterding, David. 2007. *Singapore English*. Edinburgh: Edinburgh University Press. https://www.jstor.org/stable/10.3366/j.ctt1r21h4

Eckert, Penelope. 2003. Elephants in the room. *Journal of Sociolinguistics* 7: 392–431. doi: 10.1111/1467-9481.00231

Eddington, David, and Dirk Elzinga. 2008. The phonetic context of American English flapping: Quantitative evidence. *Language and Speech* 51 (3): 245–66. doi: 10.1177/0023830908098542

Foo, Amanda L., and Tan Ying-Ying. 2019. Linguistic insecurity and the linguistic ownership of English among Singaporean Chinese. *World Englishes* 38 (4): 606–29. doi: 10.1111/weng.12359

Gonçalves, Bruno, Lucía Loureiro-Porto, José J. Ramasco and David Sánchez. 2018. Mapping the Americanization of English in space and time. *PLoS ONE* 13 (5): e0197741. doi: 10.1371/journal.pone.0197741

Gordon, Elizabeth and Margaret Maclagan. 2004. Regional and social differences in New Zealand: Phonology. In Edgar W. Schneider, Kate Burridge, Bernd Kortmann, Rajend Mesthrie and Clive Upton (eds.), *A handbook of varieties of English, phonology* (vol. I). Berlin: De Gruyter, 603–13. doi: 10.1515/9783110208412.1.64

Gupta, Anthea F. 1989. Singapore Colloquial English and Standard English. *Singapore Journal of Education* 10 (2): 33–39. doi: 10.1080/02188798908547659

Hannisdal, Bente. 2020. A corpus-based study of /t/ flapping in American English broadcast speech. In Anne Przewozny, Cécile Viollain and Sylvain Navarro (eds.), *The corpus phonology of English: Multifocal analyses of variation*. Cambridge: Cambridge University Press, 256–76.

Hänsel, Eva C. and Dagmar Deuber. 2013. Globalization, postcolonial Englishes, and the English language press in Kenya, Singapore, and Trinidad and Tobago. *World Englishes* 32 (3): 338–57. doi: 10.1111/weng.12035

Haugen, Einar. 1938. Notes on "Voiced t" in American English. *Dialect Notes* 6: 627–34. doi: 10.1515/9783110879124.72

Honeybone, Patrick. 2012. Lenition in English. In Terttu Nevalainen and Elizabeth C. Traugott (eds.), *The Oxford handbook of the history of English*. Oxford Handbooks Online, 773–787. doi: 10.1093/oxfordhb/9780199922765.013.0064

Horvath, Barbara M. 2004. Australian English: Phonology. In Edgar W. Schneider, Kate Burridge, Bernd Kortmann, Rajend Mesthrie and Clive Upton (eds.), *A handbook of varieties of English, phonology* (vol. I), 625–44. Berlin: De Gruyter. doi: 10.1515/9783110197181-041

Kachru, Braj B. 1985. Standards, codification and sociolinguistic realism: English language in the outer circle. In Randolph Quirk and Henry Widdowson (eds.), *English in the world: Teaching and learning the language and literatures*. Cambridge: Cambridge University Press, 11–36.

Kretzschmar, William A., Jr. 2004. Standard American English pronunciation. In Edgar W. Schneider, Kate Burridge, Bernd Kortmann, Rajend Mesthrie and Clive Upton, *A handbook of varieties of English, phonology* (vol. I) 257–69. Berlin: De Gruyter. doi: 10.1515/9783110208405.1.37

Ladefoged, Peter. 1997. Linguistic phonetic descriptions. In William J. Hardcastle and John Laver (eds.), *Handbook of phonetic sciences*. Hoboken, NJ: Wiley-Blackwell, 589–618.

Leimgruber, Jakob. 2011. Singapore English. *Language and Linguistics Compass* 5 (1): 47–62. doi: 10.1111/j.1749-818X.2010.00262.x

Leimgruber, Jakob. 2012. Singapore English: An indexical approach. *World Englishes* 31 (1): 1–14. doi: 10.1111/j.1467-971X.2011.01743.x

Lim, Lisa. 2004. Sounding Singaporean. In *Singapore English: A grammatical description*. Amsterdam: John Benjamins Publishing Company, 19–56.

Low, Ee Ling. 2020. English in Singapore and Malaysia: Differences and similarities. In Andy Kirkpatrick (ed.), *The Routledge handbook of world Englishes*. Oxford: Routledge, 298–318.

Meyerhoff, Miriam and Nancy Niedzielski. 2003. The globalisation of vernacular variation. *Journal of Sociolinguistics* 7 (4): 534–55. doi: 10.1111/j.1467-9841.2003.00241.x

Milroy, Lesley. 2007. Off the shelf or under the counter? On the social dynamics of sound changes. In Christopher M. Cain and Geoffrey Russom (eds.), *Managing Chaos: Strategies for Identifying Change in English*. New York: Mouton de Gruyter, 149–72. doi: 10.1515/9783110198515.3.149

Milroy, James and Lesley Milroy. 1985. *Authority in language: Investigating Standard English*. London and New York: Routledge. doi: 10.4324/9780203124666

Niedzielski, Nancy and Howard Giles. 1996. Linguistic accommodation. In Hans Goebl, Peter H. Nelde, Zdeněk Starý and Wolfgang Wölck (eds.), *Kontaktlinguistik—Ein internationales Handbuch zeitgenössischer Forschung* [Contact linguistics—An international handbook of contemporary research]. Berlin and New York: De Gruyter Mouton, 2008, 332–42. doi: 10.1515/9783110132649.1.5.332

Nycz, Jennifer. 2019. Media and second dialect acquisition. *Annual Review of Applied Linguistics* 39: 152–60.

Park, Joseph S., and Lionel Wee. 2009. The three circles redux: A market-theoretic perspective on World Englishes. *Applied Linguistics* 30 (3): 389–406. doi: 10.1093/applin/amp008

Platt, John T. 1975. The Singapore English speech continuum and its basilect "Singlish" as a "Creoloid." *Anthropological Linguistics* 17 (7): 363–74. https://www.jstor.org/stable/30027290

Platt, John T. 1977. A model for polyglossia and multilingualism (with special reference to Singapore and Malaysia). *Language in Society* 6 (3): 361–78. doi: 10.1017/S0047404500005066

RStudio Team. 2021. *RStudio: Integrated development environment for R*. Boston: RStudio, PBC.

Sayers, Dave. 2014. The mediated innovation model: A framework for researching media influence in language change. *Journal of sociolinguistics* 18 (2): 185–212. doi: 10.1111/josl.12069

Schneider, Edgar W. 2003. The dynamics of New Englishes: From identity construction to dialect birth. *Language* 79 (2): 233–81. https://www.jstor.org/stable/4489419

Singapore Department of Statistics. 2019. *Yearbook of Statistics Singapore 2019*. https://www.singstat.gov.sg/-/media/files/publications/reference/yearbook_2019/notes.pdf/.

Singapore Department of Statistics. 2021. *Census of Population 2020: Statistical Release 1*. https://www.singstat.gov.sg/-/media/files/publications/cop2020/sr1/cop2020sr1.pdf/

Starr, Rebecca L. 2019. Cross-dialectal awareness and use of the bath-trap distinction in Singapore: Investigating the effects of overseas travel and media consumption. *Journal of English Linguistics* 47 (1): 55–88. doi: 10.1177/0075424218819740

Starr, Rebecca L. 2021a. Changing language, changing character types. In Lauren Hall-Lew, Emma Moore and Robert J. Podesva (eds.), *Social meaning and linguistic variation: Theorizing the Third Wave*. Cambridge: Cambridge University Press, 315–37. doi: 10.1017/9781108578684.014

Starr, Rebecca L. 2021b. Transnational dialect contact and language variation and change in World Englishes. In Alexander Onysko (ed.), *Developments in research on World Englishes*. London: Bloomsbury, 149–72. doi: 10.5040/9781350167087.ch-008

Stuart-Smith, Jane. 2006. The influence of the media. In Carmen Llamas, Louise Mullany and Peter Stockwell (eds.), *The Routledge companion to sociolinguistics* (1st ed.). London: Routledge, 140–48.

Stuart-Smith, Jane. 2011. The view from the couch: Changing perspectives on the role of the television in changing language ideologies and use. In Tore Kristiansen and Nikolas Coupland (eds.), *Standard languages and language standards in a changing Europe*, edited by. Novus Press, 223–39.

Stuart-Smith, Jane. 2012. English and the media: Television. In Alexander Bergs and Laurel J. Brinton (eds.), *English historical linguistics: An international handbook*, Series: Handbücher zur Sprach- und Kommunikationswissenschaft 34(1). Berlin: Mouton de Gruyter, 1075–88.

Stuart-Smith, Jane. 2014. No longer an elephant in the room. *Journal of Sociolinguistics* 18 (2): 250–61.

Stuart-Smith, Jane, Rachel Smith, Tamara Rathcke, Francesco Li Santi and Sophie Holmes. 2011. Responding to accents after experiencing interactive or mediated speech. *Proceedings of the 17th International Congress of Phonetic Sciences* (ICPhS), Hong Kong, 1914–17. http://www.icphs2011.hk/ICPHS_CongressProceedings.htm/

Stuart-Smith, Jane and Claire Timmins. 2014. Language and the influence of the media: A Scottish perspective. In Robert Lawson (ed.), *Sociolinguistics in Scotland*. Hampshire: Palgrave Macmillan, 177–96. doi: 10.1057/9781137034717_9

Tan, Chor Hiang and Anthea Fraser Gupta. 1992. Post-vocalic /r/ in Singapore English. *York Papers in Linguistics* 16: 139–52.

Tan, Ying-Ying. 2012. To r or not to r: Social correlates of /ɹ/ in Singapore English. *International Journal of the Sociology of Language* 218: 1–24. doi: 10.1515/ijsl-2012-0057

Tan, Ying-Ying. 2016. The Americanization of the phonology of Asian Englishes: Evidence from Singapore. In Gerhard Leitner, Azirah Hashim and Hans-Georg Wolf (eds.), *Communicating with Asia: The future of English as a global language*, eds., 120–34. Cambridge: Cambridge University Press. doi: 10.1017/CBO9781107477186.009

Trudgill, Peter. 1986. *Dialects in contact*. Oxford: Blackwell.

Trudgill, Peter. 2014. Diffusion, drift, and the irrelevance of media influence. *Journal of Sociolinguistics* 18 (2): 213–22. doi: 10.1111/josl.12070

Turk, Alice. 1992. The American English flapping rule and the effect of stress on stop consonant durations. *Cornell Working Papers in Linguistics* 7: 103–33. doi: 10.5281/zenodo.3735148

US Department of State. 2021. Singapore. From Countries and Areas search. Last modified October 1. https://www.state.gov/countries-areas/singapore/

Vaux, Bert. "Flapping in English." Paper presented at the Annual Meeting of the Linguistic Society of America, Chicago, January 2000.

Wee, Lionel. 2004. Singapore English: Phonology. In Edgar W. Schneider, Kate Burridge, Bernd Kortmann, Rajend Mesthrie and Clive Upton (eds.), *A handbook of varieties of English phonology* (vol. 1). Berlin: Mouton de Gruyter, 1017–33.

Wells, John. 2011. Strong and weak. *John Wells's Phonetic Blog*, March 25. http://phonetic-blog.blogspot.com/2011/03/strong-and-weak.html/

Zue, Wictor W. and Martha Laferriere. 1979. Acoustic study of medial /t,d/ in American English. *The Journal of the Acoustical Society of America* 66 (4): 1039–50. doi: 10.1121/1.383323

Chapter 10

Making Things Easier: The Pragmatism behind Second Dialect Acquisition

ABBY WALKER
Virginia Tech

Introduction

When speakers move to new dialect regions, their pronunciation can, but does not always, shift away from their native dialect (D1) to be more similar to the new ambient dialect (D2). Researchers have considered many factors that potentially influence whether or how much a D2 is acquired, including the age of migration (e.g., Chambers 1992; Kerswill 1994; Payne 1980), the amount or nature of D2 input (e.g., Nycz 2013, 2019), the profile of particular linguistic variables (e.g., Chambers 1992; Trudgill 1986), and the attitudinal orientations of the migrant to the regions or dialects (Rys 2007).

One factor that is not as frequently considered in second dialect acquisition (SDA) research is what second language acquisition (SLA) researchers have called "instrumental motivation," which refers to "the practical value and advantages of learning a new language" (Lambert 1974, 98). This term is often used to include factors like monetary or academic incentives (a person needs to learn a language for a job or for a grade) and is in contrast to "integrative orientation," which is a "sincere and personal interest in the people and culture represented by the other language group" (98) and is much closer to the attitudinal factors commonly considered in SDA. While integrative orientation is often framed as more important than instrumental motivation for SLA, research has shown that instrumental motivations can impact language learning outcomes (e.g., Gardner and MacIntyre 1995).

The most obvious reason that pragmatic factors surrounding communication are not typically considered in SDA is because of the most critical difference between SDA and SLA: mutual intelligibility. By common definition, speakers of different dialects of the same language understand each other, while speakers of different languages do not. Therefore, SDA researchers have noted that there appears to be "little communicative value in acquiring a D2" (Siegel 2010, 116) and therefore migrants have "no need to explicitly learn new lexical items or their component phonemic categories" (Nycz 2019, 1483). Relatedly, SDA is typically understood to be driven largely by subconscious changes that speakers make over time (e.g., Chambers 1992)—a passive response to a change in the nature of linguistic input—and conscious performance of a D2 is typically cleft from second dialect acquisition and called *imitation* (Siegel 2010, 64–66; Trudgill 1986, 12). Therefore, changes that speakers very consciously and deliberately make are not usually the focus of SDA research, where, like most sociolinguistic research, the most privileged form of data is unconscious speech (Labov 1984, 29).

In this chapter I argue for us to take more seriously the role that instrumental factors could have in second dialect acquisition. I do so based on the self-reflective comments of regional migrants, the classic subjects of second dialect acquisition studies. This type of metalinguistic commentary has been understudied not just in SDA but also in linguistics as a field (for a discussion, see Wright 2022, 16–21, 30–36). This neglect is in part because of a heavy focus in sociolinguistics on form over content (Labov 1972), and evidence that people are not always accurate in (Trudgill 1972), aware of (Labov 1972), or do not have the vocabulary for (Preston 1996) talking about their language usage. In the current chapter, we may have additional concerns that instrumental motivations are likely more consciously available for comment than other factors and that speakers could also assign themselves instrumental motivations post hoc to explain why their speech has (not) changed. I make these caveats and still proceed, for two reasons. First, in his seminal work on second dialect acquisition, Trudgill (1986, 32) defends using anecdotes "since if, on a particular topic, we have many of them and they all point in the same direction, then we cannot ignore them." Second, researchers have argued that people's conscious knowledge and understanding of language use are valuable in their own right, for example, as a way to reveal ideologies and to see how non-linguists cognitively organize and reason about variation (Preston and Niedzielski 2010).

When we do ask (these) migrants about what they've changed in their speech and why, while they do sometimes mention factors like exposure and, rarely, attitudes, most often what they talk about appears very instrumental in nature: they changed (or maintained) their speech in pursuit of pragmatic goals like being understood, getting work, or avoiding being teased. One speaker, interviewed as part of this larger project,[1] stated that they were "very much about" assimilating because "you kind of make things easier sometimes." The insights from these migrants remind us that SDA happens in interactions and that the migrant is not just a receptacle for D2 input but that their speech—be it D1-like, D2-like, or something in between—is also being received by others. Moreover, seriously considering their comments forces us to think more carefully about mutual intelligibility, performance, and our definitions of what does and doesn't count as second dialect acquisition.

The Migrants in This Study

The speakers in this study consist of English expats living in the United States, and US expats living in England, and therefore British and American English are both the D1 and the D2 in this study, depending on the speaker. The standardized forms of each dialect (Southern British English and Mainstream US English) differ substantially from each other at every linguistic level: there is phonetic variation on almost all vowels (Wells 1982, 118–23); a number of phonemic differences (e.g., rhoticity, the BATH-TRAP split, the COT-CAUGHT merger); lexically specific pronunciation differences, often regarding stress (e.g., *garage, advertisement*); lexical differences (e.g., *boot/trunk, elevator/lift, gas/petrol*); syntactic differences (e.g., *I've not* vs. *I haven't*); semantic differences (e.g., *fit, quite*); and pragmatic differences (e.g., those discussed in Murphy and De Felice 2018). While the standardized forms of each dialect both have institutional backing and domestic status, it seems that generally British English is considered a higher-prestige dialect (e.g., Garrett, Williams and Evans 2005), and certainly that is the way in which the participants in this study experience the two dialects (Walker 2014, 134–36).

The migrants in this study (table 10.1)[2] were interviewed as part of my dissertation (Walker 2014), and the 19 English migrants were living in and interviewed in Columbus, Ohio, while the 21 US migrants were living in and interviewed in London, England. Interviews were conducted in a variety of locations, including university lab spaces, participant homes, and pubs or cafes, and they immediately followed an integrated listening (in noise) and speaking experiment (a wordlist reading task).[3] The results of those experiments suggest that both groups find it easier to understand their D2 than non-migrants do (Walker 2018) and that both groups exhibit some second dialect acquisition in the wordlist task, though the changes are relatively small (Walker 2019).

Interviews were usually between half an hour and an hour long. The bulk content of the interview covered topics related to England and America, including English and American sports, reflecting my interest in topic-based style-shifting between the two dialects (Love and Walker 2013; Walker 2019). Toward the end of the interviews, I specifically asked participants about their accent and whether they thought they

Table 10.1. Summary of speaker attributes, by speaker category (range of values in parentheses)

Speaker attributes	English expats	US expats
Number of participants	19	21
Men:women	10:9	4:17
Average age	46 (20–71)	41 (23–74)
Average age of immigration	31 (9–60)	30 (18–49)
Average # of years in US	15 (1.5–50)	NA
Average # of years in UK	NA	10 (.25–49)

changed their speech, over time or in the moment. The exact wording of the questions (and which questions I asked) differed across participants, but as an example of the nature of this part of the interview, here, in order, are (tidied) questions I asked participant 309 (a US expat):

> Do you feel like your accent has changed at all?
> Any words that you've noticed you've changed?
> What causes you to jump back and forth?
> Do people ever comment on your accent when you go back home?
> Are there any particular sounds—now I'm being a linguist—that you know are consistently different between British and American English?

In other interviews I sometimes asked people directly if they were ever misunderstood and what the reaction to their accent had been in the D2 region. Sometimes, participants initiated some discussion of dialect shifts earlier in the interview, and frequently, when I debriefed participants on my particular interest in style-shifting, they would offer more commentary. It is worth noting that I am a New Zealander living in the United States and so both saw myself, and believe I was seen by participants,[4] as sharing some SDA experiences, and cultural connections with both types of expats (as being from the Commonwealth, and as being a US resident).

Metalinguistic Insights from Migrants

In the following two sections, I pull quotes from these interviews to illustrate and explore two different types of pragmatic considerations migrants talked about when I asked them explicit questions about whether they had changed their accent or not. The first section deals with insights that referenced intelligibility, and the next covers insights that reflected more social responses from their interlocutors.

Changing Speech to Be Understood

When most speakers talked about changes they had noticed or consciously made in their speech as a function of moving across the Atlantic, they framed it as being in service of being understood. Many of their examples centered on vocabulary choices (e.g., *chips/fries, torch/flashlight, cellphone/mobile*), or the pronunciation of specific lexical items that differ substantially between British and US English (e.g., *water, tomato, garage, ranch*). The changes they had made were not in anticipation of imagined difficulties but in response to actual difficulties that they (sometimes frequently) had encountered (1–3).

1. I remember the first year I lived in New York City, going into a drug store and asking where the vitamin [vɪtʰəmən] section was. And the woman asked me like five times, "The what? The what?" And I kept on saying, "The vitamin section, the vitamin section." And finally I just said, you know, "Where are the vitamins [vaɪrəmənz]?" And she was like "Oh the vitamins! They're over there." And I think that was like a conscious choice to start using the word vitamin [vaɪrəmən]. (511, English expat)

2. I can't tell people what my name is, because when I say, "Tara" [tʰæɹə], they get really confused. They're like, "Terror? . . . are you threatening?" I'm like, "No, no, it's Tara." And they're like, "Sarah!" And I'm like "No, like that, but with a T." "What?" . . . And I introduce myself as Tara [tʰaɹə] here. (312, US expat)

3. There are certain words that, well, for instance if I go into a bar and I just want like water, and I say, "Can I have water? [wɔtʰə]," everyone is like "What? Like, what are you asking for?" And I'm like "water!" [wɑɾɹ], like and then they get it. (527, English expat)

Critically, a number of speakers underlined how functional these changes were: they were interactionally specific (4, 5), and explicitly just about being understood and *not* to change their accent (6).

4. When I got to the market, I definitely order a pound of tomatoes [tʰəmatʰouz] . . . which when I come home they're tomatoes [tʰəmeiɾouz]. (314, US expat)

5. I don't kind of consciously speak one way or the other, but I was with a student the other day, an American student. . . . And she said that I had an English accent when I spoke to English people like to the waiter, but then an American accent when I talked to her. (308, US expat)

6. I do alter or accommodate . . . in a service encounter . . . but not to change my accent as such. (320, US expat)

In a particularly illustrative example (7), an English migrant frames the conscious adoption of the American pronunciation of *tomato* as something they do because they simply will not be understood otherwise ("if I have to"). But they make clear that they are not trying to sound American, and, when telling the story, they sidenote another US pronunciation change that they wouldn't make.

7. Well because I've taught here for a long time, and I interact with Americans more, I've taught myself—so if I'm in restaurant, to order, or getting fast [fast] food—so I wouldn't say fast [fæst] food, I mean, I'm not going to pretend to be an American—but I will say tomato [tʰəmeiɾou] if I have to. (523, English expat)

It is not surprising then that the majority of places where interviewees talked about making these changes were in service contexts—at coffee shops, restaurants, bars, markets—where they were interacting with strangers (who would not know their dialect background) and where the interaction was fast and transactional in nature (see also Trudgill 1986, 23). That is, as English expat 508 said, they are being motivated by "choosing the words to get through the conversation as fast as possible."

The fact that these described changes are largely lexically specific and interactionally shallow is part of the reason that they are typically not considered particularly important in SDA (Siegel 2010, 116)—it is unclear whether these are part of systematic changes to a person's pronunciation, for example. Another reason they feel exceptional is that these changes often sound very performative: hyper-D2 pronunciations where the speaker is temporarily putting on an accent, both in the sense of how they sounded to me when speakers were giving me examples and how the speakers themselves talked about them, as separate and distinct from their real voice (8–9). Pulling on my own insights as a New Zealander living in the United States, in service encounters I've realized I need to say *tuna* as [tʰunə] (instead of [tʃunə]), but even after a decade it feels very intentional and performative when I do so.

8. I mean I'm looking at [a word in the reading task]. I think I say butter [bʌɾ̩]. Uh, but I could sometimes hear myself saying butter [bʌtʰə] . . . to be understood. (314, US expat)
9. In my real voice or to be understood? (535, English expat, asked during the reading task)

But there are also many instances of people who talk about the role of intelligibility in much broader terms, both in the sense of the changes they made to their accent (10, 11) and in terms of the circumstances under which they made these changes, often attributed to being requirements of their jobs (15, 16). That is, they framed intelligibility as driving systematic changes to their accent as a function of long-term interactional situations they were in. Additionally, some speakers suggested that conscious changes they made to be more intelligible lead to unconscious changes later (12, 13).

10. I actually had to flatten a lot of it, of myself, when I first came over here 'cause people couldn't understand what I was saying. (530, English expat)
11. I really did find myself Americanizing the way I spoke because people seriously did not understand what I was saying. . . . I did make a conscious effort to, to mollify how I was speaking. (520, English expat)
12. You want to be understood—it starts consciously but becomes unconscious. (301, US expat[5])
13. My accent has changed a lot 'cause when I first moved over, I made a conscious effort . . . to be understood. So that meant certain changes were immediate, like I stopped saying *cellphone* and I started say *mobile*. Really simple, and initially that's all that changed was my choice of vocabulary. . . . But I noticed about two years in that my vowel sounds started to change. (318, US expat)

Separate from what participants report changing in their speech and when, it is also worth noting the heavy importance they put on easy communication. Speakers often framed being understood as a non-negotiable outcome that must be achieved (14–17);[6]:

14. Essentially everyone just wants to be understood correctly . . . and that's what I want to be, is I want to be understood by the people I'm talking to. (301, US expat)
15. Sometimes when you're at work, because people are talking really fast and you need to get things done. (526, English expat)
16. I teach for a living, so yeah I have to stand up in front of 30 people and they have to understand me. (509, English expat)

17. For the most part it's a question of choosing to say them [US vocabulary items] because you're just—it's just easier to be understood. (508, English expat)

And many made clear that not being understood was unpleasant. Participants talked about needing to repeat themselves often (18, 19), which was irritating, tiring, or even "a nightmare" (525, English expat). Other speakers talked of their negative emotional reactions to not being understood (20, 21) or of not understanding (22, in this case, not recognizing lexical items).

18. [AW: Are you ever misunderstood?] Oh yeah, all the time . . . there are times where I have to repeat myself like three or four times, but it's quite rare. (312, US expat)
19. I think I ran into a lot of problems when I first moved here with people . . . asking me to repeat things and I just got irritated enough with that, that it's probably why I started changing my [accent]. (515, English expat)
20. You just want people to understand you and it gets really tiring. (301, US expat[7])
21. A lot of people don't understand me and it kind of upsets me sometimes. (525, English expat)
22. I had um an expat moment, where we were stood in front of a pub, thinking "Oh let's go for lunch." And I looked on the pub menu . . . I didn't know what a single item on the menu was and I burst into tears, 'cause I was like "I can't even order lunch." . . . So those moments were few and far between but when they happen they are incredibly emotional; it's weird. (318, US expat)

Other Pragmatic Reasons to Avoid/Maintain the First Dialect

Some of the other factors cited by participants as impacting their accent shift or maintenance also seemed pragmatic in nature. The most easily classified of these, given typical examples of instrumental motivation, were related to money: some migrants reported instances where the use of the D2 (23) or their D1 (24) had financial consequences.

23. Because so many people in Britain think you have money if you're from America, sometimes I consciously try and dilute what I'm saying so I don't get [ripped off]. I bought an automobile tire yesterday morning . . . and uh I was trying to speak softly in a non-Kentucky accent to the guy because he will say "ninety-five" or "a hundred and five quid" instead of "eighty-five quid" for that tire if he thinks you're a septic tank yank 'cause you have money. (302, US expat)
24. My radio work for the most part relies on my sounding American. I mean if I didn't sound American there are probably fifty Brits who are as clever as I am. (314, US expat)

The other reasons given by participants for changing or maintaining their accents could be described as what Kerswill (1994, 60) called "pressure to modify speech." In Kerswill's study of Stril speakers in Bergen, Norway, he used this term to capture explicit instructions from bosses to lose the Stril dialect but also migrant avoidance of teasing or stereotyping. For the US expats in particular, they were navigating a lot of negative stereotypes about Americans—for example, that they were rich (23), stupid, or tourists—and many saw their accents as activating this baggage. In other cases, speakers talked simply about not wanting the attention and/or othering that comes with having an unexpected accent (25, 26), and one speaker connects this desire explicitly to "disguising" their English accent (27).[8] In her assessment of similar comments by Canadians living in America, Nycz (2016, 70) notes that this doesn't seem to be about dialect-related shame, so much as wanting to not "derail a conversation" toward a discussion of where the speaker is from.[9]

25. There's always that horrible moment in a new class, when—you know, some people I haven't met before—when a professor will say something and I'll have to respond and it's just that awful moment the first time I speak, I can just—the class goes silent and everybody turns around to look at me because it's a different accent. (508, English expat)

26. That's the thing, everywhere you go you'll sound different. . . . You don't want to always stand out. Sometimes it's okay, but you know, I just would rather sometimes be able to blend in, and as soon as I open my mouth, I can't blend in. (303, US expat)

27. To a certain extent I will just try and disguise my accent sometimes. You know, when I get off the bus and say, "Thanks" [in US accent] and then I sound like Brooklyn or something. . . . So sometimes yeah, I'm just, I don't wanna be spotted. I don't wanna be picked out, I don't wanna be asked again after seventeen years here, "Where are you from?" (507, English expat)

The examples above illustrate pressures to lose the D1, but many speakers also felt pressure to maintain their D1 and *not* acquire the D2, mostly coming from D1 people they were still in contact with (28–31). Another reason to maintain the D1 was because of various privileges people felt it afforded them in the D2, as an outsider (32, 33).

28. I get real, real grief when I go home. . . . [M]y brothers give me real grief. Because I inflect. (508, English expat)

29. When I'm talking to my brother . . . because he'll accuse me of sounding like a yank which is regarded as being a negative thing over there and so I would take pains to really anglicize my voice. (520, English expat)

30. I'm really scared to go home and hear my family make fun of me. . . . [Y]ou don't understand how [younger brother] made fun of me so bad when I went home, like everything I said. (315, US expat)

31. I try when I speak with my parents not to sound like an asshole because that's what . . . an American who sounds English sounds like to an American. (303, US expat)

32. I think it's in some ways it's easier . . . when you have an accent, because . . . people are expecting you to say things um, it's like they're listening for them . . . like I think if you have a British accent and you mumble like it's more confusing. (310, US expat)

33. It's hard to be an eccentric in our own land but you can be in a foreign land
     and people will excuse your eccentricities on your foreignness, you know?
     (511, English expat)

I treat these pressures to modify/maintain speech as instrumental motivators
because they are not framed as being driven by internal orientations or attitudes of
the migrant but instead by external responses that the migrants are trying to avoid
or exploit. Kerswill (1994) similarly distinguishes these pressures from attitudinal
factors and finds that the degree to which participants felt this pressure aligned with
how much they acquired salient morpho-lexical features of the Bergen dialect.[10] At
the same time, other writers have treated factors like peer pressure as connected to a
speaker's identity (Siegel 2010, 170–71), that is, as something reflecting the internal al-
legiances of a speaker. And it is true that which external pressures we feel, or feel most
keenly, will likely reflect internal orientations and values (see also the "Instrumental
Dialect" subsection below). The fact that SLA researchers have found high correlation
between instrumental and integrative motivations is further evidence that the two factors are not entirely dependent (Gardner, Smythe and Lalonde 1984).

Implications for Second Dialect Acquisition Research

English and American expats talk about the changes they are aware that they have
made to their speech in largely instrumental terms, driven by practical considerations of the consequences of D1 or D2 word or pronunciation choices. Specifically,
participants talk about using the D2 in order to be understood, and to avoid negative
stereotypes or being noticed, and they talk about maintaining their D1 to avoid being
teased back home, and for financial or social gain associated with being an outsider.

As mentioned earlier, it should be noted that instrumental motivations may be
more consciously available for commentary, so it's unlikely that well-studied factors like exposure, attitudes, or phonological systems don't matter, or don't matter as
much, just because they were less mentioned. But the consistency of these comments
also indicates that instrumental factors deserve more consideration in SDA research,
and I discuss some of these implications in the sections below. Moreover, while some
of the changes discussed so far are usually considered too superficial to count in
SDA—specific lexical items in limited domains, often very consciously performed
and distinct from the speaker's "real voice"—in the "Usage versus Acquisition" subsection below, I talk through ways in which these productions have implications for
SDA, both as a phenomenon and as a defined field of study.

Mutual Intelligibility Is Not Equivalent Intelligibility

Broadly put, speakers of British and American English understand each other; these
are mutually intelligible dialects. The migrants interviewed here did not need to formally study the D2 or be immersed in the D2 in order to talk to D2 speakers, just as
British and American tourists do not need or expect translation help on holiday. But
critically, being mutually intelligible is not the same as being equivalently intelligible, especially when listening conditions are not optimal (e.g., Clopper and Bradlow

2008; Floccia et al. 2006; Labov and Ash 2014), and this includes the dialects under question here (Walker 2018). SDA contexts are ones of cross-dialectal communication, then, and in the case of British and American English, participants experience the two dialects as substantially different (34–36).

34. We speak the same language but we don't. Entirely. (318, US expat)
35. But the language is so completely different, that . . . you know you get here and you're like well sure there's a few words, and then you start to realize, no, it's significantly different. (304, US expat)
36. Two countries separated by a common language, eh? (520, English expat)

Moreover, while communication difficulties can sometimes be funny anecdotes, they can also be socially fraught. This can be seen in the comments of the expats themselves (see the "Changing Speech" subsection below), where they talked about how frustrating and upsetting miscommunications could be. It is also evident from a growing body of literature on the topic: listeners may judge speakers they find hard to understand more negatively (Dragojevic and Giles 2016; Dragojevic et al. 2017; Lev-Ari and Keysar 2010; Rickford and King 2016; though see Vaughn and Whitty 2020), and online commentary about subtitling practices reveals that marking someone as hard to understand is generally considered offensive (Yu et al. 2022).

This is all to say that, based on prior research and based on what these speakers are telling us, I follow Shockey (1984) in arguing that intelligibility or comprehensibility is likely a large factor in many observed SDA patterns. It is of particular interest that many speakers described themselves as making the bare minimum changes to their speech in order to be intelligible. In some cases, this was framed as just changing a specific troublesome word in shallow interactional contexts, but in other cases it was framed as not losing but "mollifying" or "flattening" their D1 accent as a whole. This mirrors recent work from my lab suggesting that changes made by self-identified bidialectal US Southerners from their Southern to Mainstream US English modes did not entirely stop them from sounding Southern to outsiders but did seem to remove intelligibility costs for outsiders (Walker, van Hell and Bowers 2018).

These *just enough* changes may help explain why many studies investigating SDA can demonstrate that migrants have changed their speech statistically, but the effect sizes of these changes are often really quite small (e.g., Nycz 2013; Walker 2019). Intelligibility may also contribute to why some features are more likely to shift than others: some researchers have argued that salient features often change more easily than non-salient features (Trudgill 1986, 11; though see Nycz 2016) and Auer, Barden and Grosskopf (1998) have posited that part of what creates salience is comprehensibility (see also Trudgill 1986, 21). In short, dialect differences that cause communicative challenges are likely to be noticed.

Becoming Accented

The considerations interviewees mentioned when they talked about reasons they changed or maintained their accents sound largely like the concerns of speakers of non-standardized dialects: the onus is on them to be understood (Lippi-Green 1997,

70), and they are very aware of the ways in which the associations of their dialect might impact how people receive them in social and practical ways (e.g., Smitherman 2006; Wright 2022). In fact, for many speakers in this study—who are mostly white, middle class, and educated—what they report experiencing is akin to *becoming* accented but at a later stage of life than we typically associate with speakers of non-standardized dialects.

More integration between traditional SDA studies that involve migration, and studies of bidialectalism that usually involve education, is therefore warranted. These situations both involve substantial exposure to two (or more) dialects, and comparing speech production and perception outcomes across these situations will help us understand how exposure to variability shapes production and perception (see Walker and McAllister 2023). For example, in investigating the outcomes of long-term exposure to multiple dialects, how much does the age and circumstance around first exposures matter, how much do attitudes and dialect prestige matter, and how much does the contextual separation of the two dialects matter?

One thing that bidialectal research has focused on heavily is style- or code-switching (e.g., Charity Hudley, Mallinson and Bucholtz 2022), but this has received much less attention in SDA research (though see Johnson and Nycz 2015; Walker 2019) and rarely involves recording speakers in multiple environments and/or with different interlocutors (Kerswill 1994, 149; Lin 2018; cf. Sharma 2011; Rickford and McNair-Knox 1994). Indeed, a few speakers in my study specifically used the term "code-switching" to describe their behavior. Theoretically, this raises the question of what we're trying to capture in second dialect acquisition—how close a migrant gets to a D2-like accent in their most D2-like mode, how much D2-like features appear in their most D1-like mode (i.e., Trudgill 1986, 40), and/or what their combined baseline productions are—but also highlights the value of looking at their linguistic behavior more holistically.

Usage versus Acquisition
As noted in the "Changing Speech" subsection, some speakers' reported use of the D2 could be described as performative—a highly conscious, categorical shift into an extremely D2-like pronunciation that doesn't appear to reflect their regular speech; in many cases, it even appears limited to a single lexical item. The question is whether this *usage* has any bearing on discussions of *acquisition*. Indeed, the whole of Siegel's quote regarding instrumental motivations in SDA reads, "With regard to SDA, it seems the perception may be that there would be little communicative value in acquiring a D2, *except for a few lexical items* or pronunciations that could lead to misunderstanding" (Siegel 2010, 116; emphasis added). That is, the sorts of performative uses of the D2 mentioned by participants in this study are not unknown to researchers but are usually considered exceptions to general second dialect acquisition processes.

The distinction between usage and acquisition is demonstrated best in discussions of actors using non-native dialects for certain roles. Siegel (2010, 64–66) argues that this sort of performance is not acquisition, reflecting familiarity but not "linguistic proficiency" (65; see also Trudgill 1986, 12). As his argument continues, two more contrasts between performance and acquisition are implied. First, that SDA involves the desire to acquire the D2, and second, that acquisition involves sustained, consistent use of D2: "Actors' aims are normally not to acquire the dialect, but to use it for a performance, and therefore they would have difficulty sustaining the use of the dialect outside their performance. In fact, some actors have difficulty sustaining their dialect imitations even through the duration of their performances" (65).

This reasoning behind separating performance and acquisition does not hold. First, almost none of the speakers in my study, and many other SDA studies,[11] are *aiming* to acquire the D2. Some are even vehemently against it; when US expat 315 asked me if I thought she sounded English and I said, "Yes, variably," she responded with "Oh no! I sound English. I don't want to sound English," and kept coming back to this genuine concern for the next five minutes of our conversation. Second, much of second dialect acquisition research has shown how inconsistent and contextually variable D2-usage is by migrants (see Siegel 2010, 22–55 for a summary),[12] and Rampton (2013) shows that the use of D2[13] features in stylized performance can both be momentary and still also reflect long-term exposure to the D2. In practice then, it's not clear that what it means to "sustain" a dialect is well defined and/or shared across SDA research, especially given that the majority of studies look at summative usage rates without a careful analysis of how this is maintained by speakers across time or context. Even for research that does track use across situations, we still lack clear criteria for what counts as sustaining the D2: if a speaker uses low-but-detectable rates of a D2 variant across multiple contexts, is that sustained? If they shift between very high and very low amounts of D2 variants across contexts, is that sustained? If they always pronounce a particular word with a D2 variant—but only really that word—is that sustained?

This is not to say that usage, especially performed usage, *is* acquisition.[14] Rather, one purpose of this critique is meant to motivate researchers (including myself!) to think harder about what the distinction actually is. In my estimation, the key difference appears to be one of consciousness, with a primary interest in people's utterances when they are paying the least attention to their speech (Labov 1972; Sharma 2018).[15] However, it is worth noting that even vernacular-loving sociolinguists have argued for collecting both more and less conscious speech forms to compare patterns across them, suggesting that rather than excluding highly conscious performances, we should analyze them in tandem with other speech samples.

Whether we want to include a very self-conscious "tomato" that is only used at the farmer's market as an example of SDA or not, these imitative tokens might still be of interest to us as paths through which D2 pronunciations first enter a speaker's repertoire. In the case of SDA, we (implicitly or explicitly) assume that part of the reason that migrants' speech changes is purely from substantial exposure to a D2 that begins to shape their speech production. However, we know that people understand and recognize a great deal more variation than they themselves produce, and some models of the production-perception loop posit that this means we have different representations for perception and production (Baese-Berk 2010; Garrett and Johnson 2013). Even within the migrants in the current study, the (admittedly few) measures of SDA in their speech did not correlate with their performance in a listening task: changes in perception appeared to be happening independently of changes in production (Walker 2018).

The question then becomes, What causes something that you have heard a lot to become something that you yourself say? This is especially important when we consider that D1 and D2 forms are not socially neutral; for a speaker to produce a D2 form is for them to *sound* like a D2 speaker in some way, and certain variables—for example, BATH realizations—are wildly loaded to participants (Walker 2019, 152). Exemplar accounts of language, which would posit frequency effects (see Nycz 2013), also critically allow for tokens to be tagged with relevant socioindexical information (Foulkes and Docherty 2006). Under this account, one way that D2-tokens start to enter a speaker's repertoire is if D2 speakers start to be tagged as similar to the migrant in some way, or D2-variants acquire new, desirable meanings (for example, intervocalic /t/-flapping is not associated with sounding *American* but maybe with sounding relaxed). Explicit performance of the D2 could be one way that even the most socially marked tokens enter a speaker's repertoire. If a speaker is forced to produce a particular pronunciation in order to be understood, this realization is now, by definition, something that the speaker says, and these performative, mercenary utterances could be the mechanism through which certain pronunciations enter a person's speech production repertoire. Reflecting on changes in intervocalic /t/ in his own speech, Trudgill (1986, 23) states: "I can attest that one factor that without doubt precipitated the introduction of flaps into my own speech in America was the number of people who thought, for example, if only for a second, that I wanted a *pizza* rather than that my name was *Peter.*" The keywords in this quote are "precipitated the introduction," which imply that the conscious need to be understood motivated the initial use of a D2 variant, but once introduced, the variant was used in other contexts. Chambers (1992) has already hypothesized that SDA of sounds happens through a process of lexical diffusion, stating that "speakers must *sporadically acquire* new pronunciations . . . as the basis for generalizing a rule" (695; emphasis added). The point here is that the sporadically acquired new pronunciations are likely to be in the words that cause the greatest communication difficulties.[16]

Instrumental Dialect Needs Will Be Very Situation Specific

More recent discussions of motivation-related concepts in SLA (including "orientation" and "investment") have focused on how these factors are very situated in broader sociopolitical dynamics and also are something that can change within a given person across spaces and time (see Peirce 1995; Ushioda 2012). Therefore, the role that pragmatic concerns have in whether a speaker acquires the D2 or maintains their D1 are going to be very situation and person specific.

We see this specificity in the current study. There are many similarities between both groups of expats, including some of the pressures they feel in regard to changing their accent, for example, to be understood or to avoid being noticed. But there are as well differences between being a British expat and an American expat that also manifest in the cost-benefit of their D1. Specifically, Americans were trying to avoid negative stereotypes associated with an American accent in ways that English migrants were not. Similarly, there will be situations in which a person's D1 is relatively easy for D2 listeners to understand, for example, because of heavy media exposure or economic and political relationships between countries, and situations where a speaker's D1 will be relatively obscure to D2 listeners. For example, in Walker and Drager (2018), we found that New Zealanders performed similarly with American vs. NZ voices in a lexical decision task, but US listeners did much worse with NZ vs. American voices. Presumably then, New Zealanders in the US would encounter more miscommunication issues than Americans in New Zealand would, so intelligibility would be more of a factor for the former vs. the latter group.

In his analysis of the factor "Pressure to Modify Speech," Kerswill (1994, 106) finds that women and people who migrated at an earlier age had higher scores, highlighting the ways in which dialectal pressures may be non-random: certain types of people might either be more subject to, may more keenly feel, or may be more likely to report, various pressures to maintain or lose their D1. The role of age in Kerswill's study was particularly interesting, as it could reflect how pressure can be age graded and how pressure can change over time. For example, if speakers move to a new dialect region at a younger age, they might be more teased by their peers about their accent than people who move when they are older. It could also be that their own sense of self is more/less stable and therefore more/less subject to change. One US migrant in my study was now living in England for the second time in her life, in her 30s. The first time, she had been in her early 20s, and she felt like her age influenced how likely she was to change her accent (37).

> 37. I think [my accent's] still quite American, and other people tell me it's still quite American. . . . And I think it's 'cause I'm older. . . . [W]hen I was living here and I was twenty, I remember certain words becoming much more English. (312, US expat)

The other possibility is that attitudes toward the D1, or toward variation in general, change in the D2 community over time. This is one explanation Kerswill (1994) gives for the interaction he finds between age and dialect pressure in his study: that there used to be more bigotry against a Stril accent in Bergen in the past but that at the time of his study, the dialect was less stigmatized (113). Speaker 312 also talks about how dialect change happening over time may contribute to changes in intelligibility-related issues (38).

> 38. It's harder with I think older people, um . . . it's hard for me to understand some of the older people. . . . [O]ur generation is sort of a lot easier to understand. (312, US expat)

To summarize this section, it is unlikely that any pragmatic pressures driving second dialect acquisition are universal, applicable to all D1-D2s, to all people, or even in all domains and time periods of a single person's life. This point requires researchers to understand the broader contexts of the D1-D2 relationship, and of the types of interactions a person is regularly involved in. One way to get this information, as I hope is clear from this chapter, is just to ask.

Conclusion

In this study I center the metalinguistic reflections of English and US migrants. Their observations remind us that second dialect acquisition is not simply a passive response to a new ambient dialect but the product of interactive experiences with D2 (and still D1) speakers. Migrants tell us that their conscious dialect choices are largely driven by the responses of their interlocutors, either in terms of whether the interlocutor will understand them, or whether the interlocutor will positively or negatively judge them. That is, they often frame their dialect choices as pragmatic ways to achieve communicative or other goals. Importantly, their responses also point to weaknesses in second dialect research, in understating the role of intelligibility in cross-dialectal communication, and in weak and sometimes contradicting definitions of what we include within second dialect research. At the same time, they also highlight interesting avenues of future work, and point to what could be learned by more connection with SLA research, bidialectal/non-standardized dialect research, and performance research.

Notes

1. This was speaker 038, who was a non-migrant, US fan of English Premier League football (Walker 2014).
2. I did not formally collect information on ethnicity and education, but most (though not all) of people in both groups were white and university educated.
3. In a very few cases, where I was running two people at once, one of the participants completed the interview before the experiment.
4. During the recordings, many participants comment on my accent and the degree to which I've acquired an American accent. One Brit called me "an absolute, cut down the line mix" of a US and New Zealand English speaker.
5. This comment is derived from my notes; it was a comment the speaker made after I had turned off the recorder.
6. This may seem obvious to readers, but there are many examples where people don't actually prioritize intelligibility over other social considerations, for example, the act of "smiling and nodding" when you don't understand someone.
7. This comment is derived from my notes; it was a comment the speaker made after I had turned off the recorder.
8. Another alternative mentioned by a few speakers was just to avoid talking altogether.
9. Shockey (1984, 92) similarly states that she derives "no particular pleasure from sounding different from my colleagues or from being identified as foreign in every encounter involving speech."
10. The exact role of the factor was complicated, given its high correlation with age-of-migration and gender (see the "Instrumental Dialect" subsection).
11. There are also speakers who *do* want to acquire the D2/lose their D1. For example, in Kerswill (1994, 60), one immigrant to Bergen is cited as saying, "I did not dare utter a word until I was sure I could speak the Bergen dialect."
12. English Expat 302, who said he changed his accent sometimes to be understood and fit in, explicitly talked about how he could not sustain a US accent.

13. In that study, the speaker was a L1 Punjabi speaker who learned English later in life, and I use "D2" here to refer to when his English (L2) most resembled Anglo vs. Indian English pronunciations.

14. It would be very interesting to systematically investigate whether using a non-native dialect while acting has any impact on a speaker's speech outside of the role. There are also some reasons to think usage and acquisition are not wholly separate phenomena. For example, Trudgill (1986, 12) finds similarities between the sounds that change in *imitation* and those that change in accommodation.

15. The perceived difference is probably exacerbated by historical differences in the traditions of research on performance and on SDA. These differences are primarily about the populations and situations under study: work that is typically considered as SDA research has primarily looked at the impact of migration on conversational speech, while work looking at dialect performance looks at the accuracy of (non-migrant) actors in capturing the D2.

16. This study also mirrors work in sociolinguistics suggesting that there are carrier words that initially contain the most advanced variants of changes in progress (Drager 2015; Eckert 1996; Kiesling 2004), and work in phonetics suggesting that words most likely to be misunderstood (low-frequency words) lead in a push-chain-shift (Hay et al. 2015).

References

Auer, Peter, Birgit Barden and Beate Grosskopf. 1998. Subjective and objective parameters determining "salience" in long-term dialect accommodation. *Journal of Sociolinguistics* 2 (2): 163–87. doi: 10.1111/1467-9481.00039

Baese-Berk, Melissa M. 2010. *An examination of the relationship between speech perception and production.* Unpublished PhD dissertation, Northwestern University, Evanston, IL.

Chambers, Jack. 1992. Dialect acquisition. *Language* 68 (4): 673–705. doi: 10.2307/416850

Charity Hudley, Anne H., Christine Mallinson and Mary Bucholtz. 2022. *Talking college: Making space for Black Language practices in higher education.* New York: Teachers College Press.

Clopper, Cynthia and Ann Bradlow. 2008. Perception of dialect variation in noise: Intelligibility and classification. *Language and Speech* 51 (3): 175–198. doi: 10.1177/0023830908098

Drager, Katie. 2015. *Linguistic variation, identity construction and cognition.* Berlin: Language Science Press.

Dragojevic, Marko and Howard Giles. 2016. I don't like you because you're hard to understand: The role of processing fluency in the language attitudes process. *Human Communication Research* 42 (3): 396–420. doi: 10.1111/hcre.12079

Dragojevic, Marko, Howard Giles, Anna-Carrie Beck and Nicholas T. Tatum. 2017. The fluency principle: Why foreign accent strength negatively biases language attitudes. *Communication monographs* 84 (3): 1–21. doi: 10.1080/03637751.2017.1322213

Eckert, Penelope. 1996. (ay) goes to the city: Exploring the expressive use of variation. In Gregory R. Guy, Crawford Feagin, Deborah Schiffrin and John Baugh (eds.), *Towards a social science of language: Papers in honor of William Labov.* Philadelphia: John Benjamins, 47–68. doi: 10.1075/cilt.127.06eck

Floccia, Caroline, Jeremy Goslin, Frédérique Girard and Gabrielle Konopczynski. 2006. Does a regional accent perturb speech processing? A lexical decision study in French listeners. *Journal of Experimental Psychology: Human Perception and Performance* 32 (5): 1276–93. doi: 10.1037/0096-1523.32.5.1276

Foulkes, Paul and Gerry Docherty. 2006. The social life of phonetics and phonology. *Journal of Phonetics* 34 (4): 409–38. doi: 10.1016/j.wocn.2005.08.002

Gardner, Robert and Peter MacIntyre. 1991. An instrumental motivation in language study: Who says it isn't effective? *Studies in Second Language Acquisition* 13 (1): 57–72. https://www.jstor.org/stable/44487535

Gardner, Robert, Padric C. Smythe and R. N. Lalonde. 1984. The nature and replicability of factors in second language acquisition. *Research Bulletin No. 605.* Department of Psychology, University of Western Ontario.

Garrett, Andrew and Keith Johnson. 2013. Phonetic bias in sound change. In Alan Yu (ed.), *Origins of sound change: Approaches to phonologization*. Oxford: Oxford University Press, 201–26. doi: 10.5070/P78587g0jg

Garrett, Peter, Angie Williams and Betsy Evans. 2005. Attitudinal data from New Zealand, Australia, the USA and UK about each other's Englishes: Recent changes or consequences of methodologies? *Multilingua* 24 (3): 211–35. doi: 10.1515/mult.2005.24.3.211

Hay, Jennifer, Janet Pierrehumbert, Abby Walker and Patrick LaShell. 2015. Tracking word frequency effects through 130 years of sound change. *Cognition* 139 (June): 83–91. doi: 10.1016/j.cognition.2015.02.012

Johnson, Daniel E. and Jennifer Nycz. 2015. Partial mergers and near-distinctions: Stylistic layering in dialect acquisition. *Penn Working Papers in Linguistics: Selected Papers from New Ways of Analyzing Variation (NWAV) 43*, 21 (2): 109–17. https://repository.upenn.edu/pwpl/vol21/iss2/13

Kerswill, Paul. 1994. *Dialects converging: Rural speech in urban Norway*. Oxford: Oxford University Press.

Kiesling, Scott F. 2004. Dude. *American Speech* 79 (3): 281–305. doi: 10.1215/00031283-79-3-281

Labov, William. 1972. *Sociolinguistic patterns*. Philadelphia: Philadelphia University Press.

Labov, William. 1984. Field methods of the Project on Language Variation and Change. In J. Baugh and J. Sherzer (eds.), *Language in use: Readings in sociolinguistics*. Englewood Cliffs, NJ: Prentice-Hall, 28–53.

Labov, William and Sharon Ash. 2014. Understanding Birmingham. In C. Bernstein (ed.), *Language variety in the South revisited*. Tuscaloosa: University of Alabama Press, 508–73.

Lambert, W. E. 1974. Culture and language as factors in learning and education. In F. F. Aboud and R. D. Meade (eds.), *Cultural factors in learning and education*. Bellingham: Western Washington State University, 91–122.

Lev-Ari, Shiri and Boaz Keysar. 2010. Why don't we believe non-native speakers? The influence of accent on credibility. *Journal of Experimental Social Psychology* 46 (6): 1093–96. doi: 10.1016/j.jesp.2010.05.025

Lin, Yuhan. 2018. *Stylistic variation and social perception in second dialect acquisition*. Unpublished PhD dissertation, The Ohio State University, Columbus.

Lippi-Green, Rosina. 1997. *English with an accent: Language, ideology, and discrimination in the United States*. London and New York: Routledge.

Love, Jessica and Abby Walker. 2013. Football vs football: Effect of topic on /r/ realization in American and English sports fans. *Language and Speech* 56 (4): 443–460. doi: 10.1177/0023830912453132

Murphy, M. Lynne and Rachele De Felice. 2018. Routine politeness in American and British English requests: Use and non-use of please. *Journal of Politeness Research* 15 (1): 1–24. doi: 10.1515/pr-2016-0027

Peirce, Bonny Norton. 1995. Social identity, investment, and language learning. *TESOL Quarterly* 29 (1): 9–31. doi: 10.2307/3587803

Nycz, Jennifer. 2013. Changing words or changing rules? Second dialect acquisition and phonological representation. *Journal of Pragmatics* 52 (June): 49–62. https://doi.org/10.1016/j.pragma.2012.12.014

Nycz, Jennifer. 2016. Awareness and acquisition of new dialect features. In Anna Babel (ed.), *Awareness and control in sociolinguistic research*. Cambridge University Press, 62–79. doi: 10.1017/CBO9781139680448.005

Nycz, Jennifer. 2019. Linguistic and social factors favoring acquisition of contrast in a new dialect. *Proceedings of the International Congress of Phonetic Sciences 2019*, Melbourne. 1480–84.

Payne, 1980. Factors controlling the acquisition of the Philadelphia dialect by out-of-state children. In William Labov (ed.), *Locating language in time and space*. New York: Academic Press, 143–78.

Preston, Dennis R. 1996. Whaddayaknow?: The modes of folk linguistic awareness. *Language Awareness* 5 (1): 40–74. doi: 10.1080/09658416.1996.9959890

Preston, Dennis R. and Nancy Niedzielski (eds). 2010. *A reader in sociophonetics*. Berlin: Mouton de Gruyter.

Rampton, Ben. 2013. Styling in a language learned later in life. *The Modern Language Journal* 97 (2): 360–82. https://www.jstor.org/stable/43651644

Rickford, John and Sharese King. 2016. Language and linguistics on trial: Hearing Rachel Jeantel (and other vernacular speakers) in the courtroom and beyond. *Language* 92 (4): 948–88.

Rickford, John and Faye McNair-Knox. 1994. Addressee- and topic-influenced style shift: A quantitative sociolinguistic study. In D. Biber and E. Finegan (eds.), *Sociolinguistic perspectives on register*. New York: Oxford University Press, 235–74.

Rys, Kathy. 2007. *Dialect as a second language: Linguistic and non-linguistic factors in secondary dialect acquisition by children and adolescents.* Unpublished PhD dissertation, University of Ghent. doi: 10.1353/lan.2016.0078

Siegel, Jeff. 2010. *Second dialect acquisition.* Cambridge: Cambridge University Press. doi: 10.1017/CBO9780511777820

Sharma, Devyani. 2011. Style repertoire and social change in British Asian English. *Journal of Sociolinguistics* 15 (4): 464–92. doi: 10.1111/j.1467-9841.2011.00503.x

Sharma, Devyani. 2018. Style dominance: Attention, audience, and the "real me." *Language in Society* 47 (1): 1–31. doi: 10.1017/S0047404517000835

Shockey, Linda. 1984. All in a flap: Long-term accommodation in phonology. *International Journal of the Sociology of Language* 46: 87–95. doi: 10.1515/ijsl.1984.46.87

Smitherman, Geneva. 2006. *Words from the mother: Language and African Americans.* Oxford: Routledge.

Trudgill, Peter. 1972. Sex, covert prestige and linguistic change in the urban British English of Norwich. *Language in Society* 1 (2): 179–95. doi: 10.1017/S0047404500000488

Trudgill, Peter. 1986. *Dialects in contact.* Oxford: Basil Blackwell.

Ushioda, Ema. 2012. Motivation: L2 learning as a special case? In Sarah Mercer, Stephen Ryan and Marion Williams (eds.), *Psychology for language learning.* London: Palgrave Macmillan, 58–73. doi: 10.1057/9781137032829_5

Vaughn, Charlotte and Aubrey Whitty. 2020. Investigating the relationship between comprehensibility and social evaluation. *Journal of Second Language Pronunciation* 6 (3): 483–504. doi: 10.1075/bct.121.10vau

Walker, Abby. 2014. *Crossing oceans with voices and ears: Second dialect acquisition and topic-based shifting in production and perception.* Unpublished PhD dissertation, The Ohio State University, Columbus.

Walker, Abby. 2018. The effect of long-term second dialect exposure on sentence transcription in noise. *Journal of Phonetics* 71 (November): 162–76. doi: 10.1016/j.wocn.2018.08.001

Walker, Abby. 2019. The role of dialect experience in topic-based shifts in speech production. *Language Variation and Change* 31 (2): 135–63. doi: 10.1017/S0954394519000152

Walker, Abby and Katie Drager. 2018. The role of canonicity vs. experience-based expectations on speech processing. Poster presented at the 16th Biennial Conference on Laboratory Phonology (LabPhon), Lisbon, June 19–23.

Walker, Abby and Alexander McAllister. 2023. (Un)Varied experiences: How exposure to variability impacts speech perception. To appear in Manuel Diaz-Campos and Sonia Balasch (eds.), *The handbook of usage-based linguistics*, 491–508. Hoboken, NJ: Wiley and Sons.

Walker, Abby, Janet van Hell and Mike Bowers. 2018. The effect of style-shifting on speech perception. Paper presented at New Ways of Analyzing Variation (NWAV), New York, October 18–21.

Wells, John C. 1982. *Accents of English.* Cambridge: Cambridge University Press.

Wright, Kelly. 2022. *Black professionalism: Perception and metalinguistic assessment of Black American speakers' sociolinguistic labor.* Unpublished PhD dissertation, University of Michigan, Ann Arbor.

Yu, Jessie, Molly Purtill, Lily Carroll, Sara Carter, Jessica Taylor and Abby Walker. 2022. Ideologies of intelligibility onscreen: The sociolinguistics of intralingual subtitling. *University of Pennsylvania Working Papers in Linguistics* 28, no. 2 (September): 181–190. https://repository.upenn.edu/pwpl

Contributors

Areej Al-Hawamdeh is an assistant professor of English language and linguistics at the Department of English Literature and Language, Jerash University, Jordan. She teaches sociolinguistics, the history of English, phonetics and phonology, and research methods. Her research investigates variation and change and dialect contact in modern Arabic dialects, with special focus on Jordan.

Enam Al-Wer is a professor of linguistics at the University of Essex, UK. She was the recipient of the Leverhulme Trust Senior Research Fellowship from 2017 to 2020. Her primary research interests revolve around variation and change in modern Arabic varieties, specifically focusing on dialect contact and the emergence of new dialects. Through her extensive published work, she sheds light on the intricate sociolinguistic dynamics shaping the development of the Amman dialect, a central Jordanian variety.

Karen V. Beaman is a lecturer of sociolinguistics at the University of Tübingen, Germany. Her primary research is a comparative study of Swabian, a dialect spoken in southwestern Germany, which combines a 35-year panel study with a five-generation trend study. Her work investigates language variation and change in both real- and apparent-time, with particular focus on how factors of identity, mobility, and social networks drive or inhibit change.

Daniel Erker is an associate professor of Spanish and linguistics at Boston University. He is the director of the Spanish in Boston Project, a federally funded research initiative studying the sociolinguistic behavior of Spanish-speaking Bostonians. His research investigates a broad array of variable phenomena, ranging from micro-linguistic variation in speech sounds to macro-linguistic trends such as the intergenerational maintenance of immigrant languages.

Víctor Fernández-Mallat is an associate professor in the Department of Spanish and Portuguese at Georgetown University. His research concentrates on bidialectal profiles in Spanish speakers in the United States who are in dialect contact situations, the social meanings conveyed by different Spanish forms of address, and the impact (or lack thereof) of diversity, equity, and inclusion (DEI) initiatives on language attitudes.

Juan M. Hernández-Campoy is a professor in sociolinguistics at the University of Murcia, where he imparts knowledge on a range of subjects including sociolinguistics, English varieties, the history of English, and sociolinguistic research methods. With a focus on language variation and change, his research areas encompass sociolinguistics, dialectology, and sociostylistics. He has made significant contributions to our understanding of style-shifting practices and the historical development of dialects through his extensive work on the Spanish spoken in the Autonomous Community of Murcia.

Yoojin Kang is a researcher at Cheongju University. Her research interests include how adult mobile speakers acquire new dialect features and how linguistic structures are represented in the minds of speakers, with a focus on examining how linguistic representations are linked to social meaning.

Wesley Mark Lincoln is a doctoral student at the University of Pennsylvania. His research interests include sociophonetics in Singapore English, Romance languages, and Singapore Hokkien. His current work applies evolutionary thinking to the study of language variation and change.

Michael Marinaccio is a master's student in linguistics at the University of Malta. His research centers around the morphology of nominal inflection in Maltese, with a special focus on the integration of Romance loanwords into the nonconcatenative morphological system characteristic of Semitic languages. He aims to continue his research on morphological variation within languages such as Maltese that make use of different morphological systems.

Jennifer Nycz is an associate professor of linguistics at Georgetown University. Her research focuses on accent change in mobile speakers of English, the phonetic and phonological impacts of new dialect input on vowel systems, and how place identity influences the way people use language.

Livia Oushiro is a professor in the Department of Linguistics and the director of the Laboratory VARIEM (Variation, Identity, Style, and Change) at the Universidade Estadual de Campinas, Brazil. Her research focuses on the interplay between patterns of variation and group identity, including analyses of lectal cohesion, sociolinguistic perception, and lectal accommodation in the speech of Brazilian internal migrants in contact situations.

Allison Shapp is an assistant research scientist and adjunct professor at New York University. She is interested in how people use linguistic variation in different modalities to construct aspects of identity, with particular focuses on the sociophonetics of New York City English in the city and its suburbs, variation in Liberian Englishes, and Computer-Mediated Communication.

John Victor Singler is professor emeritus of linguistics at New York University. His overriding research interests are (1) contact linguistics, especially pidgin and creole linguistics, (2) variationist sociolinguistics, and (3) language in Liberia. His current research focuses on sociophonetics and the sociohistorical context of dialect contact in Liberia.

Rebecca Lurie Starr is an associate professor in the Department of English, Linguistics and Theatre Studies at the National University of Singapore. Her research focuses on children's sociolinguistic development, language variation, and change in multilingual settings, and the sociophonetic construction of style.

Laura Torrano-Moreno is currently working under a Visiting Teacher Programme in Tampa, Florida, while serving for the Education Department of the Government of the Region of Murcia in Spain. Her research interest lies in variationist sociolinguistics, with a particular focus on studying language variation and change in an isolated local community in Murcia, southeastern Spain.

Abby Walker is an associate professor of language sciences in the English Department at Virginia Tech. She is interested in how dialectal variability is cognitively represented, and how differences in dialectal exposure lead to differences in speech production and perception.

Index

Note: Page numbers followed by *f* or *t* indicate material in figures or tables respectively